CHRIST WITHOUT ABSOLUTES

In memoriam

J.A.T.R.

Christ Without Absolutes

*A Study of the Christology
of Ernst Troeltsch*

SARAH COAKLEY

CLARENDON PRESS · OXFORD

1988

Oxford University Press, Walton Street, Oxford OX2 6DP
Oxford New York Toronto
Delhi Bombay Calcutta Madras Karachi
Petaling Jaya Singapore Hong Kong Tokyo
Nairobi Dar es Salaam Cape Town
Melbourne Auckland
and associated companies in
Berlin Ibadan

Oxford is a trade mark of Oxford University Press

Published in the United States
by Oxford University Press, New York

British Library Cataloguing in Publication Data
Coakley, Sarah
Christ without absolutes; a study of
the Christology of Ernst Troeltsch
I. Title
209'.2'4   BX4827.T7
ISBN 0-19-826670-7

Library of Congress Cataloging in Publication Data
Coakley, Sarah, 1951-
Christ without absolutes: a study of the Christology of Ernst Troeltsch / Sarah Coakley.
Bibliography: p.   Includes index.
1. Jesus Christ—History of doctrines—19th century. 2. Jesus Christ—History of
doctrines—20th century. 3. Troeltsch, Ernst, 1865-1923—Contributions in Christology.
I. Title.
BT198.C54   1988   232'.092'4—dc19   87-31021
ISBN 0-19-826670-7

Set by Burns & Smith, Derby
Printed in Great Britain
at the University Printing House, Oxford
by David Stanford
Printer to the University

Preface

I owe a very great debt of gratitude to those who have helped me in my work on this book and encouraged an interest in Troeltsch which goes back now a number of years. In particular I thank my erstwhile supervisor, Professor Maurice Wiles of Oxford, for all his support and careful criticism; and Professors Stephen Sykes (Cambridge University) and Anthony Dyson (Manchester University) in their roles as examiners of my doctoral dissertation. My colleague at Lancaster Dr John Powell Clayton, along with Dr Friedrich Wilhelm Graf (University of Munich) and Dr Walter Wyman (Whitman College, Washington), all read the manuscript with meticulous care. Their comments evidenced in themselves a fascinating diversity of cultural perspectives, and were invaluable. To them I offer especial thanks.

I also want to mention a number of others, who at various stages of the enterprise supplied either criticisms of earlier drafts, or bibliographical suggestions, or material that I would otherwise have been hard put to obtain: Robert Morgan (Oxford University); Emeritus Professor James Luther Adams and Professor Gordon Kaufman (Harvard Divinity School); Professor George Rupp (Rice University); the late Professor Walter Bense (University of Wisconsin); Professor Jack Meiland (University of Michigan); Professor Joseph Runzo (Chapman College, California); Professor Brian Gerrish (University of Chicago); Professor Trutz Rendtorff (University of Munich); Dr Hans-Georg Drescher (Pädagogische Hochschule Ruhr, Dortmund); Professor Jakob Klapwijk (University of Amsterdam); Dr Ernst Bammel (Cambridge University); and Dr Patrick Sherry and Professor James Richmond (Lancaster University). I thank them all, and no less Elaine Barlow-Morris and Anne Dalton for their excellent typing. Audrey Bayley and Anne Ashby at the Oxford University Press, too, have been patience and kindness itself.

For those actively engaged in Troeltsch research, or otherwise disposed to follow up such things, it may be useful to know that there are a number of further references, and a larger bibliography, in my doctoral thesis in its original form, 'The Limits and Scope of the Christology of Ernst Troeltsch' (Cambridge Ph.D., 1982), lodged in the Cambridge University Library. This book is a slightly revised version of that piece of work. Part of my article 'Theology and Cultural Relativism: What is the Problem?' (in *Neue Zeitschrift für systematische Theologie und Religionsphilosophie*, 21 (1979)) is now reproduced in Chapter 1 of this book, and I am grateful that the editors and publisher were happy to see this done. Professor James Luther Adams, and Dr Geoffrey Green of T. and T. Clark, Edinburgh, have graciously given permission for some quotations to be made from the proposed forthcoming collection of Troeltsch translations by Adams and Bense. I am also grateful to acknowledge permission from Duckworth, London, and their American distributor Presbyterian Publishing House, Atlanta, to quote from three of the Troeltsch translations in Ernst Troeltsch, *Writings on Theology and Religion*, ed. R. Morgan and M. Pye (London, 1977); from the editor of the *Unitarian Universalist Christian* in Boston, Mass., to quote from the translation of Troeltsch's 'On the Possibility of a Liberal Christianity' in the *Unitarian Universalist Christian*, 29 (1974); and from J. C. B. Mohr (Paul Siebeck), Tübingen, to quote from the English translation of Troeltsch's *The Absoluteness of Christianity and the History of Religions* (Richmond, Va., 1971).

Most of all, however, I want to thank my husband Chip, whose patience, help, and encouragement cannot really be adequately quantified; and our small daughter Edith, for suffering many maternal absences and distractions; and with them a host of others, chief among them my parents, who have in very practical ways done more than they know, and without whose support and chivvying, threats and prayers, this book would probably not even now be ready for publication.

S.C.

Lancaster
17 February 1987

Contents

References and Abbreviations

The following abbreviations have been made in the text and notes referring to (1) selected journal and encyclopaedia titles, and (2) works of Troeltsch which are repeatedly cited. Other *secondary* works are cited using the Harvard (author-and-date) system, whereas other works by Troeltsch are cited with the date for easy reference in the Troeltsch section of the bibliography. Further details of all the works cited (including the books and articles mentioned below) may be found in the appropriate section of the bibliography at the end of the book. ET stands throughout for English translation.

1

AJT	*American Journal of Theology*
CW	*Die christliche Welt*
ERE	J. Hastings (ed.), *Encyclopaedia of Religion and Ethics* (1908–26)
GGA	*Göttingische gelehrte Anzeigen*
NZST	*Neue Zeitschrift für systematische Theologie und Religionsphilosophie*
PJ	*Preußische Jahrbücher*
RGG	F. M. Schiele and L. Zscharnack (eds.), *Die Religion in Geschichte und Gegenwart* (^{1}1909–14)
TA	*Theologische Arbeiten aus dem rheinischen wissenschaftlichen Predigerverein*
TLZ	*Theologische Literaturzeitung*
ZTK	*Zeitschrift für Theologie und Kirche*
ZWT	*Zeitschrift für wissenschaftliche Theologie*

2

A^1	*Die Absolutheit des Christentums und die Religionsgeschichte* (^{1}1902)
Abs.	*The Absoluteness of Christianity and the History of Religions* (^{3}1929; ET 1971)
Chr. Th.	*Christian Thought: Its History and Application* (1923, repr. 1957)
'Essence'	'What does "Essence of Christianity" Mean?' (^{2}1913; ET in ed. Morgan and Pye, 1977)
Gl.	*Glaubenslehre* (1925, repr. 1981)

GS   *Gesammelte Schriften* (1912–25)
'Half C.'   'Half a Century of Theology: A Review' (^{2}1913; ET in ed.
           Morgan and Pye, 1977)
'On Poss.'   'On the Possibility of a Liberal Christianity' (1910; ET in
           Unitarian Universalist Christian, 1974)
'Sig. HJ'   'The Significance of the Historical Existence of Jesus for
           Faith' (1911, ET in ed. Morgan and Pye, 1977)
ST   *The Social Teaching of the Christian Churches* (1912; ET 1931,
           repr. 1960)

Introduction

THE problem of Christian faith's relation to history is a profound one which exercises all thinking Christian believers. But the issues at stake are complex. There is of course the perennial debate about how much we can verify historically about Jesus, and what part that historical data should play in any doctrine of Christ. But there are also more searching and radical philosophical questions: about the nature and corrigibility of any historical knowledge, and about the possibly time-bound quality not only of cherished doctrinal formulations, but of Jesus himself. Here the ambiguous threat of 'historical relativism' rears its head; and its putative effects on Christology are obviously of prime significance.

Ernst Troeltsch (1865–1923) was a polymathic figure: philosopher, historian, sociologist, politician, and theologian. He is chiefly remembered in theological circles for his assiduous study of the effects of a 'modern' historical outlook upon Christian dogmatic claims, his commitment thereby to a form of 'historical relativism', and his search for a fruitful *rapprochement* between theology and the emerging social sciences. The violent reactions these interests provoked in the succeeding generation of 'dialectical' theologians on the Continent is well known and scarcely needs another rehearsal.[1] Troeltsch's theology according to Emil Brunner sank 'into a sea of relativistic scepticism' (Brunner 1929, 7), and amounted to 'the renunciation of all that is specifically Christian' (Brunner 1934, 69). Karl Barth accused Troeltsch's *Glaubenslehre* (his lectures on systematic theology) of a 'dissolution into endless and useless talk' and of ending on 'the rocks, or the quicksands' (Barth 1956, 387). Troeltsch's Christology, more especially, has been the target of emotive criticism, and this time not just from the dialectical theologians.

---

[1] See among recent literature Groll 1976, *passim*, for a detailed study of Barth on Troeltsch; and also Dyson 1974, 53 ff., and Morgan in ed. Clayton 1976, 33 ff., for more general discussions in English.

It has been said to involve a 'pantheism of history' which cannot be truly 'Christian' (Bultmann 1969, 32), to allow no proper revelation of God in Jesus (Pannenberg 1970, 57), to be 'in no sense . . . a Christology' (Reist 1966, 192), and to be 'weak', 'inadequate', or otherwise seriously defective (Morgan in ed. Clayton 1976, 67–8 and in ed. Morgan and Pye 1977, 39, 224).

Strangely, however, no one has previously devoted a study to Troeltsch's Christology in its completeness,[2] or taken the trouble to analyse carefully the plethora of factors (among which relativism loomed large) which led to Troeltsch's abandonment of a traditional 'incarnational' model. Criticisms of his Christology tend to set out from assumed premises, an approach which leads to inevitable prejudgement. It is true that there is much in Troeltsch's view of Christ which is questionable or dated, and even more that is tantalizingly sketchy and elusive; but our aim is not to defend it *in toto* or to revitalize it in its original form. Much more crucial are the systematic issues it enshrines: the question on the one hand of what shape a Christology may take when the challenges of 'historical relativism' are seriously entertained, and, on the other, of what inputs into Christological construction are suggested by a rich engagement with the social sciences, especially with sociology and psychology. These remain pressing issues for modern Christology, and it is here that Troeltsch's own challenging responses, however fragmentary and debatable, demand proper reflective scrutiny.

But it is useless to talk vaguely of the threat of 'historical relativism' without precise understanding of the philosophical issues at stake. That is why this book begins (Chapter 1) with a detailed *analytical* account of the nature of Troeltsch's relativism. Much previous Troeltsch scholarship has been too easily content, when discussing this crucial aspect of his thought, to reiterate his own language and categories without adequate critical scrutiny, or to assess it only on the basis of selected, earlier writings from his literary corpus. Here, instead, we analyse with precision the

---

[2] There have of course been discussions of *aspects* of Troeltsch's Christology before, the better ones being the more recent. The fullest and most challenging is Gerrish 1975, which is discussed in some detail in ch. 5 below. For other discussions see Apfelbacher 1978, 227 ff.; Gerrish in ed. Clayton 1976, 128 ff.; Morgan in ed. Clayton 1976, 67 ff., and in ed. Morgan and Pye 1977, 39 ff. and 219 ff.; Rupp 1977, 25 ff.; Fischer 1967, 39 ff.; Ogletree 1965, 62 ff.; and Wolfe 1916.

full development of his thinking on relativism, and are thereby enabled to see how his own position changed over time, and how it compares with various forms of relativism being canvassed to-day in a different philosophical milieu.

From this vantage-point it becomes possible to see how relativism, the dominating intellectual interest of Troeltsch's career, was set to be a highly significant factor in his rejection of 'incarnational' Christology. But this was not the only factor. Chapter 3 ('Troeltsch on God, Redemption, and Revelation') also helps to explain this rejection; and Chapter 4 ('Troeltsch and the "Cumulative Case" against Incarnational Christology') maps out, and evaluates, the full range of reasons which com-pelled Troeltsch in this direction, but not without a preliminary scrutiny of the confusing ambiguities of the term 'incarnation'. In the mean time, Troeltsch's more positive Christological stance begins to emerge. Chapter 2 looks at the previously unstudied Christology of his earlier career (with special reference to the two different editions of *The Absoluteness of Christianity*), and charts his eventual break with 'Ritschlianism'. And Chapters 5 and 6 ex-amine the mature Christology of the *Glaubenslehre* and related writings dating roughly from 1909 to 1913, especially the articles for *Religion in Geschichte und Gegenwart*, and two important lectures of 1910 and 1911 ('On the Possibililty of a Liberal Christianity' and 'The Significance of the Historical Existence of Jesus for Faith'). On this basis it becomes possible to give a reasoned criticism of Troeltsch's complete Christological position, based on all the material available, and also, in passing, to correct some of the misplaced criticisms that have been made of it in the past.

Hermann Diem remarked some twenty-five years ago of Troeltsch's Christology that 'It is . . . clear that the questions which Troeltsch had thought out so radically and thoroughly were by no means settled, and must be taken up again somehow or other' (Diem 1959, 9).[3] This book is written in that conviction: that however unwelcome Troeltsch's criticisms of more time-honoured models of Christology may seem to some, and however

---

[3] In Britain the appearance of *The Myth of God Incarnate* (ed. Hick 1977) may be said to have suitably fulfilled Diem's prophecy. Rather astonishingly, considering the parallelism of themes, the authors of that book made very little reference to German liberal Protestantism in general, and none at all to Troeltsch. Some comparisons be-tween the themes of the book and Troeltsch's position can be found in ch. 4.

threatening his challenge to the 'absolute' form of revelation traditionally claimed for Jesus Christ, the issues he raised are not ones which can simply be averted. They do, at the very least, demand facing and answering. Moreover, as we shall see, the results are by no means all negative: the turn to 'social psychology' as a Christological tool is not, we shall argue, a reductionist counsel of despair, but a move of great positive potential, and one which still remains to be worked through fully and systematically. Far from reducing Christ to a time-bound prophet of merely contingent historical interest (and many wrongly assume that this is what he did), Troeltsch in fact suggested a mode of apprehension of Christ that was both spiritually and imaginatively enriching, and yet also compatible with the relativism he felt bound to espouse philosophically.

Thus, although Troeltsch was clearly writing in a context rather different from our own, his Christological reflections still repay study: his labours on the topic of relativism, his various reasons for rejecting a traditional 'incarnational' Christology, his awareness of the challenges of the 'other' world religions, his seminal insights into the psychological and social ramifications of Christology, and so too the shape and limitations of his own Christological alternative—all these remain worthy of critical reflection, and indeed highly instructive for the making of Christology today.

I

The Nature of Troeltsch's Relativism

TROELTSCH'S work has come to be regarded by theologians as a kind of symbol of serious engagement with problems of history, and especially those of 'historical relativism'. The 'shadow of Ernst Troeltsch' has justly been said to haunt all contemporary attempts to clarify the relation between Christian belief and history (Harvey 1967, 3 ff.). It is certainly true that the problem of 'historical relativism' was the dominating intellectual interest of Troeltsch's career, and any treatment of a particular aspect of his thought must take this interest into account. Thus at the outset of this book an overview and analysis of Troeltsch's understanding of this vexed problem will be provided. Later, in Chapter 4, it will be demonstrated how the shape of Troeltsch's Christology was deeply affected by his 'relativism'.

But 'relativism' is a highly ambiguous word: what, for instance, are the precise meanings of 'historical relativism', 'cultural relativism', 'historicism', and so on, and how are they logically interconnected? Since all these terms have themselves been used in a variety of ways, there are no agreed definitions with which to proceed, and the picture is confused. Further complexities arise in Troeltsch's case, and for two reasons: firstly because Troeltsch developed and changed his position in the course of his career; and secondly because he himself failed on occasions (as we shall show) to separate types of relativism which are logically distinct.

The object of this chapter is none the less to try to delineate the precise nature of Troeltsch's position. This will be attempted first by developing a scheme of distinguishable types of relativism, and second by using this scheme to judge the nature and coherence of the claims canvassed by Troeltsch at different times. What will not be attempted here, however, is any definitive conclusion about the 'success' or 'failure' of Troeltsch's programme *in toto*; such conclusions are a commonplace of Troeltsch research,[1] but very often judgement is passed without clear

---

1 See e.g. Bodenstein 1959,esp. 206–9; Reist 1966, 197–201; Klapwijk 1970, esp. 443–9.

analytical reflection on the nature of Troeltsch's views. Even the literature in English is fairly liberally dotted with reiterations of the language and arguments of *Der Historismus und seine Probleme* (*GS* iii. 1922), some good, some bad.[2] But what they all lack, unfortunately, is the propensity to step back from Troeltsch's own mode of expression to a position where a precise philosophical analysis of what is being claimed can be made. The provision of that sort of analysis is the (relatively modest) aim of this chapter. The broader claim, going on from there, is that it is only against this backdrop that the major constraints and influences on Troeltsch's Christology can be assessed adequately.

Before embarking on any of this, however, it is only fair to set Troeltsch in his own historical context by noting something of the variety of meanings already ascribed to the encompassing term *Historismus* in the period in which Troeltsch himself wrote on the subject. A considerable amount of research has been done on this recently by intellectual historians, and the results need only be summarized here. It is clear from the examples given by Georg Iggers,[3] among others,[4] that the word *Historismus* could apply to at least four distinct areas, not always clearly distinguished: it could connote a particular *methodology* for historical work; it could suggest something about the possibility of knowledge in general (an *epistemological* thesis); it could make a variety of *metaphysical* claims; or it could consist primarily of an *ethical* viewpoint. We may cite just a few examples. Meinecke's use, for instance, focuses primarily on a methodological issue. *Historismus* implies an 'individualizing' rather than a 'generalizing' approach to history: it rejects the positivist attempt to subsume historical data under scientific laws of regularity. But as such, according to Meinecke, it represents 'one of the greatest intellectual revolutions that has ever taken place in Western thought'.[5] As Meinecke was perhaps more aware than others, what might start

---

[2] The best (unfortunately unpublished) is Dyson 1968. Also useful and clear, but briefer, are Ogletree 1965; and sections in Iggers 1968, and Dyson 1969 and 1974. Reist 1966 is probably better known but dreadfully unclear at points.

[3] See Iggers 1968, *passim* but esp. 287–90; and id. 1973.

[4] e.g. in English: Dyson 1968, 32–68; Lee and Beck 1953–4; Rand 1964; Meyerhoff 1959, esp. 1–25; and Richardson 1964, 104 n. 3, who distinguishes eight possible meanings of 'historicism'. The most recent, and comprehensive, survey of the meanings of 'historicism' is however in Dutch: Klapwijk 1970, 1–50, esp. 45–50.

[5] Meinecke 1972, liv–lv.

as a methodology for historians could easily be taken to imply much more far-reaching consequences. A methodological view could spill over, for instance, into a metaphysical one (Meinecke 1972, xlix–l). Iggers cites an unusually early example (from 1848) of a definition of *Historismus*, as a purely metaphysical position: *Historismus*, according to Braniss, is the view that rejects the thesis of an unchanging 'Being' as the essence of reality.[6] But *Historismus* could later also be used to describe a great variety of metaphysical theses: it could simply mean that everything (unrestrictedly) was subject to change, or it could imply with that that everything in history was 'individual' or 'unique' in some sense;[7] it could further mean that, despite the appearance of flux and change in history, general 'ideas' could be seen to be knitting the process together.[8] But the optimistic interpretation could be challenged by a very different, and rival, one, which introduced the specifically ethical definition of *Historismus*. Iggers gives an early citation from Eugen Dühring (1866) in which *Historismus* is attacked as renouncing all 'convictions and principles'. This is a form of ethical relativism. Perhaps not surprisingly, it has been shown that this pessimistic definition was canvassed far more widely in the period following the Great War of 1914–18, and this no doubt partly explains why the subject has often since then been approached with a mixture of contempt and fear.

Merely these few brief examples will make it clear that the four areas I have distinguished (those of historical method, metaphysics, ethics, and epistemology) were far from being kept separate in the minds of nineteenth-century protagonists of *Historismus*. Metaphysical themes lurk in what appear to be attitudes merely to historical method or ethics. Further, the failure to spell out the precise epistemological consequence of the various understandings of *Historismus* is the most striking feature of all. Let us take a preliminary look at Troeltsch's own (most explicit) definition of *Historismus* as an example. *Historismus*, he says, is

---

[6] Cited in Iggers 1973, 456–7. Iggers makes a point of refuting the common assumption that the term *Historismus* originated only in the late 19th cent: 'In fact the term is considerably older and was well established in Germany by the middle of the nineteenth century.'

[7] See the citations in Lee and Beck 1953–4, 571.

[8] An early example of *Historismus* so defined is again given in Iggers 1973, 457: in 1850 I. H. Fichte (the son of the philosopher) described 'true historicism' as seeking 'the practical ideas which operate everywhere in human consciousness'.

'the fundamental historicizing (*Historisierung*) of all our thoughts about man, his culture, and his values' (*GS* iii. 102), or again, 'the fundamental historicizing of our knowledge and thought' (ibid. 9). This is clearly intended as the definition of a quite general attitude to the world (*Weltanschauung*); but what epistemological claim is it making, and how does the epistemological stance connect with the ethical claim about the 'historicizing' of *values*? Troeltsch's vagueness, as we have seen, was characteristic of most of his contemporaries' conceptions of *Historismus*, so we cannot chide him too strongly. None the less, in order to lay the groundwork for an assessment of Troeltsch's relativism today it is crucial to press for more clarity in the epistemological area; and to aid this we shall now suggest a schema of different possible kinds of 'relativism', giving particular attention to relativism as an epistemological thesis, and providing some illustrations from current exponents of relativism in its various forms.[9]

I

What would clearly be impractical would be to try to list every conceivable kind of relativism. The alternative, and more manageable, procedure that I offer here is that of noting five areas of possible variation for any thesis of relativism. Thus I aim to provide five tests by which we, as interpreters, may discover what sort of relativism is being canvassed in any given case.

1. The first area of variation is the most crucial, because, among other things, it enables us to distinguish between true cases of relativism and only apparent cases. Let me call this the variable concerning the *status* of any given form of 'relativism'. First here I want to note (and then set on one side) certain positions which are commonly assumed to be forms of relativism, but which on closer inspection turn out to be something different and indeed not worthy of further philosophical concern. An off-the-

---

[9] The classificatory exercise which follows owes much to discussion and correspondence with Jack W. Meiland and Joseph Runzo, whose influence and help I gratefully acknowledge (and whose recent work, ed. Meiland and Krausz 1982, and Runzo 1986, may also serve as excellent introductions to the problems of relativism). This section of the chapter originally appeared as part of my article 'Theology and Cultural Relativism: What is the Problem?' (Coakley 1979, see 224–36), which goes on to apply these tools of analysis to various confusions about relativism in recent British theology.

cuff, or popular, definition of 'relativism', for instance, might well be that it is the view that 'truth is relative to a context'. But this is vastly ambiguous. What different sorts of claims might shelter under this (umbrella) definition, and what differing status might they have? Some may turn out, on closer inspection, to be something quite innocuous, in the sense of philosophically un-controversial; let me call this different, and uncontroversial, thing 'relationism'.[10]

Consider, under this heading, three truisms. There is, first, the truism that certain propositions that are true today, or true here in Lancaster, may not be true tomorrow or indeed true to-day in Gretna Green (or where you will). Let me, for the sake of a tag, call this the 'truism of context'. At the moment it is true, for instance, that there are more white people in the United Kingdom than black. But it is quite conceivable that that position may not hold in two hundred years' time. Truths about popula-tion *relate to* different circumstances; but this is indisputable and clearly no thesis of relativism is implied. A second truism that might however be more easily confused with relativism is this: circumstances often lead people to make statements which they believe to be true at the time, but which later turn out to be erroneous. The mistake can often partly, or even wholly, be ex-plained in terms of the *relationship* between the errant belief and the prevailing circumstances. But again no thesis of relativism follows. Let me call this the 'truism of the development of knowledge'. Maurice Wiles, for example, to take a case from cur-rent British theology, seems to be more of a 'relationist' in this sense about Christian doctrinal truths than a relativist proper. For he argues in *The Making of Christian Doctrine*, for instance, that the early Fathers made mistakes (albeit understandable ones, in their cultural and philosophical milieu) and that we are now in a better position to see the truth about the doctrine of the Trinity, for example, than they were.[11] Thus, however much Wiles is

---

[10] It will be clear, I hope, that I am using the term 'relationism' differently from Karl Mannheim's use in *Ideology and Utopia* (Mannheim 1936, esp. 78 f.).

[11] See Wiles 1967, 159: '. . . I have suggested a number of points at which the reasoning used [by the Fathers] seems to me to be open to serious criticism. . . . few will, I imagine, be prepared to claim that the reasoning of the Fathers in these matters is wholly free from blemish.' Wiles's position is not without ambiguity, however, because there are occasions when he can sound like a relativist proper, e.g. ibid. 158: 'To suggest that it represents a failure in thought is to suggest that the Fathers should have been other people than they were or indeed could have been.'

sympathetically aware of the cultural restraints which made the Fathers argue as they did, he is not necessarily a relativist. He is simply stating how the Fathers' errant beliefs were *related* to their particular frameworks.

A final truism, which again does not involve relativism, I shall call the 'truism of relatedness'. This is just the obvious fact that all truths are related to some sort of context or another. It is true, for instance, that I live near the gasworks, and this is related (among many other things) to the fact that I earn only a modest salary as a junior lecturer. Everything is related to something. But this, again, is indisputable and must not be confused with the (much disputed) thesis of relativism.

Further, and finally, we must be careful not to confuse a particular *methodology* commonly espoused in the social sciences with relativism proper. This is what I shall choose to call the 'methodology of relationism', although I am aware that this position is quite commonly (and to my mind confusingly) dubbed 'relativism'. This methodology is founded on the insistence that social or historical or religious phenomena be studied at least in the first instance in their own terms. What follows from this is the stricture that we should not, for instance, rush in with Frazerian arrogance and denounce 'primitive' societies' belief in magic before we have looked to see what *they* think magic is; or again, that we should not assume when doing sociological analyses of religion that religious beliefs are fundamentally erroneous and reducible to instances of social pressure of one sort or another.[12] Now it is crucial to note that what we are discussing here is a methodological point; it is the demand for sympathetic understanding of alien material. It is what Dilthey was after in his doctrines of *Verstehen* and *Nacherleben* (Dilthey 1927, 191 ff.); it is what Collingwood more questionably required in his insistence that the historian should actually 're-enact' the thought of the past figure he studies (Collingwood 1946, 282 ff.); and it is similar again to the suggestion of Ninian Smart (following Husserl and van der Leeuw) that value judgements be 'bracketed' in the phenomenological study of religion (Smart 1973, 32 ff., 56 ff.). But none of these methodological stances inexorably leads to relativism proper, although it must be admitted that practitioners

---

[12] See Hamnett 1973, who urges this point against much current sociology of religion.

of a relationist method such as this often find themselves lured towards relativism.

Thus, although we have seen that all these forms of 'relationism' as just described could subscribe to the vague proposition, offered above, that 'truth is relative to a context', I propose that we reserve the title 'relativism' itself for something more controversial. What then is 'relativism proper'?

In its epistemological form, this more controversial position, which I suggest we call 'epistemological relativism' (i.e. relativism about knowledge), has the following logical structure: 'proposition p is actually "true"[13] (not, note, merely thought true) relative to, or in virtue of, framework f'. The crucial defining characteristic here is the idea that (for the epistemological relativist) truths are to one degree or another actively *constituted* by the prevailing framework, context, or paradigm; and that is what truths are on this view: intra-theoretic truths. It is not just (as in the case of 'the truism of relatedness') that truths are arrived at against a particular backcloth; nor is it (as in 'the truism of the development of knowledge') that certain things are—perhaps wrongly—thought true because of the prevailing context. Rather truth is, actually and constitutively, relative to a framework; and since the relativist does not believe that all can share the same framework, nor that there is any privileged position available from which absolute truth may be surveyed (because relativistic truths *are* intra-theoretic), it follows that there is the possibility, though not the strict necessity, that truths from different frameworks may be disjunctive or contradictory. This then is 'epistemological relativism' on my definition.

Some examples will help to give this substance. Peter Winch, I would argue, is an example of one who in the realm of social science has slid into 'epistemological relativism' as a result of his commitment to what I have called the 'methodology of relationism'. Thus in his *The Idea of a Social Science* his primary concern is methodological:

A psychoanalyst who wished to give an account of . . . neuroses amongst . . . the Trobriand Islanders could not just apply without further reflection the concepts developed by Freud for situations arising in our own

---

[13] I retain inverted commas here because (as we shall discuss below) 'truth' may be understood in a variety of ways by the relativist.

society. He would have first to investigate such things as the idea of fatherhood amongst the islanders and take into account any relevant aspects in which their idea differed from that current in his own society. (Winch 1958, 90).

So far so good. But Winch makes a move into a different position when he declares that the social scientist should at no point obtrude his own conception of truth on to the alien material he interprets.[14] The material will have its own inherent concept of truth or rationality, he argues, and that the interpreter must abide by, even if it is not his own. The latter position (made most explicit in his essay 'Understanding a Primitive Society') is a form of 'epistemological relativism'. The classic case here is Zande magic. Zande magic, or so Winch implies, is 'true' *for* the Azande,[15] and the European observer is in no position to declare it untrue by misapplying his alien notion of scientific truth.

Let us take one more example of epistemological relativism, this time from the realm of philosophy of science. T. S. Kuhn and P. Feyerabend, for instance, argue that scientific truths are 'paradigm-dependent', that is, that truths established in scientific activity are 'true' only in virtue of the paradigmatic assumptions on which the particular research is conducted. There is, according to these two exponents, no 'neutral observation language' by which one may win over a scientist from one paradigm to another on objective rational grounds. Going from one paradigm to another is more like a conversion experience; and thus, as Kuhn puts it, 'If I am right, then "truth" may, like "proof" be a term with only intra-theoretic applications' (ed. Lakatos and Musgrave 1970, 226).

Such then is what I mean by 'epistemological relativism', something to be clearly distinguished from the truisms we have

---

[14] See Winch 1958, 87, for example, which appears to make this move. More explicitly, see Winch's essay 'Understanding a Primitive Society' in ed. Wilson 1970, esp. 89, 91.

[15] Winch's position here is not without ambiguities. On my analysis, he appears to be juggling with three possible relativistic notions of truth: (*a*) a coherence theory, which leaves no room for checking with an external reality; see Winch 1958, 15, and his later reply to I. C. Jarvie in ed. Borger and Cioffi 1970, 257–8; (*b*) a modified form of the correspondence theory of truth, whereby a society's concepts significantly *structure* the input from outside, but a form of checking is possible; see ed. Wilson 1970, esp. 81, 82, 83, 90, 94; and (*c*) truth (especially in the case of magic) as practical *efficacy*; see ibid. 103 ff. On this last view magic is not a hypothesis about a state of affairs (ibid. 103), but a 'form of expression' to help one make 'sense of human life' (ibid. 106).

considered under the heading 'relationism'. But also to be distinguished from it (and this is our last point under this first heading of relativism's status) are various *metaphysical* theses which sometimes also shelter under the title of 'relativism'. One such metaphysical thesis (which does not necessarily imply a concomitant commitment to epistemological relativism) is the view that all historical occurrences are irreducibly unique and individual. Troeltsch, as we shall shortly see, held this view, and in the earlier part of his career called it 'relativity'. But the thesis of 'relativity', in this rather specific, metaphysical sense, should not be confused with the epistemological thesis of relativism; and although many commentators assume, in Troeltsch's case, that the two must have always gone together, we shall show in due course that there is reason to doubt this.

Another metaphysical theory, finally, which is sometimes, but not always, held alongside epistemological relativism may be called 'perspectivism'. When used to undergrid a concomitant form of relativism, perspectivism is a metaphysical substructure designed to explain how truths from different frameworks (which may well be disjunctive) fit together. One form of the theory is well evoked (though not without some ambiguity) by the story of seven blind Indians all grasping different bits of an elephant. Each of the seven claims about the elephant is, as it turns out, true. Each is true about an aspect, or *perspective*, of the elephant's anatomy. But if you happen to be one of the blind men, then your bit of 'truth' about the elephant is at least in prima-facie contradiction with your fellow blind men's constructions. What is true about the tail is not (apparently) true about the left tusk, but both claims turn out to a sighted person to be true perspectives of the elephant as a whole.

But not every form of perspectivism assumes that different parts of reality (or, in this case, of the elephant) are being grasped from different perspectives; a distinction gleaned from Nicholas Rescher (see Rescher 1978, 233 ff.) is useful here. What he calls the 'complex reality view' (a subset of perspectivism in our terms) does indeed see reality as consisting of parts, and then claims that the different truths (from different frameworks) give access to different parts of reality. Another possible form of perspectivism, however, is what Rescher calls the 'perspectival reality view'. On this view different truths (again from different frameworks) are seen as truths not just about a part of reality, but about the whole of reality. On this view, then, each perspective is a perspective on the whole of reality, and—it is claimed—'everybody . . . is right from the perspective of his own methodological approach' (Rescher 1978, 235). Now in practical terms what distinguishes the epistemological relativist who does not adopt a form of perspectivisim from one who does is the degree to which he is tolerant of truths forged in other, competing, frameworks. It is often assumed that all relativists are by definition committed to open-minded tolerance of diverse views; but this does not necessarily follow. Only the relativist who also (implicitly or explicitly) holds to some sort of theory of perspectivism is so committed, as will now be clear: it is peculiarly the view of the perspectivist that *all* (relative) truths are in some sense ultimately true.

We have now seen how crucial it is both to be able to distinguish true from only apparent forms of epistemological relativism, and also to recognize various kinds of metaphysical thesis which may be masquerading under the same title. This first, and complex, question of the status of different types of 'relativism' is by far the most tangled of the five variables I wish to expound. We can deal with the four others rather more summarily.

2. The second variable for relativists is this: we must ask in what *sphere*, or realm of discussion, the relativism is deemed to apply. We have so far only discussed the broad logical form of epistemological relativism; now we need to press the relativist further: which truths are you saying are relative? Some examples might be: true historical judgements, truths about human nature, religious truths, hermeneutical or literary truths, or (more radically) truths about perceptions and logic. The last two cases are particularly controversial. The perceptual relativist argues that what is visually true for me may not be for you (or for a New Guinean tribesman, for example). The logical relativist argues that even the most basic laws of logic are intra-theoretic. These particular forms of epistemological relativism may indeed by especially difficult to defend:[16] my point, however, is that not all epistemological relativists may be committed to them:

---

[16] This point is argued with some cogency by Lukes in ed. Wilson 1970, 194–213, esp. 208 ff.

relativism, I suggest, need not be an all-or-nothing affair. We need to beware, then, of anti-relativist critics like Roger Trigg who try to herd all relativists into one category, mistakenly insisting that all relativists must be perceptual relativists and hence (so Trigg argues) committed to ultimately indefensible positions (see Trigg 1973, 14–26, esp. 25). A blanket rejection such as Trigg's rests, of course, on the (Kantian) assumption that all our knowing is structured by, and filtered through, the same fundamental epistemic process; yet it is precisely this contention that the relativist begs to question, and the issue is one that calls for debate: it cannot simply be prejudged in favour of what Rorty has called 'mainstream' or 'systematic' Western philosophy, with its slavish commitment to the 'Kantian grid'.[17]

Likewise, we need to note that, alongside epistemological relativism of various kinds, types of ethical and aesthetic relativism may also be canvassed in a similar logical form (what is ethical (or beautiful) is so in virtue of, or relative to, framework *f*), and it may be that here, too, one form of relativism may be favoured without commitment to others. A recent example of this is provided by Steven Lukes (Lukes 1974, 165–89), who has made out a case for ethical relativism (for in the sphere of morality he says he can find no 'Archimedean point' from which to detect absolute value), but at the same time argues strenuously against a particular form of epistemological relativism.[18] He himself finds a certain prima-facie tension in this disjunction of views (ibid. 185 ff.), but I think he is right to say there is no logical contradiction involved.

Whether ethical relativism is seen merely as a variation on, or subset of, epistemological relativism will of course depend on one's meta-ethical theory. If ethical questions are ultimately questions of fact, then ethical relativism is really just a form of epistemological relativism; whereas if one holds a non-cognitivist view of ethics, then we are talking about a completely different

[17] See Rorty 1980, 367, 364. (Rorty's position, however, more radically calls for the rejection of *any* notion of a 'framework' or filter through which knowledge is processed.)

[18] He in fact calls it 'cognitive relativism': see Lukes 1974, 168 ff. However, his reasons for rejecting it ('I claim that there are conditions of truth, rules of logic and criteria of rationality which are universal and fundamental', ibid. 171) only score against forms of epistemological relativism which (*a*) extend as far as the spheres of logic and perceptions, and (*b*) deny *any* form of correspondence theory of truth.

range of application.[19] The range of application involved becomes particularly difficult to assess, however, in the case of relativism applied to the more general category of 'value', at least as the word was used by German exponents of *Historismus* in the last century. We may perhaps say, though, that 'value relativism' constitutes a more inclusive (and therefore more vague) form of 'ethical relativism' as we have defined it. For a 'value', at least as Troeltsch and some of his forebears and contemporaries in his German tradition of historiography understood it, could be simply or primarily an ethical proposition; but it could in addition, it seems, connote any viewpoint or proposition or activity of potential cultural importance or significance.[20] Talk about 'values' is thus a slippery business; in Troeltsch's case, the sense is often the first, more restricted one, although there are examples too of the more inclusive connotation.[21] But at the least the *logical* form of 'value relativism' is clear enough: 'value v is actually ethical/important/significant relative to, or in virtue of, framework f'.

3. We have argued that it is not intrinsically incoherent for the relativist to restrict his relativism to particular spheres of application. Our third variable now involves some further distinctions within the category of epistemological relativism. For relativism about knowledge can be applied not only to different spheres of study, but also—I would argue—can come in different *strengths*.

---

[19] This point is made by Runzo 1986, 74 n. 35, drawing on Frankena's distinction between 'definist', 'intuitionist', and 'non-cognitivist' meta-ethical theories (in Frankena 1973).

[20] See Iggers 1968, for useful citations on the various usages of the word 'value' by e.g. Dilthey (140 f.), Rickert (152 ff.), Weber (160), and Troeltsch himself (178 ff.). The inclusive sense is particularly obvious in the case of Rickert, who goes so far as to say that '*Every* cultural event (*Kulturvorgänge*) embodies some value recognized by men, for the sake of which it was either brought about or, if it had already come about, is cultivated' (cited in Iggers 1968, 154, my italics).

[21] For examples of the more strictly ethical sense in Troeltsch see e.g. art. 'Historiography' in *ERE* vi. 722ᵃ ('We must interpret history by the degree in which it approximates to ethical values, and at the same time we must derive these ethical values from history') and *GS* iv. 13 ('a theory of cultural values or of ethics'). In contrast, the more inclusive sense is used throughout *The Absoluteness of Christianity* (during a period when Troeltsch was self-admittedly under a strong influence from Rickert). See e.g. *Abs.* 88–90, where it is clear not only that the term 'value' subsumes and includes *religious* truth, but also (ibid. 89) that 'values' are deemed to have an independent existence of their own and to operate as metaphysical forces. For another inclusive use of the term 'value' see 'Essence' 64, where the 'value . . . of Christianity' is taken to mean anything from the history of Christianity 'which is of *importance* for the present and the future' (my italics).

Consider first a weak version of epistemological relativism (let us call it 'plain epistemological relativism'). Here the relativist argues that what *is* true is true in virtue of a framework *f*, but he does not commit himself to saying that even the criteria for truth are so relative. Certain types of 'historical relativism' (though this is another slippery term) fall into this category. Thus, to take a contemporary theologian as an example here, Wolfhart Pannenberg argues that, as the process of history broadens out, historical judgements have continually to be reformulated from new perspectives or frameworks.[22] On these assumptions one might argue, then, that what is true about the French Revolution today is significantly different from what was (actually) true about it in, say, 1790, before some of the further ramifications of its significance could be assessed. Now we notice that this sort of relativism need not imply a different set of *criteria* for detecting historical truth from the different perspectives.

A stronger form of epistemological relativism, then, is one which insists that even the criteria for 'truth', indeed even perhaps the very notions of 'truth' and 'reality' themselves, are internal to the framework or context. To return to Peter Winch, this appears to be his position when he argues in 'Understanding a Primitive Society' that 'what is real and what is unreal shows itself *in* the sense [a particular] language has. Further, both the distinction between the real and the unreal and the concept of agreement with reality themselves belong to our language' (ed. Wilson 1970, 82). Now let us call this stronger position 'criterial epistemological relativism'.[23]

But we must go further and note that yet a stronger version of epistemological relativism sometimes appears to be canvassed by relativists, and this is commonly known as 'incommensurability'. This is the view that certain frameworks have such different notions of truth or rationality that they cannot even

---

[22] Pannenberg urges that it is necessarily part of the historian's task to evaluate the events he studies; hence there is no such thing as a 'brute fact'. See his remarks in ed. Robinson and Cobb 1967, 126–7, and also Pannenberg 1970, 98–100.

[23] Of course the issues about 'criteria for truth' might be taken in more than one way: either as 'what it is to be true' or as 'how to establish what is the case'. Either alternative, if deemed to be 'relative to a framework', would constitute a case of 'criterial relativism'. (It should be noted that Runzo 1986 terms *this* form of relativism 'epistemological relativism', and what I have called 'epistemological relativism' he calls 'cognitive', or 'conceptual', relativism. The distinction is the same, although the terminology is different.)

understand each other. They are rendered incommunicado, as it were, by the failure of their different languages or concepts to mesh with each other in *any* sense.[24] Let us however note two significant things about 'incommensurability': (*a*) it is in the interests of anti-relativists to imply that all relativists hold this thesis, because then they are in a good position to denounce relativism *in toto* as patently absurd (see again, for instance, Trigg 1973, 14–16, 24–5, 152, 165, etc.); and (*b*) it is perfectly true that 'criterial epistemological relativists' such as Winch, Kuhn, and Feyerabend, and even I think D. Z. Phillips in the sphere of religious truth, on occasions appear to be propounding this form of 'incommensurability';[25] but on closer inspection it becomes obvious that none of them can keep it up, even if they want to.[26]

[24] It is only fair to point out that the term 'incommensurability' is used by some to mean something slightly less strong than my definition: 'failure of complete translatability' is then their meaning. This appears to be what Kuhn means by it, for instance (see ed. Lakatos and Musgrave 1970, esp. 266–8), and sometimes Feyerabend, who hovers between the weaker and stronger meanings (see ibid. 219–20, 227–8).

[25] For suggestions of 'incommensurability' in Winch, see ed. Wilson 1970, 8 ('we might well be able to make predictions of great accuracy. . . and still not be able to claim any real understanding of what those people were doing') and ibid. 83 ('what are we to make of the possibility of understanding primitive social institutions . . . ? I do not claim to be able to give a satisfactory answer to [this] question.') For (the earlier) Kuhn, see Kuhn 1962, 149 ('in a sense that I am unable to explicate further, the proponents of competing paradigms practise their trade in different worlds'). For Feyerabend, see again ed. Lakatos and Musgrave 1970, 219 ('succeeding paradigms can be evaluated only with difficulty and . . . may be altogether incomparable'), and also Feyerabend 1975, 271 ff., esp. 284. D. Z. Phillips also occasionally comes close to the thesis of incommensurability: see Phillips 1970, 4 ('the criteria of meaningfulness cannot be found *outside* religion'), and Phillips 1976, 183 ('To say, ''There is no God'' is more like rejecting a whole mode of discourse than expressing an opposite view within one. In saying this . . . questions arise as to whether, if a whole mode of discourse is said to be rejected, a person can be said to understand what he rejects.').

[26] Only Feyerabend, I think, wants to (see again nn. 24, 25), but even he can talk of comparing paradigms in some sense, because it is clear that he thinks it possible for a scientist to understand and weigh the merits of two conflicting theories on a rational basis, even if the theories 'do not share a single statement'. (See his 'Problems of Empiricism', in ed. Colodny 1965, 214). In Kuhn's case, shared goals are provided for competing paradigms, and these obviously provide at least a bridgehead of commensurability between theories (see ed. Lakatos and Musgrave 1970, 261). Winch talks of the importance of the anthropologist 'learning from' other cultures, and making their 'beliefs and practices intelligible to himself and his readers' (ed. Wilson 1970, 106, 78), and this I believe is more truly characteristic of Winch than his occasional flirtations with 'incommensurability'. Likewise, D. Z. Phillips's whole approach is committed to the task of *understanding* the meaning of religious statements: 'It is not the task of the philosopher to decide whether there is a God or not, but to ask what it means to affirm or deny the existence of God' (Phillips 1965, 10); and more recently he has admitted that 'there is no sharp line between belief and unbelief' (Phillips 1976, 187), which rules out the model of sharply demarcated systems of language.

Why? Because this position, as I have defined it, *is* absurd. No two frameworks or paradigms are so bounded that *no* communication or understanding can take place. If that were the case, then presumably we would not even know that the alien framework existed, because it would, literally, be 'beyond our ken'.

Here, then, is a form of relativism which is admittedly indefensible: total incommensurability between frameworks is a nonsense; but this is not to say that we have necessarily dismissed 'criterial epistemological relativism' of some sort. In the sphere of linguistic relativism, for instance, George Steiner's *After Babel* seems to me to score some very telling points against Chomsky in its illustrations of a certain indeterminacy between different languages (see Steiner 1975, esp. 105 ff.). Everyone who has learnt a foreign language knows that some words or concepts will not adequately translate into English. But this remaining 'lack of fit' need not, of course, result in complete mutual incomprehension. Likewise, Quine has discussed in *Word and Object* (Quine 1960, 51 ff.) the putative case of an English-speaker confronting a native whose language he knows not a word of, and attempting communication. This does turn out to be possible, because both can reidentify the same object (a 'rabbit' to us, but 'Gavagai' to the native); none the less we are left uncertain, says Quine, whether the native is actually seeing the same thing. There may be an area of remaining indeterminacy here, despite the fact that some sort of communication is clearly possible. (And indeterminacy, on my terms, would count as a form of 'criterial' relativism.)

4. Our fourth variable concerns the understanding of *truth* being proposed in any case of relativism, and this, as we shall see shortly, is particularly important for a clear understanding of the nature of Troeltsch's position. Let us distinguish here, first, between 'the Truth' (in the sense of an external state of affairs—for clarity's sake I shall here capitalize the 'T') and 'truth' or 'truths' in the sense of true statements enunciated by the knowing subject. When the epistemological relativist talks of 'truth being relative to a framework', it is truth in the latter sense that is in question. But this truth may be understood in a number of ways.

The relativist may, for instance, adopt some sort of 'pragmatist' theory of truth (meaning by 'true' valid, or fruitful, or meaningful, or useful); or he may, instead or in addition, apply a 'coherence' theory of truth (designating as 'true' that which coheres with other 'truths' already accepted). S. J. Tambiah's approach to the anthropologists' debate about magic is a nice instance here (in ed. Horton and Finnegan 1973, 199–229). Magic in 'primitive' societies, he argues, is not to be construed as misplaced pre-scientific activity. Rather, it is *valid* for the participants because (so Tambiah postulates) magical acts are actually equivalent to what J. L. Austin called 'performative' or 'illocutionary' utterances (see Austin 1962). In other words, we are not dealing in the sphere of magic with propositions about states of affairs, because 'Magical acts are ritual acts and ritual acts are in turn performative acts whose positive and creative meaning is missed and whose persuasive validity is misjudged if they are subject to that kind of empirical verification associated with scientific activity' (ed. Horton and Finnegan 1973, 199).

Some types of relativism, then, by appealing to pragmatist or coherence understandings of truth, may circumvent the question of Truth as an external state of affairs altogether.[27] But we should not suppose that this is necessarily the case for all forms of relativism, despite assertions by such as Trigg that relativists are inexorably committed to abandoning any understanding of truth as corresponding to an external state of affairs (see Trigg 1973, 24–6, 162 ff.). For once again Trigg scores only by recourse to caricature. He is certainly right, in my view, to question the viability of a form of relativism in which no distinction at all between 'the world and experience of it' is maintained in any sphere of application, thereby forcing the relativist into a defeated solipsism when challenged to justify his beliefs (see ibid. 165–6). This we can indeed isolate as another extreme, and indefensible, construal of the relativistic option.

But in fact many epistemological relativists do operate with a (modified) form of the correspondence theory of truth, whereby what is true for them *is* true in virtue of an external state of affairs, but mediated through and constitutively affected by the particular 'framework' concerned. On this view it is maintained that there is a three-way relation between the knower, the known, and

---

[27] Rorty 1980 provides the most exciting and sustained argument along these lines, eschewing the epistemological image of 'mirroring' reality altogether, and substituting a Jamesian notion of truth as 'what it is better for us to believe' (see ibid. 10). Suffice it to say here that I cannot concur with Rorty's radical proposal that the notion of an external state of affairs can be disposed of *tout court*.

the 'framework', and that it is only in virtue of the 'framework' (in this case not a universal one as in Kant's epistemology but a variable one) that Truth may to any degree be assimilated and 'truths' thereby constituted. This position, indeed, appears to be that of even quite extreme criterial relativists such as Kuhn and Feyerabend in the vexed area of debate over scientific theory; for it is noticeable that they still make reference to some sort of givenness (albeit inchoate) with which the scientist has to do.[28] In some areas of discourse this approach seems to be at least worthy of serious consideration, and will also, as we shall see, be found useful in analysing Troeltsch's position.

A final point to be made under this heading will also be applicable in Troeltsch's case. We should note that for the relativist (and perspectivist likewise) who does entertain some form of correspondence theory of truth along the lines suggested, the position may be further complicated by larger metaphysical assumptions. That is, it may be asserted that the (external) Truth in question is itself in a process of change and development. This then of course involves the idea of change and variation occurring at two levels—the level of ontology (the developing or changing Truth) and the level of epistemology (the changing or variable 'frameworks').

5. Finally, the fifth variable in this schema for distinguishing types of relativism concerns the notion of *framework* itself. This is perhaps the nub of the problem for any relativist, for it would at least appear reasonable to expect him to provide some clear and convincing account of the 'framework' deemed to be in operation, and thus to distinguish his position, logically from the innocuous forms of 'relationism' which simply allow for the contextualization of all apprehension of truths, morality, and beauty.[29] Again, we are entitled to press the relativist: if you say truth is

[28] Thus Kuhn still refers to 'nature' as something which is in a sense neutral and waiting to be organized, despite his insistence that there is no 'basic vocabulary consisting entirely of words which are attached to nature in ways that are unproblematic and . . . independent of theory' (ed. Lakatos and Musgrave 1970, 267, 266). And Feyerabend says, 'there is still human experience as an actually existing process' which provides a point of reference in the 'selection' of a theory 'even in those cases where a common observation language does not exist' (ed. Colodny 1965, 214).

[29] Davidson 1973-4 (now reprinted in ed. Meiland and Krausz 1982) presents the classic case for the debunking of 'the very idea of a conceptual scheme' (i.e. framework) on the grounds that it is impossible (*a*) to provide clear criteria for distinguishing different such frameworks, or (*b*) to show them to be different from mere 'beliefs'. Hence, or so Davidson argues, the concept collapses into meaninglessness.

relative to a framework, then what exactly is this 'framework'? Is it, say, a language, a scientific theory or paradigm, a temporal horizon, a set of national or cultural characteristics, or perhaps even a collection of personal prejudices? One could go on multiplying possibilities here; but let me just suggest one or two systematic alternatives which are particularly important. First, we should ask who has the 'framework' being discussed: is it a framework built into the mental apparatus of individuals (in which case, which individuals?) or is it a set of social or cultural assumptions (in which case, who, again, is involved?)? Second, is the framework deemed to be a bounded one with clear-cut edges? Or is it open-ended, capable of change and modification, such that one framework may flow into, or overlap with, its successor? Third, is the framework consciously embraced, or is it supposed to be operating at some deeply unconscious level? And fourth (and connectedly), is the framework thought to be freely (as well as consciously) adopted, or is it in some sense deterministically imposed?

Now it is not at all clear, as we shall detect, that Troeltsch answers all these questions adequately.[30] But one response he does not give, to his credit, is to support the deterministic option just alluded to; for to suggest that a prevailing 'cultural' framework entirely determines the thoughts and actions of that culture surely denies the very existence of freedom (unthinkable for Troeltsch) and reduces individuals to cultural automata. Assuming that this does involve a *reductio ad absurdum*, we may identify it as a further, indefensible, form of relativism. Yet of course not all relativists need be committed to this extreme and deterministic understanding of a cultural framework.

I have now completed my task of preparatory definition. My primary intention has been to provide a means of analysing and distinguishing different types of relativism, some of which may be sensible, others not; but I have alluded along the way to at least three such types which are definitely suspect: the strong thesis of 'incommensurability'; the solipsistic sort of relativism that allows

---

[30] Although Troeltsch is certainly culpable on this score, it may indeed prove cogent (*contra* Davidson) to continue to defend the existence of frameworks without being able to provide hard and fast verification as to their exact make-up or the boundaries or demarcations between them: see ed. Meiland and Krausz 1982, 64–5, and Runzo 1986, 51 ff., for a discussion of various recent replies to Davidson on this score.

no notion of the 'given' at all; and the crassly deterministic understanding of a cultural framework. As we turn now to an analysis of Troeltsch's relativism we should note that he is lured into none of these traps. And in general it may be a surprise to find how weak a form his relativism takes.

II

For these purposes we shall examine the status of Troeltsch's relativism in three different phases of his career, picking out illustrative passages from his books and more significant articles, and attempting in each case to distinguish between methodological, epistemological, metaphysical, and ethical propositions. For the first phase we shall give attention to Troeltsch's early articles 'Geschichte und Metaphysik' (*ZTK* 1898) and 'Über historische und dogmatische Methode der Theologie' (*TA* 1900),[31] and also his lectures on *The Absoluteness of Christianity* (1902; 2nd revised edition 1912).

Troeltsch's essay on 'historical and dogmatic method' has been given a lot of prominence in recent discussion and is often referred to as a statement of his 'historical relativism'. It is true that Troeltsch does use the verb *relativieren* frequently in the article; and he describes his own position as involving *Relativierung* and *Relativität*.[32] But it should be noted that he explicity denounces the suggestion that he is espousing *Relativismus*; and one can infer from the context that by this latter term Troeltsch means ethical or value 'scepticism', probably what we would classify as 'criterial' relativism of some sort (*TA* 1900, 103 = *GS* ii. 747). This rejection of *Relativismus* should not surprise us if we take into account an important, but brief, passage in the slightly earlier essay 'Geschichte und Metaphysik'. In the closing pages of that article Troeltsch had implied a distinction between *Historismus* and *Relativismus* (*ZTK* 1898, 68-9). The former, described only vaguely at this stage as seeing the 'ideals of all times . . . as historically conditioned (*bedingte*)', can lead to the

---

[31] Reprinted in *GS* ii. 729-53, where it is wrongly ascribed to the year 1898.

[32] See e.g. *TA* 1900, 94, 107 = *GS* ii. 737, 751. As we shall see, Troeltsch is here referring to his (metaphysical) position on the 'conditioning' and 'interconnectedness' of all historical events.

distinctly dangerous conclusion of the latter, which is described as suffocating all 'productivity' and leading to the undermining of 'simple faith in generally valid norms' (ibid. 68). Again Troeltsch here seems to be primarily worried about ethical paralysis, and is concerned to combat that at all costs. Certainly, then, Troeltsch is not a *value* relativist at the time of writing these two articles. He does admit in the later essay that there are great empirical difficulties in gaining agreement on 'a scale of values', but he believes that 'ultimately the essential uniformity of human nature provides a foundation for consensus in recognizing supreme standards of value and . . . because of this foundation, the consensus will prevail' (*TA* 1900, 102 = *GS* ii. 745-6). There is no doubt, then, that at this period Troeltsch rejects 'value relativism'.

What then is thought so significant or controversial about 'Über historische und dogmatische Methode der Theologie'? As we might expect, Troeltsch's position here involves not just methodological considerations (as his title would imply) but a mixture too of epistemological and metaphysical claims, which we must attempt to unravel. The core of his argument in this essay, as is well known,[33] is his statement of three principles of historical method: first, the 'principle of criticism' (historical work yields only judgements of varying degrees of probability, not of absolute certainty); second, the 'principle of analogy' (historical events are not radically dissimilar from one another);[34]

[33] Among the most influential treatments of these principles are those of Harvey 1967, 14-19, and Pannenberg 1970, 40-50, whose expositions are not however without misleading characteristics. More recently, see Abraham 1982, 92 ff., and (best in my opinion) Apfelbacher 1978, 209 ff.

[34] I phrase this description of 'the principle of analogy' deliberately vaguely, since it is far from clear to me exactly what Troeltsch meant by it. (For the relevant passage see *TA* 1900, 90 = *GS* ii. 732-3.) This is a notoriously difficult paragraph; but it is generally assumed that Troeltsch is here discussing the problem of the miraculous, and specifically of the abrogation of natural law, and that he is ruling out the possibility of the latter a priori. But apart from one (throwaway) reference to the resurrection at the end of the passage in question, I see no particular reason to think that this is the issue Troeltsch has in mind. Even if it is, then I still doubt Pannenberg's interpretation: Troeltsch talks about 'imputing *probability*', and 'of interpreting what is unknown . . . by reference to what is known', and this does not seem to me to suggest an a priori rejection of unparalleled events, but rather a (suitably cautious) attempt to understand them. However, as I see it, the main point of the 'principle of analogy' is an *epistemological* consideration about what (minimally) must be the case for knowledge and understanding of the past to take place at all. And the 'common core of similarity' (*Gleichartigkeit*) which Troeltsch deems to be the necessary condition is surely not, as Pannenberg thinks, a means of signalling the dogmatic rejection of the miraculous, but is rather to be identified with the 'basic consistency of the human spirit'

and third, the 'principle of correlation' (historical events take place in contexts, which condition them, and which they themselves in turn affect). Is there any sense in which one who espouses these principles could be called a 'relativist'? Perhaps it will be useful to distinguish three points here.

1. Troeltsch's 'principle of criticism' certainly implies that historical judgements are subject to revision when new evidence comes up, or when the trustworthiness of old testimony is re-examined (see *TA* 1900, 89 = *GS* ii. 731–2). However, this is a non-controversial point about the method and procedure of historians, and does not imply relativism in the sense that we have defined it.

2. The 'principle of criticism' could, however, also be read as involving one form of 'epistemological relativism' as defined above: some judgements might be subject to revision not simply because of the re-evaluation of testimony, but because from new perspectives or 'frameworks' new truths might be grasped. When Troeltsch states the 'principle of criticism' at the beginning of his article, this further proposition is not made evident. However, the Hegelian metaphysic which he later espouses ('it is indispensable to believe in reason as operative in history and as progressively revealing itself'[35]) suggests that it might be appropriate to infer such a conclusion. For if one believes that Truth of a certain sort is only progressively available through history (a metaphysical proposition) then the correctness of judgements about such Truth will likewise be relative to a historical context (an epistemological proposition). What is not completely clear here, however, is whether these judgements are constitutively affected by the historial perspective or 'framework' in which they are assimilated (this would, on my terms, involve true epistemological relativism), or whether they simply occur against the backcloth of varying historical contexts (in which case this would simply be a form of 'relationism'). On the whole, from what hints we get, I am inclined to favour the former interpreta-

mentioned in the next paragraph. This would then be akin to the point made today by some analytical philosophers of history (see e.g. Walsh 1976, 63 ff.) that the historian must, and does, assume certain basic traits about 'human nature' to be constant when he plies his trade.

[35] *TA* 1900, 102 = *GS* ii. 746.

tion.[36] But it should be underlined that the 'truths' considered in this article are apparently restricted to the religious sphere. Troeltsch does not here (or indeed ever) make a *general* statement of epistemological relativism. Indeed, one of the ways of understanding his 'principle of analogy' in the present article suggests that truths about the natural world at least (that is, natural laws) are constant and not subject to revision. And certainly, as we have already seen, he here believes 'human nature' to have universal and constant characteristics. If then Troeltsch is here making a case for epistemological relativism, it is neither a very strong nor a very conscious one, and it is restricted in application.

3. What then does Troeltsch mean when he says that the historical method 'relativizes all truths by showing their mutual interdependence' (*TA* 1900, 98 = *GS* ii. 741)? This is the point where Troeltsch's methodological prescriptions fade into metaphysical propositions, as is illustrated by the principles of 'analogy' and 'correlation'. Taken together they assert both 'a basic consistency of the human spirit' and also the 'inter-action of all phenomena in the history of civilization' (*TA* 1900, 90 = *GS* ii. 733). Troeltsch himself admits rather late on in the essay that these principles issue from 'the *metaphysical* assumption that all things, including the activities of the human mind, are totally interconnected' (*TA* 1900, 99 = *GS* ii. 742, my italics). The form of this statement is unhelpfully vague (what is meant by 'totally interconnected'?), but its intent, taken in context, is clear. All that Troeltsch wishes to combat by appeal to this metaphysic is the particular sort of 'supernaturalism' espoused by his opponent here, Friedrich Niebergall. According to Troeltsch, Niebergall's ploy is to fence off certain central Christian 'facts' and make them independent from, and unconditioned by, the ordinary flow of history. Thus, when Troeltsch says that historical method 'relativizes all truths' he simply wishes to discount this particular way of artificially (or 'dogmatically') guaranteeing the 'suprahistorical core' of Christian origins. His metaphysic, in contrast,

---

[36] Troeltsch is already talking here about the need to do theology in the context of 'universal history'. This, and his concomitant remark that human activities are (ultimately?) only understandable 'within the context of the most comprehensive whole' (*TA* 1900, 92 = *GS* ii. 734), might well suggest that knowledge *is* constitutively affected by the framework in which it is assimilated; full knowledge (or absolute knowledge), on this view, is nowhere to be found except at the end of history.

visualizes history as a 'web of mutually interacting activities of the human spirit, which are never independent . . . but always interrelated' (*TA* 1900, 92 = *GS* ii. 734). This then is a metaphysical point about the nature of history, made in a polemical context. It is not, however, a thesis of relativism in our sense.

So far, then, Troeltsch's 'relativism' seems extraordinarily mild: he is not a value relativist, and if he is an epistemological relativist, it is only in a weak sense restricted to specifically religious truths. Moreover, his position changes only slightly in *The Absoluteness of Christianity*, as we shall now see. Again, three points need to be distinguished.

1. First it should be mentioned briefly that Troeltsch makes some further methodological statements. At the beginning of the book, for instance, he underlines that historians must set aside any 'naïve' or 'dogmatic' theological conceptions they might harbour; they must develop skills in 'sympathetic understanding'; and they must concern themselves not with laws and predictions but with the unique and individual (*Abs.* 47 ff., 63). All this is equivalent to what we have called the 'methodology of relationism'; no relativism is implied.

2. Further, no relativism (in the way we have defined it) follows from the *metaphysical* thesis that Troeltsch here (as before) calls 'relativity' (*Relativität*).[37] Now, however, he provides a more explicit definition: 'Relativity', he says, 'simply means that all historical phenomena are unique, individual configurations . . .' (*Abs.* 89), and again: 'The modern idea of history . . . knows only concrete individual phenomena, always conditioned by their context' (ibid. 66). Thus 'the historical and the relative are identical' (ibid. 85). This position is not too different from that of 'Über historische und dogmatische Methode', although it does emphasize more strongly the individuality of all historical events. Yet it also balances this new tendency with a more explicit appeal to an 'Absolute' that acts as the unifying force in history. It is claimed that 'absolute, unchanging value . . . exists not within but beyond history' (ibid. 90); none the less the 'universally valid . . . works teleologically within history', and so 'in the

---

[37] As before, too, *Relativität* is contrasted with *Relativismus*, which Troeltsch takes to be the dangerous form of 'scepticism' that can (wrongly) be thought to follow from an understanding of *Relativität*. See *Abs.* 86-7, cf. 89-90.

relative [i.e. in individual historical events] we . . . find a token [*Anbahnung*] of the absolute that transcends history' (ibid. 106). This metaphysic adds up to what James Luther Adams has called a 'relativized Hegelianism' (ibid. 13). On Troeltsch's reading of Hegel, the latter errs in subordinating history to a 'law-structured' universal principle (see ibid. 66). History is not for Troeltsch predetermined by an irreversible plan of development; none the less he believes that there is here a teleological development which may be discerned with the eyes of 'faith' (ibid. 90).[38]

3. The difficulties for the interpreter become severe when it is asked what ramifications this metaphysical construct has for *epistemology* and *valuation*. As so often is the case, Troeltsch himself is not concerned to separate these categories. However, the following statement makes it clear that he is certainly not an unbridled epistemological relativist: 'universal structures of law', he says, do hold 'in the form of physical and anthropological conditions, on the one hand, and in the form of basic psychological drives and sociological laws on the other'.[39] Although this is once again somewhat vague, it is obvious that at least some core truths about human nature and the natural world are deemed constant and of universal applicability.

The main subject under discussion, however, is whether religious truths (and the 'values' that Troeltsch here uses almost as a synonym for such truths) are constant, or instead relative to a context. Does Troeltsch hold a form of epistemological and value relativism here? Unfortunately a clear answer to this cannot be given, largely because the same ambiguity is created by Troeltsch's teleological metaphysic as was found in 'Über historische und dogmatische Methode'. For Troeltsch here, the 'Absolute' (or God) is the repository of all ultimate religious Truth and Value (here conceived as metaphysical states of affairs external to the knowing or valuing subject); but if this religious Truth and Value is only available up to a point at a given time, as Troeltsch claims, then knowledge and value judgements would indeed seem to be relativized by the particular context: one could

---

[38] The appeal to 'faith' here is, as we shall see in ch. 2, a backtracking to a greater admission of methodological subjectivity than Troeltsch had been willing to grant in his two preceding large essays 'Geschichte und Metaphysik' (1898) and 'Über historische und dogmatische Methode der Theologie' (1900).

[39] *Abs.* 63: 'and sociological laws' is added only in the 2nd edn. (1912).

know a truth or recognize a value only partially or restrictedly in any given context or 'framework'. On the other hand, if the partial truth that is grasped is none the less one aspect (or 'token') of an evolving Truth, and if that Truth is itself developing self-consistently (as the teleological metaphysic implies), then it is less clear whether epistemological relativism would be implied. It might be, that is, that a form of metaphysical perspectivism could be held here that did not imply a concomitant thesis of relativism. Deciding on this is made yet more difficult, however, by Troeltsch's insistence that religious truth and value are not exactly known, but rather intuited or grasped in 'faith'.

One may trace the oscillation to and from relativism in Troeltsch's own statements.[40] In the earlier part of the book he appears to hint at at least a form of *value* relativism ('Absolute, unchanging value . . . exists not within history, and can be perceived only in presentiment and faith' (ibid. 90)) and perhaps even to push as far as *criterial* value relativism ('a criterion [for evaluating the religions] is . . . a matter of personal conviction and is in the last analysis admittedly subjective' (ibid. 96)). Statements such as these are a far cry from the confident claim in his earlier article that 'consensus' will prevail on matters of values. But in the latter part of the book a different mood takes over. Troeltsch can confidently conclude that 'The "absoluteness" [of Christianity] to which this inquiry has led us is simply the highest value discernible in history and the certainty of having found the way that leads to perfect truth' (ibid. 117–18). Moreover, the suggestion of criterial value relativism is banished when Troeltsch announces that Christianity is the highest religion because it 'represents the only complete break with the limits and conditions of nature religion', and so on.[41] Here he assumes that there are public and universally agreed criteria by which to judge the relative merits and truth of the world religions.

Granted this confusion—even contradiction—evident in *The Absoluteness of Christianity* (which, despite criticism on this score, Troeltsch made even more vexed in the course of his revision for

---

[40] This ambiguity did not escape Troeltsch's contemporary critics. See Drescher's discussion of this point (1957, 75), citing Eucken's review of *The Absoluteness of Christianity* in *GGA* 1903.

[41] See more fully *Abs.* 112; also 98: the nature of the 'goal' towards which the religions are claimed to be tending 'can be known'.

the second edition[42]), one cannot conclude as easily as Runzo does of the book (1986, 66) that 'It is readily clear that . . . Troeltsch is not a conceptual relativist' and that 'in the absence of any clear or consistent expression of value relativism, it would appear . . . Troeltsch is also not a relativist about value'. Instead, the picture is simply confused: some statements suggest that Troeltsch is moving towards both epistemological and value relativism, at least in the sphere of religious truths and values, while others just as quickly dispel such a suggestion. On balance, though, the whole tenor of the conclusions of the book suggests that proper relativism is not wholeheartedly being espoused here, and that is therefore the predominant impression with which one is left.

In what we may (for these purposes) call Troeltsch's 'middle period', however (roughly up to his move to Berlin in 1915), a more radical approach gradually emerges. We shall not here attempt a comprehensive survey, but focus simply on an important shift in Troeltsch's attitude to (intra-Christian) doctrinal truth during this time.

In 1903 Troeltsch had written a long serialized article for *Die christliche Welt* entitled 'Was heißt, "Wesen des Christentums"?', which was a response in the main to Harnack's very influential lectures on the essence of Christianity (*Das Wesen des Christentums*, 1900; Harnack 1901 in ET). For his second volume of *Gesammelte Schriften*, which appeared in 1913, Troeltsch revised this article. And, almost at the same time, he wrote another essay, 'The Dogmatics of the "Religionsgeschichtliche Schule"' (published in English translation in the *American Journal of Theology* for January 1913), which also discussed the question of the 'essence of Christianity'. What we shall here be concerned to do is extract the most radical statements of relativism from these two articles, and to note, once again, how the clarity of Troeltsch's position is ill affected by a confusion of metaphysical and epistemological statements.

---

[42] In the 2nd edn. (1912) Troeltsch in general moved towards a greater admission of the subjectivity of the claim to Christianity's superiority (see *Abs.* 120, where the central two paragraphs are new additions: Troeltsch here admits that he has moved from scientific discourse to something more like a sermon). But at the same time, and bemusingly, Troeltsch leaves intact the confident claims to Christianity's (publicly demonstrable) superiority already cited.

Particularly after Troeltsch's seventy-odd revisions,[43] the 1913 edition of 'Was heißt, "Wesen des Christentums"?' is a fascinating exposé of Troeltsch's indecision. Should he move to a consistent espousal of epistemological relativism in the case of doctrinal truth, admitting that this might, in principle, lead to a range of disjunctive 'truths'; or should he still attempt to ward off that particular possibility by a continued appeal to a unified teleological metaphysic? The dilemma is the one already familiar from *The Absoluteness of Christianity* but now made all the more acute: either Troeltsch could simply admit that what is (actually) doctrinally true at any time or place is relative to that particular conceptual framework or context, and risk a plethora of mutually incompatible versions of that truth; or he could soften the relativistic blow by appealing to a Rankean 'idea' or 'force' working its way out, self-consistently, within the development of Christianity. Put yet another way, either there are successive 'essences' of Christianity, not necessarily closely similar, let alone identical, but merely in a relationship of 'family resemblance' (to use Wittgensteinian language[44]); or there is, in addition, the appeal to *one* 'essence' of Christianity, albeit a shadowy metaphysical force, which is working its way out in the process of history's development and in some sense unifying all the successive 'essences'.

In fact Troeltsch chose the latter course, and in so doing opted (in our terms) for a form of epistemological relativism complemented by a thesis of metaphysical perspectivism. The combination is not, however, a very comfortable one. On the one hand the essay is full of confident metaphysical assertions such as 'history is ceaselessly striving to realise values which have an objective, inner necessity' ('Essence' 143); and thus, in Christianity's case, 'It has to be possible for us to think of all the manifestations of Christianity as arising in series on the strength of a force or law of development inherent in the basic idea' (ibid. 137–8). On the other hand, there are strong indications of the full acceptance of epistemological relativism where doctrinal truth is concerned. Doctrinal work, as Troeltsch asserted even in the first edition of this article, takes place in a context which constitutively

---

[43] See S. W. Sykes's analysis of the two versions of the article in ed. Clayton 1976, 139–71 (and in résumé, see his note in ed. Morgan and Pye 1977, 180–1).

[44] This parallel is applied illuminatingly in Clayton 1980, 236–48.

affects the outcome; and thus 'to define the essence [of Christianity] is to shape it afresh' (ibid. 162). Even in 1903 he realized what the implications of this might be, admitting that 'the formula for the essence of Christianity can by no means be a simple concept . . . It can only be a complex idea . . . It is necessary . . . to indicate the tension between the elements' (ibid. 154). However, by the time Troeltsch revised this article in 1913 his work for the mammoth *Social Teaching of the Christian Churches* was complete, and he had become all the more aware that such 'essence' definition might produce radically disjunctive results from different standpoints. Thus he now has to assert, for instance, that:

The protestant standpoint as opposed to the catholic, the ecclesiastical as opposed to the individualistic, the sectarian as opposed to the ecclesiastical, the synthesis which views church, sect, and mysticism together: all of these [are] conceptions of the essence . . . from a particular standpoint. (ibid. 141.)

What is happening here, as we see, is the complementation of epistemological relativism with what seems to be perspectivism of the 'complex reality view' type. That is, Troeltsch is making the (metaphysical) assertion that all the varying 'essence' formulations somehow 'correspond to' (see ibid. 141) the real 'essence' of Christianity, which is itself in process of teleological development. The implication seems to be that this correspondence may only be to an *aspect* of the external reality (hence my classification of this as the 'complex reality view'),[45] since, as Troeltsch himself puts it, the external reality is itself very complex, and different apprehensions of it may only grasp it 'one-sidedly' (see ibid. 153–5). However, Troeltsch is adamant about this perspectivism in the 1913 edition: he even adds the sentence '*all* those accommodations and appropriations . . . belong to the essence' (ibid. 155, my italics) to underline the point. But there are, too, signs of strain and embarrassment at the attempt to hold to this perspectivism alongside an admittedly disjunctive form of epistemological

[45] This interpretation may also be suggested by the passage quoted by Köhler (1941, 1) at the opening of his book on Troeltsch: 'Truth is always polymorphous, never monomorphous; it manifests itself in different forms and kinds, not in different degrees'. See also the illuminating closing passage of the 'Historiography' article, *ERE* vi. 722b: 'every epoch has a relative justification, though it must, at the same time, be judged in the light of an absolute end'.

relativism. (The 'essence' of Christianity, he admits, 'must go so far as to bear opposites and tensions within itself', ibid. 153.)

What happens, then, in the *American Journal of Theology* article of the same year, at least in its English form, is that Troeltsch quietly drops the metaphysical perspectivism of 'Was heißt, "Wesen des Christentums"?' and now simply holds to the epistemological relativism alone.[46] In so doing, he tacitly admits that there is no point in searching for some one (externally given) 'essence' of Christianity; rather, each appropriation of Christianity has a truth relative to its context:

> *the essence of Christianity differs in different epochs* . . . This, and not simply the Bible or an ecclesiastical confession must be the conception of essential Christianity underlying modern dogmatics. But this essence is actually *the subjective, personal interpretation and synthesis* which present thinking derives from the entire situation with reference to *actual living issues* and for the purpose of directing future activity. Thus there is involved a general historical feeling and understanding, but also a subjective and creative interpretation and construction. (*AJT* 1913, 13, my italics.)[47]

Implicit in this quotation is another point that might be made here, and which also runs through 'Was heißt, "Wesen des Christentums"?': it becomes obvious that for Troeltsch, epistemological and 'value' relativism belong together in the sphere of Christian doctrine. In 'Was heißt, "Wesen des Christentums"?' he had already described in detail the procedure for deciding on 'essential' Christianity. Detailed and careful historical study (a veritable immersion in all the range of Christian history) must precede evaluation of what is 'essential' today. Moreover, that evaluation must be informed in turn by thoughtful reflection on the contemporary 'living issues'. In short, the method seeks to combine assessments of historical fact

[46] See *AJT* 1913, 11–12: Troeltsch considers the idea of the whole of Christianity being vivified by an 'immanent impelling power' and then rejects it. At most, he says, we can talk in an entirely formal way about Christianity's 'productive power' to respond to new contexts. Note, however, the subtle difference in impression created by the end section that is found in the German only (*GS* ii. 519–24). Troeltsch does here readopt a form of 'perspectivism' (ibid. 520), but simply says that from the limited perspective of today's culture one still hopes to participate to a degree in the 'Absolute'. He does not however any longer use the language of (one) 'essence' of Christianity working its way out through history.

[47] Also see *AJT* 1913, 20–1, and *Chr. Th.* 13: '. . . Christianity is itself a theoretical abstraction. It presents no historical uniformity, but displays a different character in every age.'

with judgements of value. Conclusions about states of affairs (both past and present) lead inexorably to practical application. Doctrinal work embraces both these activities; truth and value cannot ultimately be held apart, although the distinction must be maintained in principle.[48]

We also now see that on this view criteria for 'essential' Christianity in any given context remain constant: the requirements of historical work on the one hand, and of an assessment of present challenges on the other, have to form the basis for value judgements. But the facts to be accounted for in any given case, and the value judgements made in the light of those facts, will vary according to context. Christianity will therefore have many 'essences', many different accounts of doctrinal truth.[49]

Up till now we have detected only traces of epistemological and value relativism in Troeltsch. And these last citations represent a mixed form of epistemological and value relativism which is quite weak: it does not imply the relativity of criteria for evaluating truth or value, and so far our reflections have been restricted to the sphere of doctrinal discussion. As we turn now to the last period of Troeltsch's career, we shall see that at least two, more radical, moves have occurred.[50] First, Troeltsch has developed a general thesis of value relativism (i.e. one not restricted to doctrinal decisions); and second, we find him flirting briefly with a strong form of epistemological relativism, implying not only 'criterial' relativism, but even 'incommensurability'. We shall consider these two developments in turn.

[48] The two occasions when Troeltsch strains to separate the two tasks are to be found in 'Essence' 177–9 (in the 1913 edn. only) and 'Historiography', *ERE* vi. 721[b]. In both cases, however, Troeltsch ends up by admitting that in practice the two tasks cannot be kept separate (even though they should be kept distinct).

[49] It is true that Troeltsch may be using the word 'objective' in a slightly forced sense ('Essence' 166) when he claims that these many different accounts of essential Christianity may all have their 'objectivity'. On the other hand, I cannot concur with Sykes (in ed. Clayton 1976, 157) that all Troeltsch's 'protestations about objectivity become redundant', or with the dismissive remark of Allen 1980, 47, that Troeltsch 'ends finally with an admonition to search one's own experience'. Admittedly the argument in this essay is muddled; but the important criteria that Troeltsch provides for achieving the maximum possible balance and fairness in the task of doctrinal reformation (see 'Essence' 167: there must be a basis in conscientious historical work by those who are professionally competent) seem thoughtful and realistic, and provide an important check on rampant 'subjectivity'.

[50] I am not claiming, of course, that Troeltsch's view on ethical relativism, especially, had not already started to become apparent some time before *Der Historismus und seine Probleme* (see e.g. *ST* 1003 as just one example). His later position on the truth claims of the world religions also began to emerge before *Chr. Th.*: see 'On Poss.' 32[a].

1. We have already cited Troeltsch's definitions of *Historismus* in his large-scale work *Der Historismus und seine Probleme* (1922). What we now must decide is what forms of epistemological or value relativism, if any, are implied by the inclusive statement that 'all thought and knowledge' about 'man, his culture and his values' are 'fundamentally historicized'. It is quite possible, of course, to read this as a mere underlining of what we have called the 'truisms' of 'context' and 'the development of knowledge'. For of course, in these senses, all thought and knowledge are 'historicized': what is true in one historical situation is not true in another, and likewise, what is thought true at one time will be seen as erroneous at another. But from the argument of the book as a whole, it is readily apparent that what concerns Troeltsch primarily is the question of value relativism. The 'crisis' he is considering is one of 'historical values' (*GS* iii. 4; see also ibid. 1–11 in general); and the position he wishes to combat is that of 'unlimited relativism' or 'wretched' (*schlecht*) *Historismus*, as he calls it (ibid. 68; see also 102). It appears that by this he means, in our terminology, 'criterial value relativism': at any rate, it implies the removal of all agreed criteria for arriving at value judgements.[51]

Troeltsch's own response to the 'crisis' set out in *Der Historismus und seine Probleme* has been more than adequately documented in recent secondary literature,[52] and here we shall merely summarize. Put simply, the method already espoused by Troeltsch for identifying the essence of Christianity is here expanded to include all 'cultural values'. Historical study, according to Troeltsch, shows that there are no constant values, or 'principles' of value (*Chr. Th.* 47 ff.), so value relativism must now inevitably be the result. On the other hand, there are criteria for arriving at appropriate value judgements in any given context —for constructing the new 'cultural synthesis', as Troeltsch puts it (*GS* iii. 164 ff. and *passim*). These criteria are upheld by following the method of basing value judgements on historical

---

[51] What Troeltsch most feared was Dilthey's 'anarchy of values': 'In the case of Dilthey . . . the consequence of historicism is scepticism, the tragic sense of life belonging to a highly stimulated mentality which aimlessly moves about in the wealth of historical data' (Troeltsch's 'Adolf von Harnack and Ferdinand Christian von Baur 1921' in Pauck 1968, 109).

[52] See again esp. Bodenstein 1959; Ogletree 1965; Lessing 1965; Reist 1966; Dyson 1968; and (most fully) Klapwijk 1970.

investigation. Subjectivity and moral scepticism can only be avoided by making informed decisions, rooted in a thorough grasp of the historical developments that have moulded European culture up to the present (see esp. ibid. III-18, 703-30). What then Troeltsch is concerned with, as he puts it in his preface, is the '*formation* of a contemporary synthesis of culture *out of historical heirlooms*' (ibid. ix, my italics). The legacy of European traditions must always be accounted for. But in each new situation, a fresh ethical decision has to be made. Values are not simply 'there' (*da*) but in an important sense also 'have to be created' (ibid. 211).

Troeltsch admits the apparent subjectivity[53] of even such an informed approach to ethical judgements; but his attempt to avoid the conclusion that it is nothing but subjective rests on two postulates. On the one hand he appeals to the human faculty of conscience: it is a formal characteristic only (*Chr. Th.* 79)—that is, it does not provide ready-made standards of value—but it is the means whereby an act of decision may be made. Such a decision, according to Troeltsch,

is always and in every case an act which differs according to situation and circumstance . . . It is a relative act, which only realises absolute standards as far as possible, and *bears in its bosom its own absolute quality only in the form of decision by the personal conscience and resolution.* (ibid. 66, my italics.)

Secondly, as may not surprise us, Troeltsch undergirds his value relativism with a metaphysic, and one on the whole remarkably unchanged from that presented in *The Absoluteness of Christianity*. He describes it as a 'metalogic': a form of 'Leibnizian monadology'. The supposition is that each individual finite spirit 'participates intuitively' in the life of the divine spirit (*GS* iii. 677, and see 673-9 in general). This identity between the Absolute and the finite is entirely mysterious,[54] and the metaphysical claim *in toto* is a leap of faith.[55] But only by means of it can an ultimate value be said to be infused into individual value judgements; only

---

[53] See *GS* iii. 79-99. However, here Troeltsch attempts to show — some would object by sheer fiat — that there is none the less a kind of 'objectivity' or 'apriority' granted to such value judgements (*a*) by their being rooted in historical work, and (*b*) by their 'decisiveness' or 'self-certainty'.

[54] *GS* iii. 678: the divine and the human are united 'in a completely unknown way'.

[55] See *Chr. Th.* 67, where Troeltsch likens his metaphysical postulate to the Pauline doctrine of justification by faith.

by means of this 'myth' (which could turn out to be misguided, Troeltsch admits[56]) can fragmented ethical decisions be seen as grounded in the transcendent. What we thus see in *Der Historismus und seine Probleme* is a definite statement of value relativism (though not of criterial value relativism) undergirded and supported by a form of metaphysical perspectivism, a perspectivism however held entirely as an act of faith.

2. In the same book, however, Troeltsch is already moving towards a new form of epistemological relativism, and such as might perhaps suggest the strong thesis of 'incommensurability'. In the last chapter he discusses the problem of how wide a range of application any 'cultural values' can be deemed to have. His conclusion is that 'There is for us only a world history of Europe. The old idea of world history must accept new and more moderate form' (*GS* iii. 708). Even deciding on how European culture should develop is itself a mammoth task, and it is the most expansive one possible for us, since 'we know only ourselves and understand only our own being' (ibid. 709). On the face of it, this might be taken as a statement of 'incommensurability', indicating the impossibility even of meaningful communication between European and other cultures. Does Troeltsch really mean this?

In one of his last essays, 'The Place of Christianity among the World Religions' (*Chr. Th.* 3–35), Troeltsch expands on this theme, but now—as the title suggests—with specific reference to the truth claims of the world religions. His conclusion, in conscious contradiction of his earlier stance in *The Absoluteness of Christianity*, is that Christianity can only be said to be true 'for us':

It is God's countenance as revealed to us; it is the way in which, being what we are, we receive, and react to, the revelation of God . . . It is final and unconditional for us, because we have nothing else, and because in what we have we can recognise the accents of the divine voice. (ibid. 26.)

This is, first, a clear statement of epistemological relativism: Christianity is 'truth for us' (ibid. 34), that is, for the European context. But further Troeltsch goes on to imply at one point that no criteria can be found to judge between the truth and value

---

[56] *GS* iii. 212. Troeltsch here plays on the ambiguity of positive and negative interpretations of the word *Mythos*: see ibid. 213.

claims (which again we notice are taken together) of the world religions:

The question of their several relative values will never be capable of objective determination, since every proof thereof will presuppose the special characteristics of the civilization in which it arises. (ibid. 33.)

Indeed, it seems that Troeltsch may even be retreating to the thesis of 'incommensurability' when he continues:

The conception of personality itself is, for instance, different in the east and in the west, hence arguments starting from it will lead to different conclusions in the two cases. Yet there is *no other concept which could furnish a basis for argument* concerning practical values and truths save this concept of personality. (ibid. 33-4, my italics.)

This might be taken to imply, surely, that there is no remaining bridgehead of communication to save the religions from mutual incomprehension. Yet the consistency of Troeltsch's position must be challenged. For on his own premisses, I shall claim, both 'criterial' relativism and 'incommensurability' are inadmissible. The latter threat can already be dismissed because, as Troeltsch himself remarks in the course of his essay, people (in general) do have a 'capacity for mutual *understanding*' (ibid. 23, my italics). The same point is again conceded by Troeltsch in his excursus into metaphysics at the end of *Der Historismus und seine Probleme*. As Troeltsch here presents it, his 'Leibnizian monadology' is developed first and foremost for an epistemological purpose. It is intended to guarantee that knowledge and understanding of the 'unfamiliar' (*das Fremdseelische*) is really possible. For our knowledge of other cultures and epochs is possible, says Troeltsch, if and only if we dare to believe that all history has an ultimate metaphysical point of unity and identity (*GS* iii. 684; see also ibid. 673). But if this is the case (as Troeltsch here more asserts than argues), and if mutual understanding on a universal scale is deemed possible by him, then surely he himself rules out the thesis of 'incommensurability'.

But so, I think, on his own admission, does he rule out any form of 'criterial' relativism. For he lets slip the remark in his late essay on the world religions that 'I found Buddhism and Brahminism . . . to be really *humane* and *spiritual* religions, capable of appealing in precisely the same way to the inner certitude and devotion of their followers as Christianity . . .' (ibid. 23, my italics).[57] In short, Troeltsch allows here that there might still be appropriately universal criteria for comparing the truth and value claims of the world religions. And if we refer back to *Der Historismus*, we find that it is primarily practical difficulties, not logical ones, that keep Troeltsch from advocating an attempt at 'value syntheses' that apply to a larger context than Europe.[58] Indeed, he stresses most strongly that the drive towards doing 'universal history' is a necessary and inevitable assumption of philosophers of history, at least in theory.[59] At the time of writing *Der Historismus*, however, Troeltsch certainly insisted on a concentration on the European heritage, both because it (then, at least) represented a fairly unified and coherent tradition with relatively little influence from outside, and also because the practical difficulties of attempting a more universal coverage seemed daunting. None the less, what is empirically very difficult (as value and truth comparisons across cultural boundaries must inevitably be) need not be logically impossible. It does not seem then that Troeltsch is really committed to 'criterial relativism'.

So far we have seen that in 'The Place of Christianity among the World Religions', Troeltsch makes the following moves. He reaffirms the value relativism espoused in *Der Historismus*, and he extends this to an epistemological relativism where the truth of the world religions is concerned. What is (actually) religiously true and a value 'for us' may not be so for 'other racial groups, living under entirely different cultural conditions' (*Chr. Th.* 26). Secondly, he occasionally appears to be espousing both 'criterial relativism' and 'incommensurability'. But other statements belie this; on his own premisses Troeltsch need not retreat to these stronger forms of relativism. However, we have not yet got the whole picture. We must mention that Troeltsch again reaffirms

---

[57] Troeltsch also mentions 'the criteria of interior purity and clearness of vision' (*Chr. Th.* 34).

[58] See *GS* iii. 72, e.g.: philosophy of history logically presses out until it includes reference to humanity as a whole ('up to the final boundary, humanity'); but in practical terms this is both impossible, because of the welter of material involved, and also unnecessary for us (according to Troeltsch at the time of writing), because 'Europe' has a distinct cultural identity and history which is relatively detached from other great cultural and religious blocks (see e.g. ibid. 704, 708).

[59] See particularly 'The Ideas of Natural Law and Humanity in World Politics' (1922), an appendix by Troeltsch in Gierke 1957, 217–18. It must be said however that the status of 'universal history' is left hanging somewhat ambiguously in the last chapter of *GS* iii.

the metaphysic sketched in *Der Historismus* in the strongest terms, expressing his view that all the religions may perhaps have a 'common ground in the Divine Spirit', and all may be 'tending in the same direction' (ibid. 32). This is, however, very much a religious postulate of faith, hope and love: 'In our earthly experience the Divine Life is not One, but Many. But to apprehend the One in the Many constitutes the special character of love' (ibid. 35).

In our terminology this position seems to be the form of metaphysical perspectivism that we dubbed the 'perspectival reality view'. That is, each religion is a perspective on the whole of reality; it does not claim only to represent a part. But, according to Troeltsch, all these perspectives ultimately (and mysteriously) correspond to a transcendent metaphysical state of affairs (the 'Divine Life'). It should be noted, then, that the understanding of 'relative truth' espoused here does not do away with the notion of correspondence to an external state of affairs. The perspectivism maintains that. On the other hand, what is noticeable in this article is that Troeltsch does also add a strong appeal to 'truth' in the sense of pragmatic efficacy, or practical validity. It is through Christianity that we have 'become what we are', he says, and no one can deny the 'fruits' of European culture (see ibid. 24–6). This is a significant move, and an important addition to Troeltsch's already complex notion of religious 'truth'.

Have we now accounted for all aspects of Troeltsch's relativism? So far we have noted that by the end of his career Troeltsch held:

1. a value relativism of general applicability (but not, as far as we can see, criterial value relativism);
2. a mixed form of value and epistemological relativism as applied to the sphere of Christian doctrine; and likewise
3. a mixed form of value and epistemological relativism as applied to the sphere of the claims of the world religions.

In neither (2) nor (3) do 'criterial' relativism or 'incommensurability' appear to be involved, although, as we have seen, the evidence in the case of (3) is somewhat ambiguous. To this list we must now add three extra items for discussion, all less clearly emphasized by Troeltsch, and thrown out somewhat *en passant* in

Der Historismus und seine Probleme and *Christian Thought*. All three suggest the possibility of an extra sphere of relativism, but present problems of interpretation.

1. A form of epistemological relativism might seem, at least, to apply for Troeltsch to the truth of historians' judgements. What he says is that a historical object (*Gegenstand*) remains constant, but one can think of 'penetrating it deeper or from different sides' (*GS* iii. 43). I take this to mean that every new historical perspective may reveal a different (true) aspect of a past event; clearly, then, perspectivism is being canvassed here, and of the 'complex reality view' type. What is less unambiguously clear is whether epistemological relativism is also implied. Is it that the historian's conclusions are true only in virtue of (a degree of) correspondence to the external state of affairs (the historical *Gegenstand*); or is it that the framework or perspective also constitutively affects the 'truth' of the historian's judgements? One suspects the latter; but I am not sure that this point is entirely clarified in *Der Historismus*, so anxious is Troeltsch in this context to avoid the charge of complete 'subjectivism'.[60]

2. In *Der Historismus* Troeltsch also drops his earlier claims both for an 'essential uniformity of human nature', and for universally applicable laws of psychology and sociology. He still holds that it is appropriate to draw up such laws; but he underlines that these laws are open to change, precisely because their subject matter, human nature, is itself open to historical change and development. Thus 'it is the historian who shows the prime phenomena of history to the psychologist and sociologist, not the other way round' (ibid. 45–6; see also 35–6, 60, 705–6). Does this loss of a sense of universal truths about anthropology, psychology, and sociology imply any form of relativism? In itself, I think not: it is simply a form of the 'truism of context', stressing the mutability of truths about human nature. This is of course a highly significant change of mind for Troeltsch. But it does not, as far as I can see, involve him in any additional form of epistemological relativism as we have defined it.

3. Finally, the discerning reader will notice in *Christian Thought* Troeltsch's casual remark that 'even the validity of science and

---

[60] Mannheim 1952, 97–108, esp. 105–6, comments on Troeltsch's unclarity on this point, but he puts it down to the failure to explicate more precisely the metaphysic which is undergirding his 'perspectivism'.

logic seemed to exhibit, under different skies and upon different soil, strong individual differences' (*Chr. Th.* 23). Is *this* perhaps a statement of epistemological relativism? If it were, the relativizing of logic, at least, might be claimed to lead to a very strong form of epistemological relativism, even implying 'incommensurability'. For it has been argued, for instance, that if two conceptual systems disagreed about the most basic law of logic (that 'the truth of p excludes the truth of not p') then 'incommensurability' would ensue (Lukes in ed. Wilson 1970, 208 f.). But in fact I think this interpretation of Troeltsch must be discounted. First, where scientific paradigms are concerned, Troeltsch so often refers in his writings to the Copernican revolution, for instance, as the discounting of a previously misguided view of the universe, that we must conclude that a statement of 'relationism', not relativism proper, is here being made.[61] (It is fair, I think, to add that Troeltsch himself did not sufficiently distinguish relationism from epistemological relativism.) Likewise, in the case of logic, had Troeltsch thought that even the most basic of our laws of logic might be denied in some contexts (such indeed as might lead to 'incommensurability' between vying systems) he could hardly have had the faith, expressed in his 'metalogic', that the unfamiliar *can* always be known and understood. Admittedly, it is hard to know exactly where Troeltsch would have stood on this; but in the absence of further expansion on the point, we may conclude that his main aim here is to stress that some societies have developed systems of logic more subtle and complex than have others. That, of course, is a truism. If, however, Troeltsch does intend a statement of epistemological relativism (i.e. 'what is logically valid in one context is not so in another'), then at least it cannot, on his own premises, be so strong a form as to lead to 'incommensurability'.

We have now concluded our survey of the nature of Troeltsch's relativism. We have argued that by the last phase of his career Troeltsch was a value relativist, and an epistemological relativist as regards various specific spheres of truth (Christian doctrinal truth, inter-religious truth, and perhaps historical truth). At the same time he maintained more than one form of metaphysical

---

[61] See e.g. *Gl.* 64: 'We clearly cannot barricade ourselves against the consequences of a Copernican system . . . of necessity the geocentric and anthropocentric picture of things vanishes.'

perspectivism, designed to underpin his relativism and to rescue it from the charge of 'subjectivism'. Having clarified this, I would like to underline, in closing this rather lengthy chapter, some implications that Troeltsch's form of relativism does not entail. First, as we have seen, it does not imply any form of 'incommensurability', and thus is a much weaker (and indeed less controversial) form of relativism than that which has sometimes been suggested in contemporary debate by (for instance) D. Z. Phillips, P. K. Feyerabend, or Peter Winch, in their various fields of expertise. Second, and connectedly, the form of epistemological relativism canvassed by Troeltsch is not unrestricted in application. It does not apply, for instance, to perceptions. And it certainly does not deny the existence of objects in an outside world, as some critics assume all 'relativists' do deny (so Trigg 1983, 2). Therefore, third, it does not reject (a form of) 'correspondence' doctrine of truth. Relative truths do, according to Troeltsch, correspond to an external state of affairs (whether metaphysical or historical) even though it may be a mystery quite how they do so.

The results of our discussion in this chapter, then, show that religious truth on Troeltsch's account is an exceedingly complex and subtle phenomenon. At one level, and to some degree, what is religiously or doctrinally 'true' is true in virtue of its correspondence to an external state of affairs, whether metaphysical (the 'Divine Life') or historical. But its truth is also constitutively affected by the framework, perspective, or context in which it is enunciated (Christianity is true for Christians; defining the essence (for framework f) is shaping it afresh). Other more pragmatic criteria for religious truth occasionally offered by Troeltsch are those of creativity, constructiveness (see *AJT* 1913, 13), and to some extent firmness of conviction (see 'Essence' 166). There is also the generalized appeal to 'fruits' that becomes most explicit in 'The Place of Christianity among the World Religions'. In short, we have here a number of criteria for religious 'truth' which Troeltsch himself deliberately mixes, but never clearly lays out and analyses.

This complicated survey of the nature of Troeltsch's relativism has now set the scene for our discussion of his Christology. How was Troeltsch's Christological position affected by his continuing reflection on the problems of *Historismus*? We shall enumerate the precise ways in which Troeltsch's relativism coloured and shaped his mature Christology in Chapter 4. But for the mean time we must turn back next to a discussion of Troeltsch's early theological writings, and to the hints we get there of the beginnings of his Christological development.

2

Christology in Troeltsch's Early Writings: The Disengagement from 'Ritschlianism'

TROELTSCH'S early theological writings, or, more specifically, his published output up to the time of *The Absoluteness of Christianity* (1902), are generally regarded as the period of his disengagement from the Ritschlian theology in which he had been nurtured at Göttingen.[1] Different commentators have appealed to different moments in Troeltsch's development as decisive for his repudiation of Ritschlian tenets,[2] but in large part their disagreement seems to stem from tacit divergence on the issue of what is decisive for the maintenance of so-called 'Ritschlianism'.[3] What is of interest for our particular concerns, however, is that no one up till now has looked at this material from a specifically Christological point of view. This, then, is the first task of this

---

[1] For Troeltsch's own reflections on his debt to Ritschl see esp. 'Die "kleine Göttinger Fakultät" von 1890' (*CW* 1920); 'Meine Bucher', in *GS* iv. 3–18; and the 'Foreword' to *ST* 19–21. Arguably it is misleading to concentrate too exclusively on Troeltsch's attitude to Ritschl in this period (see ed. Renz and Graf 1982 for contributions on a variety of other teachers and influences); for our Christological concerns, however, this focus is justified.

[2] Bodenstein 1959, 13 ff., for instance, sees this break already coming with *Vernunft und Offenbarung bei Johann Gerhard und Melanchthon* (1891); Rendtorff (in ed. Greschat 1978, 276) sees it beginning in an important sense with 'Die christliche Weltanschauung und die wissenschaftliche Gegenströmungen' (*ZTK* 1893–4); Neibuhr 1924, 12, regards the whole period 1894–1903 as one of Troeltsch's 'reaction against Ritschlianism', but the most 'remarkable' change (ibid. 38) as occurring in 'Die Selbständigkeit der Religion' (*ZTK* 1895–6); Drescher 1957, 47, identifies the years 1895–8 as 'decisive' for the departure from Ritschl, but elsewhere (ed. Clayton 1976, 13–14) also says that 1902, and the production of *The Absoluteness of Christianity*, marks the transition into a new 'period of thought'. The trouble with all such periodizations of Troeltsch's career and thought is that they tend to give the impression of more conscious and consistent changes of direction than in fact occurred (we shall give a — previously uncharted — example of lack of such consistency in this chapter). Thus while appeals to 'phases' in Troeltsch's development undeniably serve useful heuristic purposes, they need to be wielded with caution, and with due regard for the continuing fluidity of Troeltsch's thought.

[3] 'Ritschlianism' is obviously a loose term, often used to encompass views held not only by Albrecht Ritschl, but also by members of his 'school'. On occasions in this chapter it has proved useful to employ the term in this inclusive sense, and then inverted commas are (advisedly) used.

chapter: to chart, in so far as it is possible from relatively scattered and brief remarks, the development of Troeltsch's Christological thought in this period, to indicate some of the possible influences on that development, and to see how his disengagement from Ritschlian traits in Christology correlates with his criticisms of Ritschl and the 'Ritschlian school'[4] in other particulars.

The second task of the chapter is more complex and concerns interpretation of *The Absoluteness of Christianity* itself. The very significant differences between the first and second editions of this influential work are scarcely ever commented on, but are particularly important in any attempt to gauge Troeltsch's Christological thinking. Comparison of the two editions reveals telling changes on many fronts, but where Christology is specifically concerned two somewhat puzzling conclusions emerge: first, that the first edition contains passages that indicate a curious 'back-tracking' into rhetorically enunciated Christology deeply reminiscent of W. Herrmann's work and decidedly out of line with principles already stated by Troeltsch in earlier articles; and second, that the second edition, perhaps even more curiously, while embarrassedly removing or tempering some of these features, leaves others intact and thus in latent contradiction with the work that Troeltsch had in the mean time devoted specifically to Christology.[5] I have thus been led to the paradoxical conclusion that one should treat Troeltsch's best-known work, in both its editions, as something of an aberration where his Christology is concerned, representing a failure of nerve, perhaps, to carry through consistently the assault on Ritschlianism that had begun with his first published work. It is this that leads me to treat even the second edition of *The Absoluteness of Christianity* (produced in 1912) as an adjunct of Troeltsch's 'early' thought, reserving discussion of what I see as his mature and considered Christology (much of which dates from 1910 to 1912) for subsequent chapters. This procedure is, I am aware, chronologically odd, but justification for it can only emerge from the substance of the material itself, to which we now turn.

Troeltsch's conscious departure from certain central

---

[4] For a useful introduction in English to the 'Varieties of Ritschlianism' see Rupp 1977, 15–20.

[5] Particularly important here are, of course, 'On Poss.' (1910), 'Sig. HJ' (1911), and *Gl.* (from lectures now established to have been given in 1912–13: see Wyman 1983, xv, 208 n. 37).

Ritschlian tenets began even with his first publication, *Vernunft und Offenbarung bei Johann Gerhard und Melanchthon* (1891), which had first been produced for his doctorate and then reworked and expanded for his *Habilitationsschrift*. It is easy to overestimate the extent to which this work took any decisive stand against Ritschl; it was, after all, as Drescher rightly highlights (ed. Clayton 1976, 4,), a piece of work on the Reformation era done entirely in the way Ritschl liked his students to proceed—to systematic questions via historical theology. Troeltsch himself, looking back in 1920 to his student days in Göttingen, acknowledges first and foremost the almost oppressive strength of Ritschl's personal influence (clearly he was not someone to cross lightly), but also, more positively, the great love of Reformation studies that he instilled in his devotees.[6] Elsewhere, though, Troeltsch could admit that one of his central disagreements with Ritschl had always been a suspicion that he had wrongly delineated the 'dogmatic tradition in its actual historical sense' (*ST*, 19); and it is in its break with Ritschl's conception of where we may locate the origins of the modern world as we know it that Troeltsch's doctorate is most significant. Troeltsch's historical periodization, then, saw Luther as far more an heir to the medieval world than Ritschl was willing to concede.[7] Moreover, Troeltsch went on to defend Melanchthon's apologetic use of medieval philosophy (on which point Ritschl had criticized him) as an inevitable part of the need for theology at any time to connect with the prevailing philosophical climate and with 'natural man'.[8] Perhaps implicitly, then, or so Bodenstein (1959, 13 ff.) argues, we have even in this first production of Troeltsch's an assault on Ritschl's restriction of the locus of revelation to the 'fact' of Jesus Christ, and an opening up to the realms of reason and metaphysics as also mediatorial of divine activity.

Be that as it may, Troeltsch's next publication, written while he was teaching as an associate professor in Bonn, is a more

[6] *CW* 1920, 282.

[7] See *Vernunft und Offenbarung bei Johann Gerhard und Melanchthon*, 207 f., 212–13; also see Troeltsch's comments when looking back at this work in 1922, *GS* iv. 7. Ritschl's position was in fact a fairly subtle one on this point: he saw Luther as having every intention of breaking with scholastic theology, but not quite fully bringing it off: see e.g. Ritschl 1972, 209.

[8] See *Vernunft und Offenbarung bei Johann Gerhard und Melanchthon*, 1–3, 93 ff., 98 ff., and esp. 101.

telling illustration of how far he had extracted himself from his Ritschlian matrix. 'Die christliche Weltanschauung und die wissenschaftlichen Gegenströmungen' (later incorporated in *GS* ii as 'Die christliche Weltanschauung und ihre Gegenströmungen') is a long article which originally appeared in two instalments in the *ZTK* (1893 and 1894). It represents Troeltsch's first concerted assault on the problem of how to relate Christianity and its claims to the realm of modern scientific and historical thought. The vastness of the topic is typical of what Troeltsch much later described as the sort of 'superhuman problems with which inexperienced youth begins' (*GS* iv. 6). Among the bold strokes that Troeltsch makes here (many of which, frankly, are mere assertions) the following tendencies do suggest some further weakening of Ritschlian influence.

The most important move, first, is that Troeltsch gives some noticeably positive support to the 'history-of-religions'[9] approach to Christianity in his occasional admission, for instance, that Christianity owes much to its original Jewish political and religious background, that it has been subject to 'development', and has been significantly influenced by other, non-Christian, importations (*ZTK* 1894, 226 = *GS* ii. 321). This is a concession whose importance is not to be underestimated from one trained in systematics by Ritschl,[10] but it clearly indicates the competing influence at Göttingen of the historian of religions Paul de Lagarde, whom Troeltsch later described as having pulled him and his friends forcefully in a direction away from Ritschl.[11] Along with this turning towards the 'history-of-religions' approach goes a much more specific embracing of the importance of historical work in general, and with that the realization of the need to understand Christianity in its complete development, not just by restriction to its origins (*ZTK* 1893, 504 f. = *GS* ii. 239).

[9] Troeltsch's friendship with Wilhelm Bousset was particularly important here in developing the ideas proffered at Göttingen by Paul de Lagarde (see *CW* 1920, 282). For a recent reassessment of the make-up of the *religionsgeschichtliche Schule* see the important essay by Graf in ed. Renz and Graf 1982, 235–90.

[10] See e.g. Ritschl's claim in 'Instruction in the Christian Religion' (Ritschl 1972, 221) that Christianity is the only 'perfect' religion, the only one 'within which the perfect knowledge of God is possible'.

[11] See *CW* 1920, 282. Troeltsch's gratitude to Lagarde was expressed in 1913 by the dedication of *GS* ii to him. The introduction, however, makes it plain that Troeltsch was not uncritical of Lagarde, and not least of his anti-Semitism (ibid. ii, p. viii).

Hence, with a particular influence from Ranke clearly acknowledged here (see particularly *ZTK* 1894, 218 = *GS* ii. 313 f.), we
find Troeltsch's essay replete with references to Christianity's
'spirit', 'kernel', or 'principle', and with the question uppermost
in his mind as to how precisely to characterize Christianity in its
total development. There are also, one notices, some fairly fierce,
and not altogether subtle, side-swipes at the crude 'supernaturalism' with which Christianity was identified in its early
forms (*ZTK* 1893, 504, 513; 1894, 176, 222 = *GS* ii. 239, 247, 271,
317), and this is a theme that Troeltsch was later to refine much
more precisely in his attack on contemporary forms of 'supernaturalism'. The attack here, though, can be seen at most as a latent possibility for future criticisms of Ritschlianism. Finally,
however, we do find the thesis that Troeltsch had maintained in
Reformation terms in his dissertation on Melanchthon given
here its corollary: if Luther and Melanchthon were in important
respects still medieval, then Troeltsch could now insist (with
Dilthey, another acknowledged influence at this time[12]) that the
roots of our modern world lie with the Enlightenment, not with
the Reformation. This certainly is a departure from Ritschl, and
in a way is the leitmotif of the whole essay, being the theme with
which it opens and closes (*ZTK* 1893, 495; 1894, 229 ff. = *GS* ii.
229 f., 325 ff.), and signifying for Troeltsch the need for a complete reorganization of theology in the light of the change. A
secondary theme, though only briefly and vaguely stated here in
closing, is that theology must co-operate with the social sciences
in general in the reconstruction that is to be faced (*ZTK* 1894,
229–30 = *GS* ii. 325–6).

If this much sounds like a departure from Ritschl, it is however
not an overstatement to say that in some other respects this essay
still reads like a Ritschlian tract,[13] and this is particularly evident
when we look at what Troeltsch has to say about the assured
superiority of Christianity and its founder (*ZTK* 1894,
224 ff. = *GS* ii. 319 ff.). Troeltsch is unambiguous here and,
though still appealing to Ranke (*ZTK* 1894, 226 = *GS* ii. 321),

[12] See *GS* iv. 8. Siemers (in ed. Renz and Graf 1982, 203–34) has however now thrown
doubt on the real extent of this influence.

[13] Here I concur with the judgement of Drescher, ed. Clayton 1976, 6, although
arguably he underestimates the extent to which Troeltsch's conscious intentions were
otherwise.

shifts into a characteristically Ritschlian gear:[14] Christianity is the final and unsurpassable revelation; it is not simply the climax of a religious development, but something fundamentally new and 'sharply' to be distinguished from Judaism; it is the only 'spiritual and ethical' world religion, which separates it completely from all 'nature-religions'. More significantly, though, for our Christological interests, is how these assertions relate to what Troeltsch wants to say about Jesus. Admittedly it is precisely here (*ZTK* 1894, 226 = *GS* ii. 321) that he makes his concessions to the 'history-of-religions' approach: it is true, he says, that Jesus' teaching reflects the apocalyptic fervour of his times, and in particular the theme of Messianic expectation. But—and this is important for Troeltsch's later deliberations on this point— it is not really Jesus' *preaching* that we need to concentrate on here so much: that, Troeltsch is interestingly willing to concede, can be found paralleled in almost every particular somewhere in contemporary Jewish literature (ibid.). However, what is new (*das Neue*) is the *personal* impact of Jesus, and with it the claim (*Anspruch*) and certainty (*Gewißheit*) of a 'final revelation of God'. Moreover, Jesus' personality is described, with no embarrassment, as 'wunderbar' (miraculous?); and Troeltsch is willing to psychologize about Jesus' Messianic consciousness (without, however, using the characteristically Ritschlian language of Jesus' 'vocation') to the effect that Jesus perceived, in the Messianic form that was culturally to hand, the unique relationship that he had with his Father, and in that relationship was conscious of the 'absolute and invincible revelation of God' which then and now provides Christianity with its real 'depth and power' (*ZTK* 1894, 227 = *GS* ii. 322).

[14] For parallels to these points in Ritschl's own work, see the following passages as examples: for Christianity as the 'perfect moral and spiritual religion' see Ritschl 1966, 3; for Christianity's relation to Judaism see ibid. 455; and for Christ 'setting himself above all the preceding prophets of the Old Testament' see Ritschl 1972, 229; for Christianity's rising above the 'natural' world see Ritschl 1966, 455, 502–3; for the qualitative uniqueness of Jesus and for his 'complete revelation of God' see Ritschl 1972, 230; for the restriction of true revelation to Christ, see Ritschl's appeal to Luther, Ritschl 1966, 212; for the theory of 'value judgements' and the inextricability of faith and subjective commitment or claim see ibid. 204 ff., 212; for the certainty or 'passionate personal conviction' of faith, see ibid. 592. For Ritschl's somewhat ambiguous position on 'miracle' see the useful article by Barnett 1979, esp. 199–200, 207, which deals with Ritschl's early debate on miracle with Eduard Zeller, as well as the relative silence on the issue in *Justification and Reconciliation*.

This passage is worthy of further reflection, because it shows, among other things, that Troeltsch had so far refused to grasp the nettle proffered by Ritschl's son-in-law Johannes Weiss in his celebrated *Jesus' Proclamation of the Kingdom of God* (1892). A slightly defensive footnote here from Troeltsch perhaps has Weiss in mind:[15] what Weiss had underscored (against Ritschl) was that Jesus, in his expectation of a *future* kingdom, was simply wrong about its imminence; and that if we use 'kingdom of God' today in the sense of the present 'religious and ethical fellowship of the children of God' we are, frankly, using it in 'a different sense from Jesus' (Weiss 1971, 135). That Weiss's view was not shared by Troeltsch is evident not only from the passage in hand, but also from his confident characterization of the 'kernel of the gospel' as 'salvation of persons, united with the holy and loving will of God in a kingdom of love' (*ZTK* 1893, 528 = *GS* ii. 261). This, of course, was precisely the sort of description of Christianity that Weiss was objecting could not be traced back to Jesus. In this, then, Troeltsch in 1894 still stands closer to Ritschl than to Weiss, though by the time he revised this article for *GS* ii (making some significant additions) he had clearly changed his mind.[16] None the less, despite this unwillingness in 1894 to face the question about Jesus being mistaken about the future kingdom, the spiritualizing tack that Troeltsch takes with regard to Jesus' Messianic consciousness (turning it into an expression of his unique relation of sonship to the Father) is actually paralleled almost exactly in Weiss at one point, and one is almost tempted to postulate a dependence.[17]

[15] *ZTK* 1894, 227 n. 1 = the first sentence of *GS* ii. 322 n. 19 (except 'in der gegenwärtigen Verhandlungen über die Eschatologie Jesu' is changed to 'in der *damaligen* Verhandlungen . . .').

[16] See again *GS* ii. 322 n. 19, where all but the first sentence is newly added in 1913. Troeltsch now fully admits that the 'decisive' contents of the gospel are shot through with apocalyptic expectation of the end of the world, and that this raised an acute problem of adaptation for later Christianity when the expectation had died away. Troeltsch also mentions William Wrede, but pronounces far-fetched Wrede's view that Jesus himself did not think in terms of Messiahship. Elsewhere in the essay, too, Troeltsch makes new additions stressing Jesus' eschatological convictions: see *GS* ii. 290, 291; cf. *ZTK* 1894, 195, 196.

[17] See the somewhat uncharacteristic passage in Weiss 1971, 128; 'Jesus' messianic self-consciousness is only understandable within the framework of his consciousness of sonship. He could understand this commission from God and make it his own only because . . . his soul in some way lived in God in a fashion analogous to nothing we can imagine. . . . He alone may and can believe himself to be the Messiah in truth and

What is clear, I hope, from this discussion of 'Die christliche Weltanschauung und ihre Gegenströmungen' is that Troeltsch can scarcely be said to have moved very far from his Ritschlian background on substantive issues such as the exclusive superiority of Christianity or the 'uniqueness' and 'finality' of Christ, and, as Drescher rightly points out (ed. Clayton 1976, 6) this view is borne out by other hints: the language of Christianity's 'claim' (e.g. *ZTK* 1894, 226 = *GS* ii. 321), the tendency to appeal to inner experience (*ZTK* 1893, 494 = *GS* ii. 228–9), the distinction between theoretical and practical value judgements (*ZTK* 1893, 505 = *GS* ii. 240), and the strong influence from the philosophy of Lotze evident in the priority Troeltsch gives to mind over nature (*ZTK* 1893, 508, 512 = *GS* ii. 242, 246).[18] It is also fairly frankly acknowledged in the introductory footnote Troeltsch wrote for this article when he revised it for *GS* ii. Here he admits that the article represents a period in which his main philosophical influences were Dilthey and Lotze, and his evaluation of Christianity as 'entirely unique' was something 'taken over from Schleiermacher and Ritschl' (*GS* ii. 227 n. 11). Both tendencies he now (in 1913) rejects.

In so far as any Christological position can be inferred from Troeltsch's next major publication ('Religion and Kirche', *Preußische Jahrbücher* 1895) the picture has not yet changed. The essay might be described, with hindsight, as a first attempt at the issues that Troeltsch was later to attack in *The Social Teaching*: the relationship between the social and the individual aspects of Christianity. The two brief allusions to Jesus however show no signs of any modification of Troeltsch's Christological views: Jesus' personality is again described as miraculous (*wunderbar*) (*PJ* 1895, 227 = *GS* ii. 157), and the note of eschatological imminence in Jesus' message is toned down by an internalized interpretation of the gospel message: 'Jesus founded no church. He only sowed the seed which would bring forth fruit in silent hearts resigned to God's will' (*PJ* 1895, 230 = *GS* ii. 160). Again, however, it is an addition made precisely here in 1913 which is significant for the lessons which by then Troeltsch had

without fanaticism, to whom it is in some measure natural that he should be entrusted with all things by God because he has opened and offered his soul to God without reservation.'

[18] See *GS* iv. 5 for Troeltsch's admission that for him 'Lotze was the controlling spirit at first' philosophically.

assimilated, especially, one suspects, from his reading of Loisy and Schweitzer.[19] In 1913 he added, extending the sentence: 'and chose a small circle of messengers who would awaken and collect the true believers for the great hour of the coming kingdom of God . . .' (*GS* ii 160).

It is also interesting to note that at about the time Troeltsch was writing 'Religion und Kirche' he was also corresponding with his close friend Wilhelm Bousset precisely on the issue of Jesus' eschatological expectations, and from this we glean the (somewhat a priori) reasons for which Troeltsch had dismissed Weiss's book. Troeltsch here charges Weiss with turning Jesus into a 'ghastly enthusiast' (*ein grauenhafter Schwärmer*), and comments that he finds 'psychologically absurd' the idea that Jesus could identify himself with a coming Son of Man. Instead, he refers approvingly to a book by Eugen Ehrhardt which tries to dissociate Jesus from apocalyptic ideas, or at most sees them used as a means to an end—'the strengthening of the inner-personal relationship with God'; similarly Troeltsch prefers to see Messiahship as only passively accepted by Jesus, again for the sake of something else—the building up of the kingdom of God. Only this solution, he says, is 'psychologically comprehensible' (Dinkler-von Schubert 1976, 28–9). The assertion is explicitly made here, in fact, that Jesus' thought was only 'very loosely' connected with Messianism (ibid. 28), and this represents something of a modification of the position in 'Die christliche

---

[19] This is not to underestimate the significance of Bousset's influence and friendship, as we shall see, nor of his reading of Weiss. But there is evidence that encountering Loisy's and Schweitzer's work made a special impression on Troeltsch. He had originally been encouraged to read Loisy by von Hügel (see letter of 10 Mar. 1903 in ed. Apfelbacher and Neuner 1974, 63 ff.) and was sufficiently impressed by him to reiterate some of his criticisms of Harnack in his article on the question of Christianity's essence (originally in *CW* 1903). In the first edition of this article Troeltsch already objected, against Harnack (and with Loisy), that 'the recognition of the essence cannot be exclusively based on the original time and on the preaching of Jesus' ('Essence' 151 = *CW* 1903, 581), and that *Jesus'* central message, 'the approaching end of the world and the coming Kingdom', cannot be what is now 'essential for us' ('Essence' 153 = *CW* 1903, 582). The difficulty of accommodating Jesus' one-sided eschatological perspective with our present one is even more emphasized in the rev. ed. of this article for *GS* ii (1913): see 'Essence' 149. In the mean time, Troeltsch had also read Schweitzer's *Von Reimarus zu Wrede* (see Schweitzer 1966), and clearly this had had a considerable impact: see 'Half C.' 71 n. 5, a note added only for the *GS* ii version. Probably, then, Troeltsch had read this book between 1909 and 1913, i.e. between the original appearance of 'Rückblick auf ein halbes Jahrhundert der theologischen Wissenschaft' (*ZWT* 1909) and its inclusion in *GS* ii (1913).

Weltanschauung', where Jesus' Messianic consciousness was freely accepted but given a spiritualized interpretation. On burning New Testament issues such as these, the Bousset correspondence well illustrates (as we shall see again shortly) the considerable extent to which Troeltsch's thought was in flux at this time.

With the appearance of his next publication, the important essay 'Die Selbständigkeit der Religion' (*ZTK* 1895-6), Troeltsch's position does, on any account, take a much more self-conscious departure from Ritschlianism, and this has led more than one exponent to see this as the crucial moment of disengagement.[20] Certainly on the methodological issue of how to study religion, Troeltsch here explicitly accuses the Ritschlian school, and its theology of 'claim', of a fatal 'subjectivism' (*ZTK* 1896, 91 n. 1). Troeltsch instead appears to have turned back to Schleiermacher for inspiration (for a hint of this see *ZTK* 1895, 367-8).[21] The scientific way to study religion, he now urges, involves two arenas of discussion: first, psychology of religion, whose job it is to demonstrate the truth and irreducibility of religion as a universal datum, the result of (an independent) divine activity, though one not demonstrably separable from the human admixture; and secondly, history of religions, whose task it is to study the world religions in their historical development, and to look for laws and connections in that development as a way through to a comparative evaluation of the competing religions' claims to truth (ibid. 370). The importance of this new methodological stance certainly must not be underestimated: against Ritschl, it involves now a full acceptance of the 'history-of-religions' approach (compared with the more muted one in 'Die christliche Weltanschauung'), and thus a ranging of Christianity alongside the other world religions on ostensibly equal terms. And there are intimations, too, of two other anti-Ritschlian themes that are to become more explicitly developed soon after: the attack, first, on what Troeltsch here calls the 'dualistic supernaturalism' of the Ritschlian school (ibid. 363), which involves the confident de-

---

[20] So e.g. Niebuhr 1924, 38-9; Drescher in ed. Clayton 1976, 7-8.

[21] Thus Drescher comments (ed. Clayton 1976, 8): 'It is above all Schleiermacher's position which we see in the background mediating a decisive influence.' But it is not until 'Geschichte und Metaphysik' (*ZTK* 1898, 27 ff.) that Troeltsch more explicitly acknowledges this influence.

marcation of areas of pure divine revelation, free from any ming-
ling with human elements; and second Troeltsch's positive
avowal of philosophy and speculative metaphysics, those enter-
prises so deeply despised by Ritschl (see ibid. 373).[22]

None the less, even on these methodological fronts, 'Die
Selbständigkeit' represents on closer inspection not a complete
escape from Ritschlian tendencies. For when it comes to the
crucial question of the supposed superiority of Christianity
Troeltsch hovers, seemingly, half-way between the Hegelian
route of seeing Christianity as the necessary peak of a unified and
objective religious development, animated by an inner dialec-
tic,[23] and Ritschlian-style appeals to 'faith' in Christianity's absoluteness as a subjective means of supporting this assertion
(*ZTK* 1896, 211 ff.). In other words, the language of 'claim' may
have largely fallen away (though see ibid. 213), but the theme
lurks; and the result is perhaps an uneasy compromise, with some
of the criteria for Christianity's superiority that Troeltsch throws
in for good measure also still reminding one of Ritschl (that
Christianity is the only religion of redemption that is truly
'spiritual' and 'ethical', for instance) (see ibid. 201).

Christologically, likewise, the essay marks a period of transition. On the whole, Christology is conspicuous by its absence,
and this in itself is surely significant: one looks in vain for any
continuing claims for Jesus' personality as 'wunderbar', or for
any appeals to faith brought about by a direct impression of him.
Instead, new notes appear in an explicit attack on the 'Ritschlian
school' (*ZTK* 1895, 373 ff.), both for limiting the sphere of
religious truth to what is mediated through the 'historical appearance of Jesus' (ibid. 373) and for the 'certainty' that is meant
to attend this exercise (ibid. 374). Later, in a footnote (*ZTK* 1896,
213–14 n. 1), Troeltsch touches briefly for the first time on the issue
of how to relate Jesus' 'person' to the Christian 'principle' (*Prinzip*) in general. He takes the view that the *Prinzip* (that which is
deemed to animate and unite Christianity in its full historical
development[24]) is just as important as Jesus' person, although the

---

[22] See esp. the celebrated 'Theology and Metaphysics' in Ritschl 1972, 151–217.

[23] See *ZTK* 1896, 200 ff. This is not to say that Troeltsch is uncritical of Hegel here:
see esp. ibid. 81, 94, and (by implication) 105–7.

[24] Troeltsch was to be more explicit about what he meant by the Christian 'principle'
in 'Geschichte und Metaphysik', *ZTK* 1898, 56 ff., where he is careful to distinguish his

Prinzip depends both for its original emergence, and for its support, on the personality lying behind it. Troeltsch denies that the two need be set in opposition. All this is important, because it shows that Troeltsch has now moved, under the pressure of his newly espoused methodology, to a position in which Jesus can no longer be made into an 'absolute truth' (cf. *ZTK* 1895, 373), no longer then into the sole source and criterion even of Christian revelation, let alone divine revelation in general. The significance granted to the developing Christian *Prinzip*, although done guardedly with no suggestion that Jesus' 'person' could ever become redundant, does indeed withhold the sort of finality from Jesus' revelation that Troeltsch had earlier been willing to grant.

This does not mean that there are not also some more cautious Christological notes sounded, *en passant*, in the essay, and that is why I say it represents a transition. It is still urged, for instance, that Jesus personally 'guarantees' the truth of Christianity in virtue of his own 'inner communion with God' (*ZTK* 1896, 200); so Troeltsch is still confidently psychologizing about Jesus here. Moreover, he is also still worrying about the extent to which one may appropriately allow Jesus to have been implicated in apocalyptic thought; he denies, for instance, that Jesus' teaching arose out of despair over the world (as did apocalyptic) but instead affirms that it arose directly out of his 'own religious life' (ibid. 197–8 n. 1). Similarly, the next year, in 'Christentum und Religionsgeschichte' (*PJ* 1897 = *GS* ii. 328–63) Troeltsch could, in one very scant Christological reference, continue to make appeal to the completely 'inward' and 'personal' nature of Jesus' authority (*PJ* 1897, 436 = *GS* ii. 350). Thus apparently he showed no qualms, yet, about the possibility of detecting Jesus' internal psychological processes.

A distinct change, then, occurs with 'Geschichte und Metaphysik', which appeared in 1898 (in *ZTK*). In some ways this essay merely drives home points already made in 'Die Selbständigkeit der Religion'; in others, it breaks significant new ground. It is perhaps important to sketch the polemical context in which it was written: Troeltsch had in 'Die Selbständigkeit'

position from that of Hegel, while at the same time acknowledging Hegel's importance in the moulding of the concept (p. 57). Troeltsch himself wishes to use the concept not to express acceptance of a 'metaphysic of the Absolute' but as a means of indicating the 'unity' (*Einheit*) and 'impetus' (*Triebkraft*) of a complex historical development (p. 56).

reserved special words of scorn for Julius Kaftan (one of the most distinguished of the 'older generation' in the 'Ritschlian school'[25]) for his attempts to dismiss the non-Christian religions as 'mere human postulates' in comparison with the 'divine communication' in Christianity (*ZTK* 1895, 375). The editors of the *ZTK* allowed Kaftan an immediate opportunity to respond (in the appropriately titled 'Die Selbständigkeit des Christentums', *ZTK* 1896), and in so doing he not only put his finger on the ambiguity in Troeltsch's methodology that we have already noted,[26] but also firmly reiterated his conviction that revelation must be limited to 'Jesus Christ, holy scripture' and that philosophy must be kept firmly out of the theological picture (Kaftan 1896, 382).

Troeltsch's reply took up both these challenges, and thus now brought to the fore the two themes which had been the more subsidiary ones in the previous article: first a negative appraisal of the Ritschlian school's form of 'supernaturalism', and then a positive acceptance of a Hegelian-style metaphysic of history, this time with no remaining appeals to 'faith' attached.[27] On the first count, it is important to note that Troeltsch is only making a fairly circumscribed attack on 'supernaturalism' here. It is not that he objects to 'supernaturalism' *in toto* (that would belie his own alternative); rather, he is motivated for the mean time mainly by his 'history-of-religions' principles. What he rejects, then, is the attempt to restrict divine activity solely to the Christian sphere, to appeal to 'an entirely idiosyncratic causality of revelation proper only to Christianity' (*ZTK* 1898, 4).[28] At the end of the essay (ibid. 68–9) he returns to this point and this time sets 'supernaturalism' over against a 'historicist' viewpoint in general. 'Historicism', he says, which certainly has its dangers (ibid. 68), but whose central tenet is that all historical occurrences are 'conditioned' (*bedingte*), is simply incompatible with the sort of 'supernaturalism' he is

[25] For some background information on Kaftan see Rupp 1977, 17 f. Kaftan differed importantly from Ritschl and Herrmann, both in his willingness to consider, at least, the 'other' religions, and in his positive appraisal of the mystical element in religion.

[26] Kaftan posed the issue thus: 'Either empirical analysis and then at the right place a transition . . . to personal conviction, to faith,—or a doctrine of religion in the sense of a metaphysics; . . . Troeltsch attempts an impossible standpoint and falls between two stools' (Kaftan 1896, 391).

[27] Instead Troeltsch prefers now to talk of 'decision' (*Entscheidung*) (*ZTK* 1898, 60–1), which anticipates the language of his later analysis of ethical relativism in *GS* iii.

[28] For more on the issue of the type of 'supernaturalism' which Troeltsch rejected, see ch. 3.

here attacking, that is, the appeal to 'inviolable' areas of divine activity.

On the other score, the question of a metaphysics of history, Troeltsch here comes (self-admittedly) very close to Hegel in his assertions about Christianity as the convergence point and (demonstrable) goal of all previous religious developments. Of the two alternatives that Kaftan had offered him, then (either a subjective 'conviction' of Christianity's superiority or a metaphysic of history), Troeltsch now unambiguously chooses the latter, though, as we shall see, this new-found adulation of Hegel was not to last more than a couple of years without rather drastic modification.

These are the central themes of 'Geschichte und Metaphysik'. But the Christological hints that attend them are of considerable importance, and indeed this essay contains much more extended Christological reflection than any of Troeltsch's previous publications. The most radical development concerns the implications for Christology of a rigorous application of the historical critical method to the study of Jesus. Since the time of Strauss's *Life of Jesus*, Troeltsch says, the conclusion had been forced on theologians that 'We catch sight of the personality of Jesus only through the veil of a tradition which conceals such basic matters as the chronology and geographical dispersion of Jesus' operation, the names of the apostles, and the data of the day of his death' (ibid. 7). The implication of what Troeltsch says here is surely that naïve appeals to direct experiences of Jesus, circumventing the laborious task of historical study, are ruled out of court. Moreover, Troeltsch sounds more sceptical now than perhaps at any other time in his career[29] about the possibility of reconstructing a complex portrait of Jesus' 'personality' with any degree of certainty.

At the same time, though, he makes new concessions about Jesus' implication in the thought-forms of his time (apocalyptic included now) and comes closer to Weiss's position on the

---

[29] Troeltsch was to appear much more confident about the reconstruction of a reasonably reliable portrait of Jesus later, particularly in 'Sig. HJ'. (For a discussion of this see below, ch. 5.) For the mean time we must note that there is in this present essay a considerable tension between apparent historical scepticism and the insistence that immediately follows (*ZTK* 1898, 7) that we can at least still be sure of Jesus' 'unique communion with God'.

kingdom than before, stressing that for Jesus everything centred on a (future) kingdom that would attend the imminent judgement and end of the world (ibid. 7). The thorny question of Jesus' Messianism, however, is here avoided, and steered off quickly in a later passage (ibid. 63). This change of direction on New Testament issues is interestingly borne out by the correspondence with Bousset at the same time (letter of 5 August 1898). Troeltsch admits here that he is still 'unclear' about Jesus' relationship to eschatology in general and Messianism and apocalyptic in particular;[30] his new scepticism, moreover, is reflected in a turning away from the attempt to psychologize about Jesus' thoughts and intentions at all: 'Rummaging about' in Jesus' self-consciousness he now considers more an issue for dogmatics than for strictly historical work (Dinkler-von Schubert 1976, 35).

What the same letter also reveals, however, is that Troeltsch is relieved to find that he is still maintaining friendly relations with at least Harnack and Herrmann (ibid. 35) despite his earlier fears, expressed in a previous letter (ibid. 31-2), that 'Die Selbständigkeit der Religion' would mean a break not only with Kaftan, but with Herrmann also.

The references to Herrmann, and the general anxiety about increasing theological isolation, cast a fascinating light on the remaining Christological passages in 'Geschichte und Metaphysik'. On the one hand Troeltsch is already very far from Herrmann's theological position: his increased critical scepticism is, as we have seen, accompanied by a greater willingness to implicate Jesus in his times and in that sense relativize him;[31]

---

[30] Troeltsch says here that on the whole he thinks Jesus' Messiahship was something that he 'just let happen' to himself (Dinkler-von Schubert, 1976, 35), which does not really amount to a 'proper Messianic consciousness'. Bousset's *Jesus* (1st German ed. 1904), later greeted enthusiastically by Troeltsch (ibid. 43), was to take a somewhat similar line, though perhaps with more willingness to 'rummage about' in Jesus' psyche than Troeltsch here seems to allow possible. Bousset argued there that Jesus 'could not dispense with the Messianic idea if he wished to be intelligible to himself. . . . the Messianic idea was the only possible form in which Jesus could clothe his inner consciousness, and yet an inadequate form; it was a necessity, but also a heavy burden which he bore in silence almost to the end of his life; it was a conviction which he could never enjoy with a whole heart' (Bousset 1906, 178, 180).

[31] This much already goes well against Herrmann's grain. In contrast to Troeltsch's reflections on the implications of Jesus in his own particularized culture, see Herrmann's insistence that the 'inner life' of Jesus can be made directly available to Christians as something both immediately compelling and quite unparalleled (Herrmann 1909, ch. 2 *passim*, but esp. e.g. 80-5). It is important to realize, however, that Herrmann

moreover Troeltsch goes on to draw out the dogmatic implications of this move when he lets drop the later remark that we
are now in no position to appeal to Jesus' 'self-testimony'
(*Selbstzeugnis*) as a proof of his 'absolute divinity' or 'sinlessness'
(*ZTK* 1898, 63).[32] Further, one of his main gibes against Kaftan is
that the historical critical method entirely disallows the neat
parcelling out of the supernatural and natural elements in Christianity in general (ibid. 6) and Jesus in particular (ibid. 7-8).
Kaftan's attack on the Logos Christology of the early Church
Troeltsch is evidently willing on the whole to accept as valid,[33] but
what Kaftan does not concede, says Troeltsch, is that without the
authoritative teaching of the Church on Logos and incarnation,
he has nothing to fall back on in Christology but a 'strong supernaturalism' which flouts the canons of historical critical work
(ibid. 65-6).[34]

Troeltsch does, it is true, share with the Ritschlians the idea
that once out of its primitive milieu the Christian message
became unfortunately 'hardened' into Church dogma (ibid. 65).
But where he now differs from Ritschl and Kaftan (and Harnack)
is in his new assimilation of the lessons of Weiss: Jesus was interested only in a future kingdom and pointed away from himself,
he says; later Christological dogma, then, not only 'hardened'
the gospel, but crucially changed its contents: instead of being
future-orientated it turned decisively to the past and 'absolutized'
the person of Jesus (ibid.).[35]

distinguishes between the 'risen Christ' (who is 'hidden' and apparently unavailable
(pp. 291, 292)) and the 'Person of Jesus', who is, it is claimed, compellingly available
(p. 291).

[32] For Herrmann on Christ's sinlessness and consciousness of the same, see e.g. ibid.
89.

[33] See what Troeltsch himself wrote on the Logos Christology two years later in *Die
wissenschaftliche Lage und ihre Anforderungen an die Theologie* (1900), 22-3, describing it as a
'compromise' with ancient philosophy. Quite what Troeltsch meant by 'compromise'
here is left unexplained, but it seems most likely in the context that he intended to convey that the Logos doctrine was an inevitable aspect of Christianity's *rapprochement* with
the prevailing culture which involved losses as well as gains. For a discussion of the
variety of ways in which Troeltsch uses the term *Kompromiß* see Clayton 1980, 55 ff.

[34] Troeltsch had already, on 5 Oct. 1896, made (one presumes) this very point to Kaftan in the public setting of a meeting of the Friends of the *Christliche Welt*, and caused not
a little embarrassment in so doing. Köhler (1941, 1) reports how, at the end of a learned
talk by Kaftan on the Logos doctrine, Troeltsch jumped up to respond, starting,
'Everything is tottering'. When Kattenbusch later denounced Troeltsch's analysis,
Troeltsch left rudely, slamming the door. (See also Pauck 1968, 65-6.)

[35] It is instructive to compare this position with that of Harnack's celebrated lectures

This much in 'Geschichte und Metaphysik' moves in a distinctly radical direction. But when Troeltsch comes to discuss once again the issue about Jesus' person and his relation to the Christian *Prinzip*, a subject which had elicited particularly vehement criticism from Kaftan (see ibid. 56), rather different notes are heard. What is so interesting here is that Troeltsch appeals, approvingly, to Herrmann's *The Communion of the Christian with God* in support of the position he outlines (ibid. 62). The fact that Herrmann could not, at least on the basis of that book, have come anywhere near accepting any of the sceptical conclusions in this article that we have already detailed[36] appears not to concern Troeltsch. Jesus' 'person', he now insists (expanding on his treatment of this point in 'Die Selbständigkeit der Religion'), can never be separated from the Christian 'principle'. This is not only because the person (an ultimately 'mysterious act of God') logically and chronologically precedes the 'principle', but also because only by returning to the person can the means of 'unfolding' the principle become apparent (ibid. 59). Christians always have to return to Jesus, then, as their only means of 'security' (*Bürgschaft*) in their relation to God.[37] Just as it was Jesus' personal impact (rather than the novelty of his teaching) which differentiated Christianity from Judaism in the first place (ibid. 61), so also now his person is the true source of irreducible, and mysterious, 'authority' (ibid. 63). The Christian 'principle' set loose from the person, then, would be 'like a sunset after the sun has gone down' (ibid. 62). None the less—and this is a very significant addition—Troeltsch ends this discussion with the remark that Christian faith always has to return to the *gospel* of

Das Wesen des Christentums two years later in 1900. Harnack of course certainly believed that the direction of patristic Christology was misleading (though inevitable) compared with the simplicity of Jesus' own teaching. But he was unwilling to get too involved in the difficulties raised by the eschatological outlook of Jesus, and interpreted his view of the kingdom in an entirely interiorized fashion (see e.g. Harnack 1901, 56). Herrmann, interestingly, was more willing to take account of the future reference in his treatment of the kingdom (Herrman 1909, 95 f.).

[36] See e.g. Herrmann's insistence that historical critical problems can be short-circuited by a direct experience of the 'inner life' of Jesus (Herrmann 1909, 76).

[37] The sentence referred to ends: 'the source and security of this relationship with God always goes back to the person of Jesus whose picture is the living and ever effective symbol, whose word is the security, and whose self-offering is the power of faith' (*ZTK* 1898, 62). This of course is very reminiscent of Herrmann 1909, 80 ff. e.g., where it is insisted that Christian teaching is of no avail without the 'Person of Jesus'.

Jesus, 'whose sense and goal God himself reveals in history, working it out in *ever new and ever deeper [ways]*' (ibid. 67, my italics). This in itself modifies in an important way the possible suggestion that Jesus' person would be the locus of final and complete revelation. Clearly, on Troeltsch's view here, *Prinzip* and *Person* must be held together.[38]

The reciprocity of *Person* and *Prinzip* was a theme that Troeltsch was to return to in his later work on dogmatics,[39] and in many ways the Christological position in 'Geschichte und Metaphysik' remarkably anticipates his later, more considered Christological thought. This theme of conjoined *Person* and *Prinzip*, along with the relativizing of Jesus to less than the complete (or 'absolute') revelation of God, the insistence on the astute application of the historical critical method in the search for the Jesus of history, and the full implication of Jesus in eschatological fervour, are all strands which reappear later. There is even a hint also here of Troeltsch's later position on the 'many Christs' (Chapter 6, below), when he throws off the enigmatic remark (*ZTK* 1898, 63–4) that what is often called 'Christology' (he uses inverted commas advisedly) is in contrast to the quest for the historical Jesus really not a science at all but a matter for 'imagination'.

But if all this is a foretaste of the future, the reference to Herrmann remains perplexing. Could Troeltsch really have approved of Herrmann's continual (and, if one is frank, uncritical) appeals to the 'inner life' of Jesus? This, and one or two remaining remarks about Jesus' 'unique relationship to God' (ibid. 7), or about his having 'completed' every revelation (ibid. 60), make one wary of saying that Troeltsch had by now sloughed off every vestige of Ritschlian influence in Christology. What seems more likely is that Troeltsch was himself as yet undecided on whether to follow through, where Christology was concerned, the full im-

---

[38] Pannenberg's criticism, therefore (1970, 57), that Troeltsch fatally separated *Person* and *Prinzip* in 'Geschichte und Metaphysik' is simply misplaced. Pannenberg says here: 'The distinction, which Troeltsch took over from Biedermann, between the person of Jesus and the Christian principle introduced into history by him, cannot but lead to the severance of the ground of faith from history.' Pannenberg fails to acknowledge here that Troeltsch implicitly criticizes Biedermann for such a tendency, suggesting an important modification of his position (*ZTK* 1896, 59). Moreover, the whole tenor of his argument, as we have seen, is designed to counteract the suggestion that Jesus' *Person* could be regarded as dispensable.

[39] See *Gl.* 346, Sig. HJ' 184 ff., and the discussion of this below, ch. 5.

plications of a 'theology of historicism' (ibid. 69), and that, perhaps for political as well as personal reasons, he was anxious for the mean time not to alienate Herrmann.

Apfelbacher (1978, 234–5) has recently brought to light a previously unpublished letter which Troeltsch wrote to Herrmann in this very year (27 October 1898), which may well add another dimension to this issue. The letter indicates that, in spite of Troeltsch's approving reference to *The Communion of the Christian with God* in 'Geschichte und Metaphysik', he was already worrying about the issue which was later to cause him to break decisively with Herrmann's Christology. In reference now to Herrmann's more recent essay 'Der geschichtliche Christus der Grund unseres Glaubens' (1892), Troeltsch asks him to clarify what he means by 'fact' and 'personality' when he refers to 'the fact of Jesus' personal life' or 'the historical fact of the person of Jesus' (ibid. 234). If by 'the fact' of the 'historical Christ' Herrmann intends the uncritical acceptance of a collection of bits of information given on authority, then Troeltsch cannot go along with him. If, however, he is referring more to the 'psychological' effects that are felt to accrue from reflection on Jesus' personality, then Troeltsch is more willing to concur (ibid. 235). Similar worries about uncritical tendencies in Christology are more scornfully expressed by Troeltsch the next year in a review of Martin Kähler's *Dogmatische Zeitfragen* (*GGA* 1899), where Troeltsch makes it clear that Kähler's escape route for avoiding the historical Jesus question is quite unacceptable to him and amounts to 'pure Biblicism' (ibid. 942; cf. 945–6).[40] All this is pregnant of future developments.

In the mean time, though, Troeltsch wrote only two more articles which are relevant for our Christological purposes before *The Absoluteness of Christianity*. One, a skirmish with another of the Ritschlian school, Ferdinand Kattenbusch (*CW* 1898),[41] made another attack on the Ritschlians for their failure to take the historical methodology seriously, but without any explicit reference to Christology. The other, 'Über historische und dogmatische Methode der Theologie' (*TA* 1900), has already

---

[40] His brief review of H. Martensen Larsen's *Jesus und die Religionsgeschichte* earlier the same year (in *TLZ* 1899, 400) also suggests scepticism about appeals such as Larsen's to Jesus' 'entirely unique consciousness of "divine Sonship" '.

[41] For the background to this see Rupp 1977, 20 f.

been treated in substance in Chapter I, but while there is fairly little here in the way of overt Christology, one or two passing hints are worthy of reflection, not least because they are important for my suggestion that *The Absoluteness of Christianity* (coming a little later in 1902) represents a back-tracking in Troeltsch's Christology.

It is important to remember that the weight of Troeltsch's polemic in this essay is directly against theologians who subscribe in principle to 'historical method', but at crucial points observe areas of security where the historical critical method is not allowed to penetrate (*TA* 1900, 97 ff. = *GS* ii. 739 ff.). But this, says Troeltsch, will not do: 'the historical method must be consistently (*voller Ernst*) applied' (*TA* 1900, 95 = *GS* ii. 738); give it 'an inch and it will take a mile' (*TA* 1900, 92 = *GS* ii. 734).[42] Troeltsch goes on to claim that the consequences of the consistent application of the method are two:

In the first place, historical criticism brings a measure of uncertainty to every single fact. . . . Now it becomes impossible to base religious fact on any single fact: faith and fact are linked by large and broad connections. their relationship is mediate, not direct.

In the second place, these connections between faith and fact are themselves not isolated and unconditioned . . . they arise out of a historical context, they share its substance, and they must be understood in relation to it. (*TA* 1900, 93–4 = *GS* ii. 736.)

This passage is important, but certainly not unambiguously clear. To my mind, Troeltsch is saying rather more than two things: first, that all historians' conclusions about 'facts' are subject to revision (new evidence may come to light, for instance); second, that no interpretation of a fact is unambiguously given; third, that even the original interpretation will be informed not just by a (hermetically sealed) 'fact', but also by culturally supplied admixture; and (at least implicitly) fourth, that any contemporary interpretation will have to take into account not only that original context of response but also the present cultural milieu. Even if I am reading in too much here, it is clear enough what Troeltsch is combating: the whole article, as we have seen, is a polemic against those who try to keep particular 'facts' safe from

---

[42] The German in fact is 'Wer ihr den kleinen Finger gegeben hat, der muß ihr auch die ganze Hand geben.'

criticism *in toto*; but there is also a rejection here of a kind of 'naïve realism' which will tolerate no ambiguity in the hermeneutical task and which likes to think that no cultural or human input need sully the response to a divine action. Both these points obviously have important implications for Christology, and, one might say, suggest a latent criticism of Herrmann.[43] At the same time, Troeltsch is most anxious to stress that his position does not disallow the 'originality', 'mysteriousness' or 'creative significance' of the great religious prophets and personalities (*TA* 1900, 94 = *GS* ii. 736). History in no way precludes 'originality' in this sense.

It is only in the light of all this that one may properly interpret the two explicitly Christological references in the article. The first occurs near the beginning when Troeltsch has been discussing the 'principle of analogy', and he says:

Jewish and Christian history are . . . made analogous to all other history. Actually, fewer and fewer historical 'facts' are regarded as exempt from the exigencies of the analogical principle; many would content themselves with placing Jesus' moral character and the resurrection in this category. (*TA* 1900, 90 = *GS* ii. 732-3.)

The muddied way in which Troeltsch has just discussed the problem of 'historical analogy'[44] certainly does not help one in trying to decide what he means here, particularly since the two exceptions he cites scarcely seem to present strictly comparable problems. None the less, the use of the passive verb, and the context of the article's polemic as a whole, surely dismiss the possibility that Troeltsch himself is willing to exclude 'Jesus' moral character' and 'the resurrection'[45] from the full implications of the historical method. Rather, he is attacking those (modified) defenders of the 'dogmatic method', who have conceded a certain amount to historical method, but still wish to erect protective

---

[43] According to Herrmann (see again e.g. Herrmann 1909, 83), the 'inner life' of Jesus directly and compellingly confronts the inner life of the Christian ('there arises *in our hearts* the *certainty* that God Himself is turning towards us in this experience'). The problem of cultural conditioning thus scarcely seems to arise.

[44] See my long footnote (n. 34) above, ch. 1.

[45] The only other remarks Troeltsch makes about the resurrection at this period are to be found in 'Geschichte und Metaphysik' (*ZTK* 1898, 60-1), but they are too brief and elliptical to tell us much about what his views were. For his later position on this, see below, ch. 6.

barriers round some more limited 'supra-historical core' (*TA* 1900, 95 = *GS* ii. 737).

The other Christological passage well illustrates the strong Hegelian influence which Troeltsch was still (self-confessedly) under when writing this article. It is in the context of his belief that 'reason is operative in history and . . . progressively revealing itself' (*TA* 1900, 102 = *GS* ii. 746) that he writes:

At only one point was [the original tie of the human spirit to nature] broken through. This point, however, was located at the centre of great contemporary and subsequent religious developments, namely in the religion of the prophets of Israel and in the person of Jesus. Here a God distinct from nature produced a personality superior to nature with eternally transcendent goals and the will-power to change the world. Here a religious power manifests itself, which to the person sensitive enough to catch its echo in his own soul, seems to be the conclusion of all previous religious movements and the starting point of a new phase in the history of religions, in which nothing higher has emerged. (*TA* 1900, 104 = *GS* ii. 748.)

Precisely what status is Troeltsch according to Jesus here? Certainly not the status of God, or of the (Hegelian) Absolute *simpliciter*, since, for all his positive espousal of Hegelian metaphysics here and in 'Geschichte und Metaphysik', one of the major points at which Troeltsch wishes to modify Hegel is in the supposition that the Absolute has already made its full and complete appearance in Christianity.[46] Indeed he has already stated in the present article his belief that the 'historical method' *in se* disallows such a possibility, and thus that it is not even necessary to appeal to a 'philosophical theory', such as Strauss's that 'the Idea does not like to pour all its fullness into a single individual' (*TA* 1900, 92 = *GS* ii. 734). This is not however intended as a rejection of Strauss, but as an implicit endorsement.[47] And thus the sort of Christology that Troeltsch is sketching here is, perhaps not surprisingly, somewhat similar to that held by Strauss in at least one phase of his career:[48] Jesus marks a new breakthrough in

[46] See 'Geschichte und Metaphysik' (*ZTK* 1898, 40 ff., 54–5); 'Über historische und dogmatische Methode der Theologie', *TA* 1900, 96, 103–4 = *GS* ii. 738, 747.

[47] For discussion of the extent to which Troeltsch's agreement with Strauss on this point affected his Christology, see below, ch. 4.

[48] Troeltsch seems to be close here to the Strauss of the 3rd edn. of *The Life of Jesus*. See Keck's survey essay on Strauss's theological development in Strauss 1977 (esp. lxvi) for this comparison, and also Hodgson's introduction in Strauss 1972 (esp. xl–xlii).

human spiritual and moral potential, which is unlikely to be superseded. His 'originality' and 'creativity', it is argued, are quantitively superior to that of other prophetic personalities, and no recourse to a subjective theology of 'claim' should be needed to support this (*TA* 1900, 107 = *GS* ii. 751). But all this, Troeltsch is careful to add, does not in any way imply that Jesus becomes immune from historical critical investigation, or that he is any the less implicated in 'the flux, the conditioning, and the mutability of history' (*TA* 1900, 104 = *GS* ii. 748).

The central theme of 'Über historische und dogmatische Methode', then, is that no area of history, however sacred to Christianity, can escape the probings of historical critical investigation, and this in itself represents (implicitly) a potent criticism of Herrmann, one that Troeltsch was later to voice in no uncertain terms. But for the mean time his Christological thought was unclarified: flirtations with Hegel and Strauss on the one hand; an attraction (or at least a politically motivated politeness) to Herrmann on the other; these were odd Christological bedfellows on any account. But while neither tendency was to be central to Troeltsch's later Christological thought,[49] it is only with this particular tension in mind, I think, that one can begin to understand the strange Christological concoction that emerged in Troeltsch's next major production, *The Absoluteness of Christianity*. In representing this first edition as a back-tracking towards 'Ritschlianism', what I primarily mean is that in some passages Troeltsch explicitly adopts a position uncannily close to Herrmann, and that this actively flouts the tenets of the 'historical method' as laid down in his most recent essay on 'historical and dogmatic method'. Certainly, then, we shall not be able to say that Troeltsch had 'disengaged' from 'Ritschlianism', at least where Christology is concerned, until after *The Absoluteness of Christianity*.

But it is only fair to mention that Troeltsch may well not have intended, at least in the planning stage of these lectures, to get involved in Christological discussion at all. It is surely significant that the 'Thesen' (*CW* 1901), which Troeltsch published in advance of the lectures to be given before the Friends of the *Christliche Welt* at Mühlacker on 3 October 1901, contain no

---

[49] This is not to say that small remains of both are not still to be found in Troeltsch's mature Christology. See below, chs. 5 and 6.

Christological reference whatsoever. And one also has to bear in mind the pressures, in a public performance such as this, both not to offend too many sensibilities and also, perhaps, to end on a suitably stirring or positive note. Be that as it may, it is noticeable that the Herrmannesque passages that strike one as so odd are all concentrated in the closing sections of the book.

The earlier strains, however, are quite different. It is as well to remember the new philosophical direction which Troeltsch took in these lectures: forsaking (ostensibly at least)[50] the Hegelian approach to the problem of the absoluteness of Christianity that he had adopted between 1898 and 1900, he now attempted to solve it by reference to Heinrich Rickert's philosophy of history and the idea of 'immanent values' in history.[51] The net result, as we have already discussed in Chapter I, was a high degree of ambiguity on the crucial issue of whether Christianity could be publicly shown to be the fullest revelation of God (up till now at least) or whether this apprehension could only be made, subjectively, from the standpoint of faith. The former tendency represents the continuance of Hegelian influence, though of course with the usual modification reinforced here that Christianity does not (and cannot, at least while history continues[52]) represent the achieved and final revelation of God. The latter tendency is sheltered now, rather dubiously perhaps, under a new Rickertian cloak of respectability, though as I shall show my own view is that there is in effect much more of Ritschl's theology of 'claim' left here than Troeltsch was willing to concede.[53]

---

[50] See *Abs.* 63 ff.

[51] Rickert's argument was that the 'values' expressed by a culture are manifestations of timeless, absolutely valid norms. For a useful exposition and critique of Rickert's *Kulturwissenschaft und Naturwissenschaft* see Iggers 1968, 152 ff. For Troeltsch's assimilation of Rickert, Drescher's treatment (in ed. Clayton 1976, 15 ff.) is very useful, though one perhaps needs to add that, although Troeltsch is indeed already manifestly influenced by Rickert in the 1st edn. of *The Absoluteness*, he says elsewhere (*GS* iv. 9) that it was not really until 1905 that he fully assimilated Rickert's views.

[52] See e.g. A^1 54 = *Abs.* 90. We note here (even in the 1st edn.) a slight modification of the more confident claims in 'Über historische und dogmatische Methode' (*TA* 1900, 104 = *GS* ii. 748) that Christianity 'seems to be the conclusion of all previous religious movements' and that 'it is *unthinkable* that something higher should emerge' (my italics). Compare with this A^1 81, 41–2 = *Abs.* 114–15, 78–9, where it is admitted, following Lagarde, that a new revelation, superior to Christianity, could emerge.

[53] The result is that Troeltsch effectively returns to the uneasy position of 'Die Selbständigkeit der Religion' (1896) on this issue, as already described. For Troeltsch's attack on the theology of claim see A^1 43–8, esp. 45 n. 1 = *Abs.* 80–3, 169–70.

Under the circumstances of this ambiguity, it is perhaps not surprising to find, on the one hand (correlating with the modified Hegelian tendency), that the earlier Christological references in the book take up the Straussian themes that Troeltsch had already rehearsed in 1900. But now the approval of Strauss is even more unambiguous:

> Strauss . . . has shown clearly and irrefutably—in opposition to Hegel—that no absolutely perfect principle of religion can be realized in history at any single point. . . . History is no place for 'absolute religions' or 'absolute personalities'. Such terms are self contradictory. (A^1 41 = *Abs.* 78.)

More clearly here than ever before, then, Troeltsch forcefully relativizes the potential of Jesus' revelatory powers. By definition, it seems, he cannot *be* God, or represent the 'Absolute' fully.[54] But as was also the case in his previous article 'Über historische und dogmatische Methode', the other side of this (Straussian) coin is the strong assertion that what Jesus none the less is is someone of '*incomparably* creative originality' (A^1 89 = *Abs.* 125, my italics) who 'soars above' ordinary humanity, and who has the power to 'renew a weary world' (ibid.). This statement, as in the earlier article, is made without any indication that a subjective element of valuation is required to inform it.[55]

That is one side of the Christology in the book, and it is in straightforward continuity with 'Über historische und dogmatische Methode'. But the other side, the surprising side strongly akin to Herrmann, is represented by passages at the end of the book such as this, which bear quotation at some length (the brackets indicate what is only in the first edition).

> . . . we are grasped by the authority of Jesus himself, to whom, as the highest religious power, we may in good conscience devote ourselves with such reverence and commitment that we forget about all the wearisome roads and detours apart from which a people enmeshed in the diversity of history cannot come to him. The religious man can and may forget the study of history at this point and live with naive absoluteness in the presence of God, all time being consumed in the vision

---

[54] For a further discussion of this point, see below, ch. 4.

[55] However, what is perhaps also significant is that the major section discussing the superiority of Christianity to the other religions (A^1 74 ff = *Abs.* 108 ff.) is completely devoid of reference to Jesus.

of the One disclosed to us as the divine goal. [Not theology and apologetics, but the simple voice of the heart free from the burden of history will pronounce the confession of Paul: no one can lay another foundation other than that which is laid, which is Jesus Christ.] (A^1 128; cf. *Abs.* 161.)

Elsewhere, just to give two more examples this time found solely in the first edition, Troeltsch can say that Christianity's 'claim' (*sic*) to absoluteness 'has nowhere yet been refuted or surmounted, and no imagination is capable of conceiving such a surmounting; and so it remains that no other foundation is laid for the soul's health of mankind except Jesus Christ' (A^1 126; cf. *Abs.* 159). And in the first edition the book ends, rousingly, with the assurance that the 'religious-studies' approach need not necessarily obstruct the possibility of returning to the 'simplicity, freedom, and clarity' of Pauline faith, since 'the surest and strongest ground of salvation is Jesus Christ' (A^1 129; cf. *Abs.* 162–3).

My reasons for suggesting that passages such as these represent a back-tracking towards 'Ritschlianism', and an affinity with Herrmann in particular, must be spelled out more clearly. The following tendencies emerge. First, as we have already seen, Ritschl's 'claim' theology, also found in Herrmann, reasserts itself,[56] but with it (second) the insistence that the impression made by Jesus *directly* affects the 'inner' person (or is received 'in our hearts').[57] This second feature is particularly characteristic of Herrmann's theology.[58] At the same time, third, a tendency to psychologize confidently about Jesus' intentions reappears[59] and with that, fourth, the eschatological dimension of Jesus' teaching all but dies away.[60] These too are tendencies found in Herrmann.[61] The following passage (oddly left intact in the second edition) incorporates all these four features:

[56] See again A^1 126 = *Abs.* 158–9; A^1 113 = *Abs.* 148. For 'claim' theology in Herrmann see esp. Herrmann 1909, 93–7.

[57] See e.g. A^1 83 ('innerlich'); 87 ('die ganze Seele'); 91 (in 'unserm Herzen') (= *Abs.* 119, 123, 126).

[58] See e.g. Herrmann 1909, 108 ff.

[59] See e.g. A^1 87, 110, 128–9 (= *Abs.* 123, 145, 161–2).

[60] However see A^1 110, 124–5 (= *Abs.* 145, 157) for the *occasional* admission that Jesus was bound up in the thought-forms of his day and that for him 'all ultimate salvation and all ultimate truth were . . . something to be awaited'. However, the important passage in *Abs.* 145 about the imminent kingdom of God is, as we shall see, only found in the 2nd edn. (cf. A^1 111).

[61] See e.g. Herrmann 1909, 84 ff. for confidence in describing Jesus' inner inten-

The naive absoluteness of Jesus is simply his faith that he has been sent by the Heavenly Father and his certainty that just as the will of the Father is the only truth by which human behaviour should be governed, so the promise of the Father is the only salvation. The justification for this claim is that it flows from the purest and most powerful religious idea in a way that encounters the inner man most deeply and compellingly. (A^1 113 = *Abs.* 147–8.)

Further Herrmannesque features are, fifth, the occasional (but none the less strong) suggestion that any revelation outside Jesus is scarcely to be admitted;[62] the stress, sixth, on the 'certainty' with which Christian faith's relationship to Jesus is attended;[63] seventh, the appeal (admittedly on only one occasion) to the 'inner life' of Jesus;[64] and eighth, and perhaps most important, the claim apparent in the passage quoted at the outset, that 'naïve' faith can forget about historical critical problems and simply relate directly to Jesus.[65] It is no wonder, then, that Herrmann responded warmly to Troeltsch's treatment of 'naïve' religion in his review of *The Absoluteness of Christianity*, despite fairly biting criticism on other scores.[66]

Whether we see the appearance of these themes in Troeltsch as an aberration, a failure of nerve, or simply an unreflective lapse into the preaching mode in the face of a conservative, but by no means uncritical, audience, there is no way that it can be reconciled with the principles that Troeltsch had laid down in his essay of 1900 'Über historische und dogmatische Methode'. In addition, it stands in at least a problematic relationship to what I have called the Straussian strand in the same work. That insisted that one must look *beyond* history for God (or the 'Absolute') and not

tions. On the question of the kingdom, as we have already seen (see above n. 35), Herrmann was admittedly more subtle than some of the other 'Ritschlians'. Sometimes he does allow for the future reference in Jesus' message of the kingdom (see ibid. 95 f.), but at other times the eschatological dimension is left out and he sounds much more like Harnack (e.g. ibid. 87: 'by the Kingdom of God [Jesus] means God's true lordship over personal life, especially in men's own souls, and in their communion one with another').

[62] See e.g. A^1 83 (cf. *Abs.* 119–20): 'über die Offenbarung Gottes in Jesus hinaus nichts Höheres zu erwarten ist'; A^1 91 (cf. *Abs.* 126–7); A^1 129 = *Abs.* 162 ('leave to Jesus the disclosure and consummation of the salvation of the future'). Also see the other passages on A^1 126, 129 already cited above. For the same strand in Herrmann see e.g. Herrmann 1909, 84, 'a Personal life that has no equal'.

[63] See A^1 83 ff., 91 = *Abs.* 119 ff., 127. Cf. e.g. Herrmann 1909, 83.

[64] A^1 91 (cf. *Abs.* 126). See Herrmann 1909, *passim* but esp. 80 ff.

[65] A^1 128 (cf. *Abs.* 161). See e.g. Herrmann 1909, 66 ff., 114.

[66] See Herrmann 1902, 330–4, esp. 334.

restrict one's gaze to Jesus; whereas the end of the book exhorts the reader to concentrate solely on Jesus in a return to 'naïve' Pauline faith.

The years that intervened between the first and second editions of this work (1902–12) brought not only clarification in Troeltsch's Christological thought but new developments in his philosophy of religion, the production of all his 'positive' contributions to dogmatics, and above all his great sociological analysis of the history of Christianity, *The Social Teaching*.[67] It is in these years, I would suggest, that the real disengagement with 'Ritschlian' traits in Christology occurred, and to a large extent one can chart that disengagement by reference to Troeltsch's explicit renunciation of Herrmann's Christological approach.

The break with Herrmann certainly did not restrict itself to matters of Christology.[68] But where the latter was concerned two decisive issues came to the fore. First, in his critique of Herrmann's *Ethik* (1901) in *ZTK* 1902 Troeltsch now strongly reasserted his belief in the eschatological 'one-sidedness' of Jesus' own ethical views, and the impossibility of accommodating them to a Kantian-style ethic of universal love.[69] Now, in a way he had not before, Troeltsch explicitly accepts the embarrassing feature of Weiss's thesis: Jesus' views about the imminent end proved to be wrong, and Christian ethics simply has to take account of that fact and adjust accordingly.[70]

Even more forceful, though, is Troeltsch's attack on Herrmann's Christology in his article of 1909,[71] 'Rückblick auf ein

---

[67] See *GS* iv. 10–13 for Troeltsch's own description of his intellectual development at this time.

[68] More fundamental were general questions about methodology and ethics. For reflections from a contemporary, see Diehl 1908. There are also useful, if brief, discussions in English in Rupp 1977, 33 ff., and in Morgan's contribution to ed. Clayton 1976, 40 f., 58.

[69] 'Grundprobleme der Ethik', *ZTK* 1902; later, with some changes, this is incorporated in *GS* ii. 552–672. See esp. *ZTK* 1902, 150 (= *GS* ii. 634) on the kingdom of God: for Jesus, says Troeltsch, 'the kingdom of God is not the relationship among men attained through a common recognition of the law of autonomy as a law implanted in our breasts by God; this is a modern abstraction, wholly removed from the naïve realism of the ancient world. Rather, it is a wonderful gift of God . . . a kingdom in which God will be seen . . .'. For further discussion see Bense 1974, 18 ff., whose translation (p. 41) I am using here.

[70] Troeltsch made his views on this similarly clear in *ST* and (the 2nd edn. of) 'Was heißt, "Wesen des Christentums"?'.

[71] *GS* ii. 193 wrongly has 1908.

halbes Jahrhundert der theologischen Wissenschaft' (in *ZWT*). The crucial passage is this:

> Particularly interesting in the case of Herrmann is the struggle between history-writing and subjective mysticism. He stresses increasingly the personal certainty of the religious life in itself. It can only be found as one's own truth and one's own experience. But it needs a power supply from history and a foundation outside itself. At the same time Herrmann has recourse again and again to the 'impression of Jesus' which can be got from the gospel, independently of all historical work. Someone who has at this point become certain of his cause does not need to concern himself unduly about what other people consider necessary on historical grounds. This 'impression' then implies a special metaphysical position for Jesus established through judgments of faith. These are quite extraordinarily difficult statements . . . (*ZWT* 1909, 127 = 'Half C.' 75.)

This is worthy of extensive quotation because it shows that now Troeltsch has unambiguously rejected the very traits of Herrmann's Christology that he had himself briefly endorsed in *The Absoluteness of Christianity*. The claim made by the 'impression' of Jesus, the 'certainty' that is supposed to attend this, the 'special metaphysical position for Jesus', and above all the flouting of historical methods by appeals to direct experiences of Jesus received independently of research: all these are now firmly rejected. And there is no mistaking the derogatory tone here. The reference to 'subjective mysticism' would have been anathema to Herrmann, who had spent so much energy in *The Communion of the Christian with God* dissociating himself from 'mystical' tendencies.[72] Moreover, in the same article Troeltsch also accuses Ritschl of taking 'the personality of Jesus out of the rest of history by means of a value judgement . . .' (*ZWT* 1909, 117 = 'Half C.' 68) and of having to 'leave the refined, relativising, . . . sceptical historical research of his day to itself' (ibid.).

Troeltsch further sharpened this criticism of both Ritschl and Herrmann when he revised this article for *GS* ii in 1913.[73] But in

---

[72] See Herrmann 1909, 29 ff. The mystic, according to Herrmann, 'leaves Christ behind' (p. 30).

[73] For new additions in connection with criticism of the Ritschlians, see 'Half C.', the para. on pp. 62–3 and 63 n. 4; on p. 64, the additional sentence starting 'In other words, Ritschl twists Schleiermacher's subjectivism . . .'; on p. 66, the two sentences starting 'On the other hand, this biblicism grounded purely in history and feeling was so unsafe

the mean time, in 1911, he had renewed his attack on Herrmann in 'The Significance of the Historical Existence of Jesus for Faith', objecting particularly to Herrmann's supposition that no one who does not 'know Christ' can have any faith in God, and countering: 'It is anything but obvious that the religious personality of the historical Jesus can be fully and clearly known and made directly and personally effective. ... This has ... certainly been rendered impossible by modern criticism' ('Sig. HJ' 188–9).

What I shall call Troeltsch's mature or considered Christological reflections are characterized at least partly,[74] then, by his dissociation from Ritschl and Herrmann on precisely the issues he saw presented by 'modern criticism': any appeals to 'impressions' of Jesus that circumvented the painstaking work of historical criticism were now taboo. This Troeltsch had clarified by 1909, but made even more explicit in 1911. Clearly, then, he was faced with an acutely embarrassing dilemma when at the end of that same year he came to revise *The Absoluteness of Christianity* for its second edition. The options were presumably these: he could leave the book as it was, as an expression of his position in 1901; or he could rewrite it entirely, bringing its Christology fully into line with the work he had done in that area in the mean time; or he could forge some sort of compromise between these two in the limited time he had available. In the event it was the last course he adopted.

The result makes strange reading—perhaps even stranger than the first edition. Troeltsch's remark in the new preface that 'The few changes in this new edition are merely stylistic' (*Abs.* 44) is deeply misleading; his admission elsewhere later that the difference between the editions reflected the 'continuing advance of . . . questioning', and that the result was 'uncomfortable', is nearer the point.[75] Outside our specifically Christological concerns there are changes that reflect Troeltsch's shift in philosophical perspective (he had become more critical of

---

against general historical methods . . .'; and on p. 75, the additional phrase 'despite every effort to make statements of faith independent of historical research'.

[74] Other major characteristics were to be, on the one hand, Troeltsch's 'social psychological' reasons for the necessity of the historical Jesus, and, on the other, what he called his 'Christ-mysticism'. For my analysis, see below, chs. 5 and 6.

[75] 'Half C.' 72. This was a footnote added only in the 1913 revision.

Hegel[76]) and a concomitant change in his views about the relation of the 'other' religions to Christianity. He is evidently now less sure that all the religions converge on Christianity and find in it their fulfilment,[77] although he lets that theme still stand alongside.[78] At the same time, he occasionally makes greater allowance than before for the subjectivity of the claim to Christianity's superiority,[79] although he lets that theme stand, too, alongside the more confident 'demonstrations' of the matter elsewhere.[80] In the same vein, he tempers his previous claims for Christianity's eternal superiority by moving to admit that on the whole Christianity's supremacy is confined to this culture and its future;[81] he also allows more pessimistically for the possibility of an ice age, or the end of our present civilization.[82] In addition, he displays a new, and somewhat defensive, attitude to ecclesiastical

[76] This is reflected in a number of ways. See e.g. the newly added footnote (*Abs.* 168 n. 4) with its explicit rejection of Troeltsch's earlier 'strongly Hegelian standpoint'; the sentence significantly added in *Abs.* 75: 'No period is a mere rung on a ladder; each one possesses, in context, its own nature and self-sufficient meaning'; and the frequent allusions to Troeltsch's article on 'Contingency' (in English in *ERE* iv. 87–9) which (implicitly at least) contains a powerful criticism of Hegel's absolute idealism (see *Abs.* 43, 101–2, 166 n. 16).

[77] See e.g. *Abs.* 127: Troeltsch now says of non-Christian 'religious developments': 'These too are all, *in their own right*, living religious movements in which God is at work' (my italics).

[78] See e.g. ibid.: 'it has become Christianity's distinctive task to make itself the crystallization point for the highest and best that has been discovered in the human spiritual world'; see also ibid. 114: Christianity is the 'culmination' and 'convergence point' of 'all the developmental tendencies that can be discerned in religion'. Both these statements are carried over unchanged from the 1st edn.

[79] See esp. *Abs.* 120: the central two paras. here are new additions, where Troeltsch admits that 'we have . . . made a transition from scientific discourse to religious', and 'we have turned to preaching', etc. See again above, ch. 1, for remarks on how this shift affects the consistency of Troeltsch's position.

[80] See e.g. *Abs.* 109–14, which is substantially unchanged from the 1st edn., and which has an almost 'colonial' tone of certainty about Christianity's superiority.

[81] Troeltsch had of course already in the 1st edn. admitted that Christianity might be superseded by a new, superior, revelation (see n. 52 above). But now see e.g. the addition in *Abs.* 94 that, 'as long, at least, as the continuity of our culture endures', Christianity will reign supreme; or the new sentences in ibid. 104–5, affirming that '*Our world of culture* . . . will never produce a "new religion"' (my italics), or the new admission (ibid. 128–9) that Christianity is the embodiment of the absolute 'in our cultural context and our moment of history'.

[82] *Abs.* 91–2 (from 'One can, it is true, have reservations' to 'the more or less clearly known history that it embraces') is a new addition, as is ibid. 115–16 (from 'Again, if every conceivable possibility is to be taken into account'). Both passages consider the possibility that Christianity, along with civilization as we know it *in toto*, could be wiped out by vast planetary or climatic changes.

authority, and specifically avoids talking about the 'Church' as if identifying with an official ecclesiastical position.[83]

These are the non-Christological themes modified in the second edition. But the Christological changes (or lack of them) are even more interesting. Extraordinarily Troeltsch lets stand, at some juncture or other, most of the themes associated with Herrmann's theology that we earlier isolated: the theology of 'claim' (*Abs.* 148, 158–9), *despite* a further rejection of it in a footnote (ibid. 172 n. 5);[84] the impression made by Jesus 'inwardly' or 'in our hearts' (ibid. 123, 126); the tendency to chart Jesus' self-conscious intentions (e.g. ibid. 145, 147); the 'certainty' of faith inspired by Jesus (ibid. 119, 121); and most tortuously of all, the appeal to experiences of Jesus unfettered by historical scholarship (ibid. 161). Here, however, Troeltsch feels obliged to add a new explanatory paragraph, clearly trying to bring what has been said into line with what he had in the mean time written in 'The Significance of the Historical Existence of Jesus for Faith' (1911) about the necessity of keeping Jesus as a focal symbol in the Christian cultus. Thus he adds a sentence about how returning to Christianity's 'foundations' is indeed 'indispensable to the cohesiveness . . . of a religious community' (*Abs.* 161).[85] But the result is at best embarrassed: for in 'The Significance of the Historical Existence of Jesus for Faith' Troeltsch had unambiguously stated that no direct relationship with Jesus was possible, but only that mediated via careful historical work; here, he is frankly stating the opposite, encouraging those with 'naïve' faith not to let 'critical historical scholarship interfere' with being 'grasped by . . . Jesus himself' (*Abs.* 160–1).

The main changes that Troeltsch does make to Christological passages attempt, in one way or another, to tone down the finality of the claims about Jesus that (at points) he had appeared to make in the first edition. Thus, for instance, the two exhortatory passages at the end of the book recommending that one finds, with Paul, a sure 'foundation', or 'ground of salvation', in Jesus

---

[83] See e.g. *Abs.* 126–7 (cf. *A¹* 91). Troeltsch replaces appeals to 'die Kirche' with references instead to 'the Christian community of life and spirit' or 'Christianity'. Also see the defensive, but witty, new footnote, ibid. 171–2.

[84] See also the new statement in *Abs.* 159: 'The validity of Christianity is verified not by arguing the nature and strength of claims to revelation, redemption, and truth but by judging what lies behind the claim.'

[85] See also the footnote here, *Abs.* 172–3.

(A^1 126, 129) are omitted. Likewise, wherever he can, Troeltsch changes appeals to the superiority of Jesus (alone) to appeals to 'personalism' or 'Christianity' or 'the prophetic and Christian world' or 'Jesus and his kingdom'. (*Abs.* 159-60, 126, 121, 126; cf. A^1 126-7, 91, 85, 91). In this way, then, the revelation previously claimed to be found solely in Jesus is significantly democratized. By the same token, the occasional reference to Jesus' 'final and definitive' truth is knocked out,[86] or else toned down by a subtle addition, such as the qualification that (at least) 'in our entire range of vision' (*Abs.* 120) there is no higher revelation than Jesus to be hoped for (cf. A^1 83). In addition, Troeltsch does score out his own previous appeal to the 'inner life' of Jesus,[87] and tries, perhaps not altogether successfully in the surrounding context,[88] to incorporate a paragraph that properly allows for Jesus' eschatological perspective. Now Troeltsch admits that 'by and large the person of Christ retired behind this reality—the kingdom of God' (*Abs.* 145; cf. A^1 111).

The trouble is, as we have shown, that the revision is not consistently or thoroughly carried through. One can only assume that it was done hurriedly or distractedly. Most of the themes paralleled in Herrmann are allowed to stand, while others are slightly modified, or new themes (like the eschatological admission) are simply pasted into the collage. The result is even more bemusing than the first edition, especially when Troeltsch appeals, in his footnotes,[89] to the very writing ('The Significance of the Historical Existence of Jesus for Faith') that would contradict much of what is said here, scoring out altogether the possibility of a direct relationship to Jesus.

---

[86] See A^1 111; cf. *Abs.* 145. Similarly, the appeal in A^1 113 to Jesus' personality as 'supreme' among the 'great fundamental mysteries of reality' is omitted in *Abs.* 148.

[87] See A^1 91; cf. *Abs.* 126: 'the inner life' is changed to 'the life and passion'.

[88] In *Abs.* 144, Troeltsch asserts the indispensability of the 'personal character' of Jesus as an exemplification of the 'universality' of his 'demand and promise'. But his new appreciation of Jesus' eschatological stress (ibid. 145) then leads him to indicate that the message of the kingdom, *rather than* the 'person of Christ', is the core of the original preaching, and that (a new passage in *Abs.* 148) it was the early Christians who were (misguidedly) responsible for transferring the point of 'absoluteness' from the kingdom to the person of Jesus. The result of these additions is that the reader of the 2nd edn. of *The Absoluteness of Christianity* is left very unclear what positive place Troeltsch now wants to ascribe to the *person* of Jesus. In fact, 'Sig. HJ' and *Gl.* provide an answer to this, as we shall see in ch. 5 below; but *Abs.* provides only confused impressions on the issue. For more on the interpretation of this new addition in *Abs.* 148, see below, ch. 4.

[89] See again *Abs.* 142-3.

If we now draw together the complex strands of this chapter, the overall results are these. The general question of the dating of Troeltsch's disengagement from 'Ritschlianism' must, first, depend on precisely what tenets of Ritschlianism are in question. Depending on whether the crucial issue is deemed to be Troeltsch's view on historical periodization, or his espousal of the 'history-of-religions' approach, or the acceptance of the implications of the 'historical method' in general, or his turn to metaphysics, or the issue of supernaturalism, or the rejection of the theology of 'claim'—the list could be extended, but on each criterion, as I have demonstrated, the decisive point of 'disengagement' would be plotted in a subtly different way. As far as my own Christological concerns go, I hope to have shown: first, that the years up to 1900 saw a gradual but steady moving away from discrete themes in the Christology of Ritschl and the 'Ritschlian school', culminating in Troeltsch's strong stand against the possibility of 'immediate' relationships to past 'facts' in 'Über historische und dogmatische Methode'; second, that the strongly Herrmann-like passages in *The Absoluteness of Christianity* represent a distinct reversion towards the 'Ritschlian school' from the position previously attained, and can perhaps only be explained in terms of personal or political motivation; third, that the second edition of the same work is a most inadequate (and indeed in Troeltsch's own words 'uncomfortable') attempt to bring the book into line with the Christology that he had meanwhile formulated; and fourth, that if we are to talk of any decisive break with 'Ritschlian' Christology, then we must probably date it in the years leading up to 1911, when Troeltsch's attacks on Herrmann's and Ritschl's Christological method became particularly sharp, and concentrated criticism on their attempts to avoid submitting the person of Jesus to the full implications of historical critical research. If Troeltsch had voiced these themes long before (as he had),[90] he had not until then been willing, as we have shown, to accept the lessons for himself.[91] Even then, as we shall

---

[90] Implicitly, as we have shown, in 'Über historische und dogmatische Methode der Theologie' (1900); more explicitly already in A^1 43 ff., esp. 48 (= *Abs.* 80 ff., esp. 83).

[91] Troeltsch's characteristic method of work is perhaps an additional explanatory factor here alongside the political motivations we have already indicated. He was, as Harnack recorded in his funeral speech for Troeltsch, a voracious reader (see Pauck 1968, 120), often quicker to consume than to digest; he wrote (and revised) fast too, often, one

explore in later chapters, Troeltsch's mature Christology does not totally dispense with the occasional Christological theme or turn of argument deeply reminiscent of his 'Ritschlian' heritage.[92] But as far as Troeltsch was concerned a break of a very conscious nature had by 1911 been made from what he called the 'intolerable' contradictions of Ritschlian Christology ('Sig. HJ' 188).

assumes, under pressure; and, as Troeltsch himself charmingly admitted, he was 'not a systematic thinker' (*GS* iv. 3). Consistency was not, therefore, his strongest characteristic.

[92] Even in 1913, it is interesting to note, Troeltsch can still refer approvingly to Herrmann's *Communion of the Christian with God* (*AJT* 1913, 18).

3
Troeltsch on God, Redemption, and Revelation

In this and the remaining chapters we shall be primarily concerned with what I have called Troeltsch's 'mature' theological reflections, dating, that is, from about 1909 onwards.[1] It is principally in his scattered articles on dogmatics for the first edition of *Die Religion in Geschichte und Gegenwart* (these contributions appeared from 1909 to 1913) and in his posthumously published *Glaubenslehre* (lectures from 1912–13)[2] that we find what Troeltsch described as his 'positive' contribution to systematic theology (see *GS* iv. 13). In this chapter we shall not attempt to solve the delicate problem of the extent to which Troeltsch regarded his dogmatic work as 'scientific' in character; nor shall we aim to provide a detailed or even rounded analysis of this dogmatic corpus;[3] instead we shall simply describe those aspects of his doctrines of God, redemption, and revelation which help to explain his rejection of an incarnational Christology. This will lead on to a precise enumeration of the reasons for this rejection in the next chapter. But here, for the mean time, we shall concentrate on

[1] I have shown in ch. 2 that 1909 brought a particularly overt rejection of the Ritschlian school's theology in 'Rückblick auf ein halbes Jahrhundert der theologischen Wissenschaft' ('Half C'.). It was also the year of the publication of the 1st vol. of *RGG*. However, we should note that several of the articles on dogmatic themes later incorporated in *RGG* (some without changes) had already appeared in 1907 (see Graf and Ruddies 1982, 80 ff.) and we should thus use 1909 only as a rough point of demarcation. Similarly, when I talk of Troeltsch's 'mature' theology I do not in any way mean to imply that from this point his thought lacks further development, as will be amply demonstrated later.

[2] Not from 1911 to 1912, as stated in the text. See again ch. 2 n. 5.

[3] For a brief discussion of the problem of the 'scientific' status of Troeltsch's dogmatics (on which point he cannot be said to have been fully consistent), see A. O. Dyson's 'Ernst Troeltsch and the Possibility of a Systematic Theology' in ed. Clayton 1976, 81–99, and (much more fully) Wyman 1983, esp. 46–57, 90–6, 120–8, 167–9, 193–203. A detailed analysis of his complete dogmatic corpus is not yet available, but useful brief discussions are to be found in Köhler 1941, 161–92, Kasch 1963, 177–210, in Gerrish's article 'Ernst Troeltsch and the Possibility of a Historical Theology' (in ed. Clayton 1976, 100–35), and in Wyman 1983, 129–69.

showing how Troeltsch's metaphysic of history is expanded into the language of Christian dogmatic theology, and then how Troeltsch uses it to do much of the work that more traditional theologians would ascribe to the doctrine of Christ.

Since doctrines of God, redemption, and revelation are of necessity closely interrelated, it is virtually impossible to deal with them in neat succession. The division of the material here is mine rather than Troeltsch's, but I trust it will conduce to clarity, as well as help to draw out some of the more controversial aspects of Troeltsch's system. Starting with a preliminary analysis of Troeltsch's concept of God and of his self-manifestation in progressive revelation, we shall then look at redemption and revelation as received by individuals, and finally return from there to examine further implications for the doctrine of God, in particular for the doctrine of the Trinity.

I. GOD AS TRANSCENDENT AND IMMANENT

When Troeltsch talks of the transcendence of God outside his specifically theological works, his language is often disconcertingly abstract, owing far more, apparently, to the influence of the German tradition of idealist metaphysics than to biblical understandings of God. Thus, for instance, the transcendent God is the 'Absolute', the 'unchanging value . . . [that] exists not within but beyond history' (*Abs.* 90); or it is an idea that arises 'out of the examination of experience and the attempt to unify it in final terms';[4] or again, in *Der Historismus*, 'the idea of God' or 'something analogous' (*sic*)[5] is necessary for the 'construction of criteria' for evaluating history (*GS* iii. 183–4).

Very different, however, is the religiously motivated insistence

---

[4] 'Religion and the Science of Religion' (1906), in ed. Morgan and Pye 1977, 118.

[5] For Gogarten this phraseology was 'idolatrous and delusive' and indicative of Troeltsch having 'abandoned theology' (see ed. Robinson 1968, 349–50). Writing in 1924 Gogarten could not refer to Troeltsch's *Glaubenslehre* in published form, but some allusion to his *RGG* articles would have helped clarify that this was not Troeltsch's last word on God. It was simply that *Der Historismus* was not the place to be engaging in 'positive' dogmatic theology. One of Troeltsch's last letters to Bousset reveals (in contrast to the dialectical theologians' characteristic propaganda on the issue) that, far from giving up dogmatic theology gratefully on his move to Berlin, Troeltsch missed it acutely (see Dinkler-von Schubert 1976, 51).

in the *Glaubenslehre* on the mystery of an indescribable Godhead: in conscious contrast to the 'pure rationalists' Troeltsch declares that 'No predications of God are possible without limiting him: as soon as we apply scholarly methods we run into the impossibility of giving expression to him . . .' (*Gl.* 53). Here there is a forceful distinction made between experience and conceptualization. The mystery of the experience of a transcendent reality defies reduction to a mere intellectual postulate: 'Religion may not be reduced to academic knowledge (*Wissenschaft*)' (ibid.). Moreover, and in addition, God's transcendence may be experienced on occasions as terrifying, awesome, and irrational (ibid. 161-2): these are traits which Troeltsch describes as necessarily following from the notion of God as invading 'will' (*Gl.* § 12). And his treatment of God as 'love', too, (*Gl.* § 14) is no less revealing of his own experience of the transcendent. Thus, with a hint of possible influence from St John of the Cross, Troeltsch strenuously denies that God's love is 'sentimental'; the approach of God may be more nearly experienced as 'frightening', 'negative', and 'powerful' than as consoling. On occasions God may have to hit hard, as with a chisel (*Meißel*), in order to rupture our 'hard shells' (*Gl.* 222).

What is quite clear here, then (as it is perhaps not in *Der Historismus*), is that Troeltsch's God is not just a hypothesis conjured up by philosophy of religion, a Kantian postulate of reason, but, on the contrary, a being with whom philosophy must come to terms as already vibrantly existent. We recall that Troeltsch had already in his early writings devoted much energy and effort to an attempt to demonstrate the transcendence of God in the sense of his extra-subjective reality or *irreducibility*;[6] now, in the *Glaubenslehre*, and in confessional vein, he clothes that transcendence in the particular attributes of 'will', 'holiness', and 'love' (*Gl.* § 12-14), all of which evoke awe and wonder. At the same time he persistently underlines the ultimate *unknowability* of God, which we may take to be a further way of construing divine 'transcendence'. Later, in his last work *Christian Thought*, his revised position on the truth claims of the world religions leads him to stress the divine transcendence in this last sense further

---

[6] See esp. 'Die Selbständigkeit der Religion' (*ZTK* 1895-6) and *Psychologie und Erkenntnistheorie in der Religionswissenschaft* (1905).

still. The 'Divine Life', as Troeltsch now refers to God, is believed to take up into itself the truths of all the great religions (*Chr. Th.* 31-2, 35). Hence, of necessity, God's essential being becomes still more ineffable and mysterious, transcending even the apparent contradictions of the great religious systems.

Thus the theme of God's transcendence, understood in a variety of ways, is undoubtedly present in Troeltsch, indeed strenuously maintained;[7] but it must be admitted that his stress on God's immanence is far more characteristic. There are at least two reasons for this. First, Troeltsch is determined to combat what he calls a 'dualistic' understanding of God. This is in the first place part of his objection in his early period to a particular sort of 'supernaturalism'.[8] His attack on 'dualistic supernaturalism' is clearly enunciated in his debate with Niebergall in 1900, and amounts to a rejection of what we would now call a 'God of the gaps'. Niebergall's God, he objects, has a 'duality in the divine nature'. He is 'involved in every vital moment' as 'the purposive will that produces the motion of the total system'. But he is also 'capable of extraordinary activities . . . that break through and abrogate the ordinary operation of the system' (*GS* ii. 743). Read in context we see that this is not so much an objection to the miraculous *per se*, least of all to the 'bursting forth' of specific divine initiatives (which Troeltsch himself, as we shall see, wishes in a particular sense to defend), but a religious objection to the idea that God has two distinct modes of activity: one relatively unimportant and humdrum, which critical scholarship is allowed to probe, and the other salvifically decisive but sealed off from critical scrutiny. The emphasis on the 'extraordinary

---

[7] It was not for nothing that von Hügel was so deeply attracted to the theme of irreducible transcendence in Troeltsch's early work. As Daly (1980, 117-39) has recently shown, what worried von Hügel more than anything else was the prospect of 'pure immanentism', i.e. the loss of the sense of the objective transcendence of God. As long as that could be secured, however, he was quite content to be strongly immanentist in tone, especially in what Daly delineates as his 'modernist' phase (1895-1910). Much the same could be said of Troeltsch's particular combination of transcendence and immanence.

[8] We have already touched on Troeltsch's objections to the Ritschlian school's form of 'supernaturalism' in chs. 1 and 2. The point under discussion here (the assertion of a 'dualism' even in the divine nature) is only one aspect of Troeltsch's objection to 'dualistic supernaturalism' (though an important one). The central criticism, from which this one follows, is that 'dualistic' or 'exclusive' supernaturalism asserts that there are some (critically inviolable) areas of pure divine activity intruded into the ordinary flow of human history. For more discussion of this see ch. 4 below.

activities' inevitably downgrades the significance of God's presence 'in every vital moment'. A similar motive fires a much later
objection to 'dualism' (in a slightly different sense) in a fascinating
little skirmish Troeltsch had in 1921 with his pupil Gogarten. Here
we get our only glimpse of Troeltsch's reaction to the emerging
'dialectical' theology. It is not 'supernaturalism' that is the problem this time, but a 'radical dualism' in the sense of an extreme
disjunction between God and his creation. Gogarten, says
Troeltsch, is an heir to Kierkegaard in his idea of God as in
'radical contrast to the world', and in his 'disregard of all mediation between God and the world'.[9] What Troeltsch objects to,
then, as we can see in both these examples, is any conception of
transcendence that undermines or compromises the possibility of
God's continual and supportive presence, of his persistent self-
mediation in history. In slightly different ways, Niebergall's and
Gogarten's 'dualism' both have this tendency, and only a firm
stand on immanence can correct it—or so Troeltsch believes.

But secondly, and apart from this theological point,
Troeltsch's metaphysic clearly conduces to an emphasis on God's
immanence. According to the 'metalogic', each individual 'participates intuitively' in the Absolute; and the relativized 'values'
available in the unfolding course of history are the result of an absolute value cohering (in partial forms) in historical events (*GS* iii.
211 ff.). Thus, in the *Glaubenslehre* Troeltsch will say that reflections on relativism lead to a particular understanding of God's
(immanent) self-revelation in history (*Gl.* 94–5). As he puts it
later in his reply to Gogarten: God's 'being and continuous
creative activity . . . are not opposed to the world as Gogarten has
it; *they carry the world in themselves:* they are themselves the life of the
world . . .' (ed. Robinson 1968, 314–15, my italics).

Troeltsch's stress on divine immanence leads naturally into a
doctrine of progressive, or continual, revelation.[10] In his article
on 'Historiography' written for Hastings' *Encyclopaedia*, he talks

---

[9] 'An Apple from the Tree of Kierkegaard' (1921) in ed. Robinson 1968, 312 (see p. 314
for the charge of 'radical dualism'). It should be added that Troeltsch himself does of
course wish to uphold a *form* of 'dualism' (i.e. a maintenance of the transcendence of
God sufficient to avoid the trap of 'monism'). See ibid. 314 f. for Troeltsch's description
of his own 'wholly instinctive and naive concept of religious dualism'.

[10] There may well be influence here from Richard Rothe, as Moltmann (1967, 225 f.)
suggests. For Troeltsch's appreciation of Rothe, see his *Richard Rothe* (1899), and esp.
34 f. for this theme.

of '. . . the absolute in the relative, *yet not fully and finally in it*, but always pressing towards fresh forms of self-expression . . .' (*ERE* vi. 722^b, my italics). In the *Glaubenslehre* progressive revelation is a dominant theme. God's revelation is not confined to the Bible, or to Jesus, but manifests itself in and through the Church's entire history up to the present (see *Gl.* 39 ff., 118 ff.). This is the 'working out of the Divine Life (*die Auswirkung des göttlichen Lebens*)' (ibid. 39). The saints, in particular, expand on and develop the revelation seen in Jesus (see ibid. 120 and 'Sig. HJ' 201). In all this, Troeltsch, as a Protestant, applauds and defends the distinctively Catholic teaching of revelation expanding through the Christian tradition (*Gl.* 47).

Several further points of clarification must now be made about Troeltsch's doctrines of divine immanence and progressive revelation. First, in Troeltsch's early writings, and for the most part during his period at Heidelberg, God's revelation is conceived of as 'progressive' in the sense of teleological. We are already familiar with this theme from *The Absoluteness of Christianity* ('the universally valid . . . works teleologically within history', etc.: *Abs.* 106) and from Troeltsch's earlier discussions of the 'essence' of Christianity.[11] In the *Glaubenslehre* too, this is still Troeltsch's understanding. It is admitted that God reveals himself in 'the most varied forms of expression' according to each 'total situation (*Gesamtlage*)'. But in these forms 'may be recognized a sequence and progression in ethical and spiritual terms' (*Gl.* 2). It is true that Troeltsch rejects what he sees as the Hegelian error of a necessary and ordered progression (see e.g. *Abs.* 66 ff.). But he is clear none the less that God's self-revelations are self-consistent and unified. By the end of his career, however, this confidence is tempered. The teleological theme has not disappeared; it is still hoped (in faith) that all religion 'has a common ground in the Divine Spirit ever pressing the finite mind onward towards further light and fuller consciousness' (*Chr. Th.* 32). But it is admitted now that the 'Divine Life' cannot be trained into one revelatory progression. For it 'constantly manifests itself in always-new and always-

---

[11] By 'earlier discussions' I mean principally the two edns. of 'Was heißt, "Wesen des Christentums"?' (1903 and 1913), which, as I argued in ch. 1, can be contrasted with the apparently more radical departure in *AJT* 1913, where the idea of one (teleologically developing) 'essence' falls away.

peculiar individualisations — and hence . . . its tendency is not towards unity or universality at all' (ibid. 14). On this, later, view, God's self-revelation remains continuous, but not 'progressive' in the sense of a consistent or unified evolution.

A second point of clarification that may be needed is that Troeltsch's stress on divine immanence and progressive revelation does not for him imply an equal, or democratic, revelation of God at all times. 'At special points' there may be 'bursts' of divine revelation (*Abs.* 69); 'from time to time' God reveals himself in a more 'clear and distinct' way than at other times (ibid. 99).[12] In short, revelations may differ in 'content, depth, and majesty' (*Gl.* 51). Thus, despite Troeltsch's assault on Niebergall and his kind, he is still willing to allow that God does not necessarily manifest himself consistently. It is not just that people are inconsistent in their response, but that God actually reveals himself more fully through some people and contexts than through others.

A third point to clarify is that Troeltsch is very insistent that the mode of divine immanence and revelation is entirely mysterious: he talks of the 'secret (*Geheimnis*)' of the connection of the human and divine (*Gl.* 41).[13] I stress this only because Troeltsch is sometimes accused of 'reading off' revelation from history, as if it were openly available for public inspection.[14] But on the contrary, revelation in history according to Troeltsch may only be perceived by faith (despite his occasional remarks in *The Absoluteness of Christianity* that suggest otherwise[15]). Troeltsch's article on 'Revelation' for *RGG* (1913) opens with a clear statement that the concept of revelation always 'belongs'

---

[12] Admittedly in these two particular passages in *Abs.* Troeltsch is employing the language of philosophy of history (of 'principles', 'universals', or historical 'goals') rather than speaking in specifically theological terms (of revelation, or acts of God). As we shall shortly demonstrate, however, it would have been unthinkable for Troeltsch to divorce human historical development from specific divine initiatives: his is not a 'deist', or absentee, conception of God. Any human religious development is always at the same time a response to the specific pressure of the divine.

[13] The same theme of the inextricability of the human and divine in revelation was, as we noted in ch. 2, already characteristic of Troeltsch's early writings, esp. 'Die Selbständigkeit der Religion' (*ZTK* 1895-6) and 'Geschichte und Metaphysik' (*ZTK* 1898).

[14] So Morgan in ed. Clayton 1976, 59; see my criticisms in Coakley 1977, 327-8.

[15] See e.g. *Abs.* 98: 'The nature of this goal [of history] can be known'; but then compare e.g. ibid. 90: the absolute can only be perceived in 'presentiment and faith'. We have already discussed this ambiguity in ch. 1.

with that of religious faith. Indeed, 'The being and working of God *cannot be read off from the world* . . . and cannot be proved unless one brings this faith with oneself as presupposed' ("Of-fenbarung", *RGG* 918, § 1, my italics).

A fourth and final point, which leads on from Troeltsch's conception of the human and divine as mysteriously intercon-nected, is the suspicion—voiced by Müller (1966, 343), and more recently by Gerrish (ed. Clayton 1976, 119 f.)—that Troeltsch's emphasis on divine immanence lapses into 'pan-theism'.[16] What is meant by 'pantheism' in this context is the loss of adequate distinction between the divine and the human. Troeltsch is however aware of the danger: as Gerrish himself shows, he repeatedly returns in the *Glaubenslehre* to the problem of distinguishing his own brand of Christian theism from 'pan-theism' or 'Buddhist monism'. The main distinction, he claims, lies in the place made in Christian theism for the distinctive worth of the individual, and his or her freedom to respond—or indeed not to respond—to the sense of God.[17] The question is really whether this distinction between God and the individual can in practice be sufficiently maintained in the light of Troeltsch's belief in their (mysterious) interpenetration. We shall return to this issue shortly, but a treatment of Troeltsch's views on redemption must precede any definitive conclusions.

II. REDEMPTION

'Redemption', for Troeltsch, means individual events of re-demption ('inner transformations'), not a representative re-demption effected through Christ's death. Troeltsch describes the traditional understanding of a once-for-all redemption as an 'impossible' belief ('Glaube und Geschichte', *RGG* 1455, §4). The reasons for this are complex, and we shall leave detailed ex-amination of them for the next chapter. But the main argument

[16] Müller, writing from a Barthian standpoint, is hostile to Troeltsch's whole understanding of dogmatics, and charges Troeltsch with 'pantheism' without any men-tion of the many passages in *Gl.* where Troeltsch tries to dissociate his position from this. Gerrish's analysis is much fairer, and restricts this charge to Troeltsch's eschatology.

[17] See the citations from *Gl.* given by Gerrish (ed. Clayton 1976, 119), namely *Gl.* 73–6, 141–2, 169–70, 184–5, 196–7, 357–9. Also relevant are ibid. 77, 157 ff.; 'On Poss.' 28ᵃ ff.; 'Erlösung', *RGG* 482–3, § 2; and *GS* ii. 826.

is already clear: God's continual presence, his *immanence*, makes
a past and distant act of redemption religiously unnecessary
('Erlösung', *RGG* 484, §3: 'die Immanenz Gottes im
Weltleben'). Redemption need no longer be seen as a cosmic
tour de force on the part of the deity, but something recurrently
available, 'an essential component of the eternal creation of
God' (ibid.). Redemption can be something newly effected for
each believer; it becomes an 'elevation and liberation of the person through the attainment of a higher personal and communal
life from God'.[18] Troeltsch regards this view as especially
characteristic of 'liberal' or 'modern' theology,[19] but he
remarks in his *Social Teaching* that it has always been found in
brands of 'mystical' Christianity.[20]

Individual redemption has four central components, according to Troeltsch (*Gl.* 328 ff.; 'Erlösung', *RGG* 485 ff., §§ 4 ff.).
First, it is a salvation from personal *suffering*—in the specific sense
of 'existential anguish (*Weltleid*)'.[21] This suffering, Troeltsch
holds, is an inevitable part of a world that is 'finite' and turned
towards the 'natural level' rather than towards the spiritual. But
suffering can actually help to precipitate redemption: in an approach which interestingly parallels a strain in the early Barth,[22]
Troeltsch remarks that 'in suffering we recognize a reminder of
the limits and insufficiency of natural being . . . suffering drives
us beyond nature and helps us turn our back upon it'
('Erlösung', *RGG* 485, § 4). Through the experience of redemption suffering is not removed ('objectively' it remains the same),
but it is seen in a new light. It is recognized not only as
'necessary', but also as (ultimately) 'transitory' (ibid., end of
§ 4).

Second, redemption means a new attitude to *sin*. According
to Troeltsch the process of redemption both highlights the full
seriousness of sin and gives assurance of 'God's grace and

---

[18] 'On Poss.' 27ᵇ; see also 'Erlösung', *RGG* 481–8 *passim*, and *Gl.* 356, etc.

[19] See 'On Poss.' 27ᵃ⁻ᵇ; 'Erlösung', *RGG* 484, § 3; 'Protestantisches Christentum
und Kirche in der Neuzeit' (1906), 426–7, 447; 'Sig. HJ' 184 f.

[20] *ST* 995–6; see also 'Sig. HJ' 186.

[21] 'World-weariness' would be a more slavish translation, but would not fully catch
the sense Troeltsch intends. There may well be echoes of Hegel's notion of 'alienation'
here.

[22] See Barth 1933, 132: God 'is to be found on the plain where men suffer and sin', etc.;
see also ibid. 155 ff.

readiness to forgive': 'By coming to know his own sinfulness, man learns to desist from relying on his own power, and by believing in the grace of forgiveness he learns to surrender himself to God' (ibid. 486, § 5).

Third, and concomitantly, redemption saves the individual from 'ethical and religious weakness (*Unkraft*)' (*Gl*. 328, 337 f.), and leads to 'a new strength for life . . . which gives us the inclination and strength trustfully to surrender our natural self to the Divine Life' ('Erlösung', *RGG* 486, § 6). These first three features of redemption all cohere together in one experience, and this experience apparently has a quality of immediacy and self-authentication or, as Troeltsch sometimes puts it, of *objectivity*. This 'objectivity', according to Troeltsch, favourably replaces that asserted for the old model of redemption: 'it becomes necessary to see the objective side of redemption in the religious experience, in the present redeeming and elevating work of God in the soul that surrenders itself to him' ('Glaube und Geschichte', *RGG* 1456, § 4).

The fourth component of redemption is somewhat different from the first three, and might seem to follow rather oddly after this emphasis on present experience. But Troeltsch insists that the source of redemptive experience is not simply the 'many impressions conveyed by life itself', although this present reference is clearly important. It must also, however, be based on 'the collective strength and experience of the Christian community', and pre-eminently on reflection on the 'person of Jesus' himself (see 'Erlösung', *RGG* 486-7, § 7). But this raises a difficulty, and one central to Troeltsch's theology. Why is Jesus thus necessary for redemption, if present redemptive experience has all the ring of self-authentication? Further, will any freely interpreted 'impression' of him do, as Troeltsch here suggests (ibid. 487, § 7), or is the 'historical Jesus' (as recovered through intricate historical analysis) also necessary in some way for redemption and faith? These are questions to which we shall have to return in detail when we examine Troeltsch's Christology in Chapters 5 and 6.

But something that is illuminating on this point, and worth mentioning now, is the firm stand Troeltsch takes in his article on the 'essence' of Christianity against the views of von Hartmann, who had categorically denied any importance of the

person of Jesus for Christianity, and relocated the 'essence' of
Christianity in the idea of the 'sameness' of God and man
('Essence' 172). Troeltsch feels sufficiently strongly on this issue
to expand the attack on von Hartmann at some length in the
second edition of the article.[23] He insists on the indispensability
of 'a redeeming personality' (ibid. 170 n. 10) and upholds, interestingly, the importance of the idea of 'the sacrifice of the one
for the many' (ibid. 173) in the face of von Hartmann's
'pessimistic pantheism', where Christology is simply taken as a
'mystical symbol' of a 'painful world-process' (ibid.) This,
then, is further evidence that according to Troeltsch redemption cannot be dissociated from reflection on Jesus, however
significant present and privatized experience may also be.

Obviously the case of von Hartmann also throws interesting
light on the issue of Troeltsch and 'pantheism'. One could
hardly hope to find a more fervent rejection of the idea of the
'sameness of God and the world' than here (ibid. 172). The
material on redemption in Troeltsch's dogmatic corpus,
however, confirms this rejection only with some important
qualifications. At the outset, Troeltsch does indeed maintain a
clear distinction between the divine and human, wielding the
traditional language of grace and freedom (see *Gl.* 359). In the
process of redemption God's initiative of grace and forgiveness
must be met by the individual's (free) willingness to respond.
But as Troeltsch describes the individual's further spiritual
development the language becomes more ambiguous. He talks
of the believer gradually growing 'through devotion *into* the life
of God' ('Erlösung', *RGG*, 486, § 6, my italics), and this is apparently no mere poetic metaphor. For in his section on
redemption and the 'final consummation' Troeltsch states his
belief that the individual soul eventually (after further growth
beyond death) 'returns definitively into the Divine Life'.[24] Gerrish is right, then, to complain that Troeltsch's *eschatology*
capitulates to absorption or a loss of clear distinction between
God and the individual. In this rather restricted and unusual

[23] Cf. *CW* 1903, 682 ff., with 'Essence' 170 ff. Even in the 1903 edn. Troeltsch asserts
in the strongest terms that 'faith in Jesus . . . is for us the prerequisite for the most essential [component] in the essence of Christianity . . .' (*CW* 1903, 683), and roundly rejects
von Hartmann's 'pantheistic' version of the incarnation.

[24] 'Erlösung', *RGG* 487, § 8. See also 'Eschatologie', *RGG* 630, § 4; *Gl.* 381-2.

sense, therefore, one may convict Troeltsch of 'pantheism', though the charge of 'neo-Platonism' might have been more apposite.[25] Yet in Troeltsch's defence it must be said that he makes a fairly clear distinction between 'earthly redemption' and the (eschatological) 'fullness of redemption' (Erlösung', *RGG* 487, § 8), and where the former is concerned the charge of 'pantheism' cannot I think be sustained.[26]

A final problem raised by Troeltsch's doctrine of redemption is one which really concerns his doctrine of humanity. Both Barth and Brunner have accused Troeltsch of not taking human sinfulness seriously (Barth 1956, 384; Brunner 1934, 137–8, and see 265–6). Is human nature ultimately sinful in Troeltsch's view, or is it really potentially divine? That, at any rate, is the dichotomy Barth would seem to force upon Troeltsch. It is true that Troeltsch's discussion of redemption reveals an ambiguity, which Barth is not slow to exploit against him. On the one hand there is talk of the 'sinfulness and egotism of the finite creature' ('Erlösung', *RGG* 484, § 3) and his need to 'learn to desist from relying on his own power . . . [and] to surrender himself to God' (ibid. 486, § 5). On the other hand, there is said to be a 'latent' capacity in humanity freely to repudiate 'self-love' and 'self-glorification'.[27] And suffering is described as prompting us 'to seek the deeper spiritual strengths *in ourselves*' (ibid. 485, § 4, my italics). But this ambiguity is of course—as Barth himself points out (1956, 384)—a corollary of Troeltsch's rejection of a

[25] See Gerrish in ed. Clayton 1976, 119–21, whose objections were anticipated by Sleigh 1923, 224 ff. Troeltsch is entirely willing to concede the *proximity* of his thought here to neo-Platonic emanationism (see *Gl.* 364, 381), but it is important to note that what 'union' or 'absorption' mean to him is the freely given alignment of the human will with God's will in love. This, in a 'timeless' context beyond death, would, Troeltsch thinks, amount to 'absorption' (see ibid. 364, 381; 'Eschatologie', *RGG* 630, § 4; and see 'Theodizee', *RGG* 1191, § 3).

[26] Troeltsch himself draws this line in the *Gl.*: there may be an element of 'pantheism' in his eschatology, he admits, but 'For the practice of the present, we hold on to theism . . .' (*Gl.* 239). It may also be of relevance to note, on the subject of Troeltsch's supposed 'pantheistic' tendencies, that he actually goes out of his way to underline that Jesus, at any rate, did not teach a mystical unification with God involving loss of individual identity (*Gl.* 197). Troeltsch then is fully aware of the speculative quality of his eschatology, and admits that here is an area of dogmatics where we are virtually compelled to move beyond what Jesus has to offer: for Jesus, the (imminent) establishment of the kingdom on earth was the central concern, and 'Eschatology in the proper sense' (life after death) 'played a rather minor role in his preaching' ('Eschatologie', *RGG* 630–1, § 5).

[27] 'An Apple from the Tree of Kierkegaard', ed. Robinson 1968, 315.

traditional atonement theory. The old model of an apparently ineradicable sinfulness, 'atoned for' or 'satisfied' by a representative death, is laid aside. Hence Troeltsch must find the means of our hope elsewhere—in our own individual experience of redemption. No wonder, then, that both pessimistic and optimistic themes coexist in Troeltsch's anthropology.[28]

III. INDIVIDUAL REVELATION

Having 'individualized' the concept of redemption, Troeltsch is left in the position of virtually equating it with that of revelation. We have already discussed Troeltsch's understanding of progressive revelation; but it is the concept of *individual* revelation which is decisive and primary for him. Personal revelation, he says, must be for him the 'overmastering (*zwingende*)' factor

[28] In part we can explain this by saying that here Troeltsch simply stands in a tradition reaching back to Schleiermacher, for whom fall and redemption are also recurrently available options (see Schleiermacher 1963, i. 244 ff. and 271 ff.). But we can say a little more here than simply ascribing an influence, despite the sketchiness of the position Troeltsch adumbrates. What is clear is that the dichotomy Barth is after (either Troeltsch should accept the radical, 'objective guilt' of humanity or admit that it has no real need of redemption *ab extra* at all (Barth 1956, 384-5)) is just not one that Troeltsch would accept as valid. Human nature according to him is neither wholly corrupt nor wholly self-sufficient. Thus the (related) problem of divine grace and autonomous human freedom is only acute, he urges, if God and humanity are set over against one another as two absolutely distinct entities (see 'Gnade Gottes', *RGG* 1473, § 4). If, however, we agree that human freedom is actually logically dependent on divine freedom for its existence, then the apparent irreconcilability between 'synergism' and a pure gift of grace is mitigated (ibid.). Luther's 'faith alone' *is* true, but in the sense that any free act which we may previously (and wrongly) have perceived as solely our own 'work' is in fact a work of God's creativity in us (ibid.). Not, Troeltsch admits, that there is not a remaining logical 'antinomy' here between divine and human freedom. But this is somewhat resolved in practical terms by the experience of the *Ineinander* of the divine and the human. At the same time, Troeltsch is deeply concerned to uphold the reality of 'radical evil' (see e.g. *Gl.* 303-4, 314, and for Barth's comments, 1956, 385), and (even from his earliest writings) to distinguish his position from that of a naïvely 'optimistic idealism' (see e.g. *GS* ii. 301). This emerges with particular force in a revealing (but little known) article 'Ostern', which Troeltsch wrote towards the end of the harrowing experience of World War I, and where he urges his readership to face up to 'the deep inner darkness of our life' (*Deutscher Wille*, 1 Apr. 1918, 6).

In sum, Troeltsch's views on freedom, grace, and sin are rather more subtle than Barth gives him credit for, and the ambiguity in his understanding of the nature of humanity is deliberately upheld, not lapsed into through failure to locate a latent contradiction.

For a full and detailed historical account of Barth's response to Troeltsch's writings see Groll 1976.

in religion (*Gl.* 47). On the other hand, as with redemption, revelatory experiences cannot occur without 'stimulus' from the resources of the Christian tradition ('Offenbarung', *RGG* 919-20, § 2), and particularly from the 'intensification and elevation of the personal life proceeding from Jesus' (ibid. 921, § 4.3). Strictly speaking, therefore, Troeltsch concludes, Christian revelation is threefold: 'fundamental in Jesus, forward developing in history, and finally . . . in individual religiosity and illumination' (ibid. 921, § 4.2). But the core definition of revelation remains the 'inner sensing and certainty' of God (ibid. 918, § 1).

For a clear understanding of what Troeltsch is referring to as 'revelation', then, we must say that he sees it first and foremost as the inextricable combination of divine act and human experiential response. It is 'a matter of the divine and human *within* each other, and it is not possible easily to separate the absolute divine truth and the human admixture' (ibid. 921, § 4.4, my italics). Revelation in this sense, however, may vary enormously in its power and depth, and in a religion such as Christianity the ordinary believer is dependent for this on the inspiration of prior revelation (in the same sense[29]) in the prophets, Jesus, the apostles, the fathers, and the saints.[30] Hence Troeltsch's distinction here between 'productive' and 'reproductive' revelation: on the whole, ordinary believers' experience of revelation is 'reproductive', dependent, that is, on a more fundamental or normative (or 'productive') revelation outside them; but even so their own experience will have an element of 'relative productivity' (*Gl.* 42).[31] Productive and

[29] See 'Religionsphilosophie' (1904), 127: revelation 'need not at all be conceived (in the wooden manner of many doctrinaire theologians) as a sum of doctrines or dogmas. It may well be viewed as the totality of a practical religious power and mood emanating from the centres of revelation which only assumes fixed form in doctrines and concepts.' Or again, 'Glaube', *RGG* 1439, § 2: 'Revelation is the productive and original appearance of new religious power, the practical elevation of life as a whole, which communicates its powers through its bearer.'

[30] See e.g. *Gl.* 41, 120; 'Sig. HJ' 201, 202-3.

[31] Troeltsch had first made this distinction between 'productive' and 'reproductive' revelation in 'Geschichte und Metaphysik' (*ZTK* 1898, 59). In the *Glaubenslehre*, it should perhaps be added, the distinction is drawn in a somewhat more subtle way, since now Troeltsch underlines that the original ('productive') revelation is always received in a particular cultural context which affects its interpretation (see *Gl.* 42-3).

reproductive revelations are not however different in kind, but only in strength or intensity. From all this we can see that Troeltsch's core understanding of revelation requires no wedge to be driven between revelation in history and revelation in present experience, as Morgan (ed. Clayton 1976, 58–9) has suggested.[32]

However, we do need to note that Troeltsch is also willing to allow 'revelation' to include the meaning of the deposit of faith in Bible and doctrine (the 'Catholic' view[33]), though only in a secondary sense. This is not to say that such reflective revelational content is not important, indeed indispensable:

> For revelation always requires some kind of documentation where the revelation can be known in classical and normative form . . . This documentation—however much freedom may be possible in its interpretation and the elaboration of its implications—still constitutes the authority that religion cannot do without, either for the formation of its community or for the conviction that its idea is to be recognised as valid truth. ('Religionsphilosophie' (1904), 128.)

In the *Glaubenslehre* Troeltsch more guardedly refers to this revelational deposit (in particular the Bible) as 'testimony' to personal revelation rather than revelation itself (*Gl.* 41). Strictly speaking it reveals only in so far as it provides a real and 'effective picture' of the original, experiential, revelation to which it testifies (ibid.). But either way, here is further evidence that the root meaning of revelation for Troeltsch is something experiential and individual.

From here we are in a position to see how 'revelation' now becomes almost indistinguishable from redemption in Troeltsch's view. This is evident from a comparison of the two appropriate contributions to *RGG*. Troeltsch apparently felt constrained, as systematics editor, to write two separate articles, 'Offenbarung' and 'Erlösung', and he duly did so. But, in the last section of the article 'Offenbarung', revelation and redemption are simply treated synonymously ('Offenbarung', *RGG* 921, § 4). It is true that the term 'redemption' is reserved for the particular religious experience of salvation from suffer-

---

[32] See again my remarks in Coakley 1977, 327–8.
[33] See *Gl.* 47: Troeltsch says here that he can only endorse this 'Catholic' view 'in part (*teilweise*)'.

ing, sin, and weakness. But this is really the only distinction from the (more inclusive) concept of revelation, since redemption is itself a 'religious experience'. Presumably Troeltsch could have reserved the term 'redemption' for the first, decisive religious experience—a moment of conversion, say. But this is not a distinction he wanted to exploit, any more than Ritschl, his teacher in dogmatics, had wished to limit the process of 'redemption' to the original verdict of justification on an individual (see Ritschl 1972, 237). Thus redemptive experience according to Troeltsch always continues and progresses ('it takes place . . . in every moment . . . we feel God to be present in the forgiveness of sins') ('Erlösung', *RGG* 486, § 5). And likewise, 'revelation' too is applied to a limitless series of 'moments' in the individual's developing religious life.[34]

Perhaps Troeltsch's equation of revelation and redemption may not so greatly surprise us when we take his most characteristic definitions of religion into account. For him, 'religion', in spite of all his keen interest in its sociological and ethical aspects, remains essentially mystical. It is, 'in the stricter sense', 'elevation to the divine in religious experience' (*Abs.* 102); it is a 'real interpenetration of the human and the divine spirit' (*Gl.* 2); in short, 'the primary phenomenon of all religion is mysticism'.[35] And while it is true that after his work for *The Social Teaching* Troeltsch was far less sanguine about 'mystical' religion having any self-sustaining power without the complementary support of community and cult (see *ST* 993-4), that is not to say that he ever abandoned his conviction that mysticism must be at the living heart of any viable religious movement.[36]

[34] Troeltsch particularly refers here to moments of prayer and meditation. See 'Religion and the Science of Religion' (1906) in ed. Morgan and Pye 1977, 92: '. . . every religious person knows the amazing variety of intensity in the various religious moments of his life . . . Everyone knows that these moments are to be found in prayer and in meditation. To these above all a theory of religion must do justice, if it is to be not a mere metaphysical system for the intellect, but a theory of religion as it really is.'

[35] Ibid. 115. Compare also 'Religionsphilosophie' (1904), 156, where Troeltsch talks of 'the basic essence of religion' as residing in 'inspiration, revelation, religious experience'. (Interestingly, Troeltsch added 'prayer and meditation' to this list in the 1907 edn.) That Troeltsch can elsewhere (*Gl.* 218) say that *redemption* is the essence of religion does not suggest a change of mind, since for him (as we have shown) mystical experience, religious experience in general, revelation, and redemption are all almost interchangeable terms.

[36] See *ST* 996. On a more personal note, one of the things Gertrud von le Fort specially underlines in her remarks on Troeltsch in her memoirs is that he was of a

Thus too it is the mystical dimension that most actively informs Troeltsch's root understanding of both 'redemption' and 'revelation'.

IV. GOD AS ACTIVE AND PASSIVE

We must now note the further features of Troeltsch's doctrine of God that arise from his understanding of individual redemption and revelation. How does God act, according to Troeltsch? As we saw in Chapter 1, his metaphysic of history — his views on 'analogy and correlation' in particular — disallows purely or overtly divine acts free from any historical and human 'conditioning'. Niebergall's God, who intervenes in a way that suspends the order of the natural world, and thus proves his acts as unambiguously and unmixedly divine, is, as we have seen, firmly rejected by Troeltsch. God's 'acts' thus become immanent in the natural world, perceived only in the religious experiences of revelation and redemption. In these experiences, as we have seen, God acts characteristically as a 'divine *love* that seeks us',[37] or as an 'invading, apprehending, *will*'.[38] It is true, as we have already noted, that Troeltsch can occasionally give the impression that a latent human capacity for redemptive advance may short-circuit the need for God's personal intervention (see e.g. *Gl.* 357-9). But this is not the full picture: Troeltsch will the next moment emphasize the active grace of God with equal, if not greater, forcefulness: '*everything* depends upon the initiative of God coming towards us . . . upon the action of God laying hold of us and giving us assurance, not upon anything we might do' ('Erlösung', *RGG* 486, § 5, my italics). 'Acts of God' on Troeltsch's definition, however, are subjectively endorsed 'occurrences', and in no way publicly, or demonstrably, divine. That certainly makes them somewhat

mystical temperament ('If one spoke to him privately, he admitted to being a mystic himself . . .' (von le Fort 1965, 89)). Apfelbacher's recent study (1978, *passim* but esp. 43 ff. and 270 ff.) presents this mystical strain as central to Troeltsch's life and thought, arguably to the extent of overstatement.

[37] 'On Poss.' 29[b], my italics; see also *Gl.* § 14 ('Gott als Liebe').

[38] *Abs.* 141 (my italics), comparing Christianity with 'ecstatic mysticism and theological pantheisms'. See also *Gl.* § 12 ('Gott als Wille und Wesen').

elusive; but it does not mean, as is sometimes supposed,[39] that Troeltsch questions their existence; on the contrary, he acknowledges that 'acts of God distinct from the ordinary course of psychic life' are at 'the heart of all actual historical religion' ('Religionsphilosophie' (1904), 132–3).

Far more interesting theologically than Troeltsch's views on God's acts, however, is his account of how God is acted *upon*. His doctrine of God's 'self-redemption (*Selbsterlösung*)' is arguably the most daring feature of his *Glaubenslehre* (as some of the early reviewers were not slow to point out[40]), and remarkably anticipates themes in later 'process theology'. What Troeltsch suggests is that every individual redemption creates a new 'reality (*Wirklichkeit*)' in God (*Gl.* 344, 360); it 'enriches' God, in that one who originally came from God has freely returned to him ('Erlösung', *RGG* 484, § 3; *Gl.* 217 ff.). Thus, through individual events of redemption we can say that God 'redeems himself'. This, claims Troeltsch, is merely the logical outcome of the Christian understanding of love: ' "God is love" means: he is the one who communicates himself in eternal creation and who in redemption *returns to himself* out of this creation in the abundance of finite personal spirits' ('Erlösung', *RGG* 484, § 3, my italics; see *Gl.* 219).[41]

Troeltsch is fully aware of the controversial aspects of his theory, its affinity with neo-Platonic emanationism in particular, and the dangers of divine impotence and restriction it brings in its wake (see ibid. 203). And he is also quite willing to concede his debt here to mystical forebears (of somewhat doubtful orthodoxy) such as Meister Eckhardt and Jacob Böhme (*Gl.*

---

[39] See e.g. Turner's misleading remarks (1978, 316) that 'Troeltsch found traditional Christology so problematical because it forces one to consider the possibility of a God who acts in human history, taking the initiative in finding man rather than leaving man to find God.' For one thing (the point in hand), Troeltsch does strongly defend the notion of an act of God; for another, the reason Turner gives is not in fact one of the ones that motivates Troeltsch's rejection of incarnational Christology (cf. below, ch. 4).

[40] See e.g. Seeberg 1926, 212 9; Althaus 1927, 593.

[41] The idea of *Selbsterlösung* is also, Troeltsch says, an implication of that remaining 'antinomy' between divine and human freedom which we have already noted (see above, n. 28). If human freedom is dependent ultimately on divine freedom, Troeltsch wants no less to argue that divine freedom is in some sense reciprocally dependent on human freedom and response (*Gl.* 203–4). The (truly) free response of the creature to the creator implies an 'enrichment' of God (ibid. 220); without that response, however, God is to a degree 'restricted' (ibid. 203).

227, 236–7) — which for Barth is tantamount to an instant self-condemnation.[42] Aware of the daring aspects of his thesis, however, Troeltsch in fact backs away at the last minute with a disclaimer of ignorance. The idea of *Selbsterlösung* must remain at the level of speculation; and in view of our restricted human understanding, Troeltsch says, God's nature is ultimately a mystery to us: 'What God is, no one will ever fathom'.[43] By his own admission, then, Troeltsch falls far short of providing a detailed or complete argument for the idea of divine *Selbsterlösung*.

But whatever the theological dangers of this doctrine, it has crucial, and fascinating, consequences for the question of theodicy. Troeltsch's answer to the problem of suffering is unequivocal. If God's love involves a close identification with his creatures, then it must also involve his suffering with them. God does not create suffering for us to endure alone: 'The notion of divine love only comes to fulfilment when we do not surrender ourselves to the illusion that God does not suffer. On the contrary, *it is an essential feature of holy love* that God himself undergoes suffering' (*Gl.* 236, my italics). Here, we note, is the strongest possible statement of divine love and passibility, and one that most interestingly foreshadows Moltmann on the same theme;[44] but what is so strikingly different from Moltmann's presentation, and in general surprising from a Lutheran, is that Troeltsch delivers his reflections on this point without a hint of a *theologia crucis*.[45] How then does Troeltsch *know* that God is characteristically loving, forgiving, and redeeming—indeed that he actually participates in the suffering of humanity? Is it

---

[42] See Barth 1956, 386: 'Does this mean that we are back at Jacob Boehme and Master Eckhard?' (The rhetorical question is not intended positively.)

[43] *Gl.* 239, quoting K. F. Meyer.

[44] See Moltmann 1974, ch. 6 and esp. p. 230: 'Were God incapable of suffering in any respect, and therefore in an absolute sense, then he would also be incapable of love', etc. More recently Moltmann has actually cited Troeltsch's *Gl.* in support of this theme (1981, 59–60).

[45] In part this may be explained as a reaction against the 'Ritschlian school'. As von Hügel (in the *TLS*) 1923, 216, reports, he and Troeltsch would agree in rejecting an over-concentration on the 'Passion . . . of Christ' as found especially in Kaftan and Herrmann's theology. In the light of this it is perhaps ironic that Harnack chose to stress the following in his funeral address for Troeltsch: '. . . he believed that the majesty and humility which shines forth from the cross of Christ is the example and power of our life; this is the practical test of the Christian faith' (Pauck 1968, 126).

purely from direct religious experience, or is it not also from another source? This leads naturally to the question of God's relationship to Christ. We shall have to leave a fuller discussion of Troeltsch's Christology until Chapters 5 and 6, but we shall now just touch on it in the context of Troeltsch's attitude to the doctrine of the Trinity.

V. GOD IN TRINITY?

Troeltsch restricts his discussion of the Trinity to a mere five pages in the *Glaubenslehre* (*Gl.* 122–6), and for the most part this cannot surprise us. For one thing there is the example of Schleiermacher, who left his own discussion of the Trinity to the conclusion of his *Glaubenslehre* (Schleiermacher 1963, ii. 738 ff.). But in Troeltsch's case the downplaying of the doctrine is not only the result, as in Schleiermacher, of its not being 'an immediate utterance concerning the Christian self-consciousness' (ibid. 730); for where Troeltsch is concerned there is not even any question of an immanent Trinity, since Christ, as we shall see, cannot on Troeltsch's suppositions be ontologically equivalent with God the Father. Hence any discussion of 'internal relations' in the Godhead is rendered otiose at the outset, and trinitarian discussion ceases to be a central part of the doctrine of God.[46] Instead, Troeltsch adopts a pragmatic approach: he suggests maintaining a form of 'economic' Trinity as 'a formula for connecting the historical and the religious in Christianity' (ibid. 122). This 'economic' approach, he contends, was the original trinitarian understanding anyway (see ibid. 123, 126). But apparently Troeltsch's 'formula' simply reduces to the rather bland contention that the manifestations of God throughout Christian history have really been 'of the nature of God himself (*aus dem Wesen Gottes selbst*)'.[47] The Spirit, of course,

---

[46] In another context Troeltsch is also willing to add the familiar criticism that the doctrine of the Trinity was in any case a product of a fusion of Christianity with Hellenistic thought, doubtless necessary at the time, but not binding now (see *GS* iv. 90; the same point is touched on in *Gl.* 123).

[47] *Gl.* 122. It should perhaps be noted that *Gottes Wesen* for Troeltsch has the rather specific sense of God's essential or *consistent* nature; this corrects the possible misunderstanding that God's 'will' might be just random; in fact it is goal-directed and consistently patterned (see *Gl.* § 12, and esp. p. 137).

has played its part in God's historical revelations. Indeed, as far as one can see, the 'Holy Spirit' is simply a metaphorical description for God's revelatory activity, though it is mentioned here, and indeed throughout the *Glaubenslehre*, without much attempt at definition.[48] Rather bemusingly, though, this Spirit is also equated in Pauline fashion with 'the Spirit of Christ'. Troeltsch, moreover, can conclude his section on the Trinity by affirming the phrase 'God in Christ, and through Christ's Spirit, in us' (ibid. 124).

What is strange here is that Troeltsch obviously thinks that he is just restating his doctrine of revelation when he reduces the Trinity to a vague 'formula for connecting the historical and the religious'. But in fact his own understanding of revelation already raises ontological questions about the relationship between God and Christ which one might normally expect trinitarian reflection to help illuminate, but which this 'formula' merely glosses over. For instance, outside the *Glaubenslehre*[49] (but in writing contemporary with it) Troeltsch can describe Jesus as 'the great divine revelation of the love of God, the assurance of forgiveness, and the value and conquest of suffering . . .' ('Erlösung', *RGG* 487, § 7). Jesus is, in short, 'the highest revelation of God accessible to us' ('Sig. HJ' 206); and further, 'it is impossible to keep alive the distinctively Christian idea of God apart from seeing its life-giving embodiment in Jesus' ('On Poss.' 30[b]). Thus, although Troeltsch still strongly rejects the full 'deification' of Christ (ibid.), it is clear that Jesus has a revelatory importance which is not of merely contingent interest; indeed, it decisively affects and colours his doctrine of God. Thus, the Father is recognized as sin-forgiving and loving '*in Christ*' (see 'Essence' 173, my italics); or again, 'Christian religious faith is faith in the divine regeneration of man who is alienated from God—a regeneration effected *through the knowledge of God in Christ*' (*AJT* 1913, 13, my italics). On his own premises, then, Troeltsch cannot so lightly brush aside the

---

[48] The closest thing to a definition of the Spirit is to be found in *Gl.* 347: 'The Spirit of Christ is . . . the animating and driving force of the community, a principle of the continual widening and deepening of the Christian understanding of God.'

[49] In the trinitarian section of the *Glaubenslehre* in question, Troeltsch just states the 'current view' (*Gl.* 123: the reference may be to Harnack) that the concept of God should be taken purely from Jesus' *preaching* about God.

Christological question bound up in any consideration of the Trinity as he attempts to do in this particular section of the *Glaubenslehre*.[50]

We have now described Troeltsch's doctrines of God, redemption, and revelation in sufficient detail to aid our discussion in the next chapter of the reasons for Troeltsch's rejection of an incarnational Christology. Some of the points which vitiate such a Christology will already be obvious. But in closing this chapter it will be instructive to point out some ways in which the three doctrines treated here already do much of the work that a Christology might more normally be expected to do.

First, the doctrine of incarnation may often be called upon to remove doubts about the compatibility of God and humanity. In the incarnation, it is argued, the transcendent God shows himself not only able, but willing, to enter into fallible human history: here he is made directly available to his creatures.[51] Yet this point, as we have seen, is already affirmed by Troeltsch in his emphasis on divine immanence, and in his descriptions of the mystical interpenetration of the human and divine in religious experience. Further, and second, the doctrine of the incarnation may well be invoked to deal with the problem of suffering. Although the world is of necessity a place of suffering, God, it is said, shows his sympathy, his willingness to share our lot, by coming among us as a man and undergoing death on the cross. Yet here again, as we have seen, Troeltsch already takes up this principle into his doctrine of God. Without reference to

---

[50] The central sections in the *Glaubenslehre* on the doctrine of God (§§ 12–14) share the same trait: Jesus' teaching is frequently appealed to, but only once (p. 224) could one say that Jesus' personal example is at all in question, and then only fleetingly. To this extent, then, Troeltsch deserves the charge that for him Jesus is only a contingent (and thus dispensable) proclaimer of a new message about God (see e.g. Müller 1966, 344). But it must be emphasized that this is not the full picture. This is indicated not only by the clear statement of the passages outside the *Gl.* just cited, but is also shown by the Christological sections of the *Gl.* itself; see § 8, esp. p. 103: the 'personality' and 'life' of Jesus, not just his teaching, are indispensable for Troeltsch's understanding of him as revealer ('prophet'), redeemer ('priest'), and mystical head of the Church ('king'). So, by his own admission, Troeltsch cannot only look to Jesus' teaching for what is characteristic of the Christian understanding of God: it is Jesus' *person* which reveals God, not just his verbal exposition. For more on this problem, see below, ch. 5.

[51] For a recent exposition of this (and the following) point in favour of an incarnational Christology, see Hebblethwaite 1977, who repeats the same points in ed. Green 1977, 103, and ed. Goulder 1979, 92 ff.

the cross, he roundly asserts that if God truly loves, then indeed he truly suffers.[52] Third, some kind of doctrine of atonement or redemption through Christ is normally an adjunct of an incarnational Christology. But Troeltsch, we note, refers us straight to the individual's experience of redemption as self-authenticating. Although this experience is precipitated and sustained by reflection on the person of Jesus, it is not directly or solely reliant on the action or influence of this historical figure. And fourth, and more generally, we may notice that Troeltsch is more than content to harbour elements of mystery and paradox within the doctrines that we have so far discussed. His concepts of God, redemption, and revelation fit so snugly with his metaphysic of history that it may be easy to overlook this factor. But as for the means of God's interpenetration with humanity, as for his immanence which yet does not destroy his transcendence, as for his freedom which creates human freedom but is also dependent on it, these ideas are upheld as the kind of impenetrable mystery and paradox which we might more normally expect to confront in Christology. Likewise, for Troeltsch (at least after his very earliest articles), what may be called 'miraculous' in Christianity lies not in Jesus' person *per se*, but in internal religious revolutions precipitated by reflection on him.[53]

Why, then, is it the incarnation which presents such a stumbling block for Troeltsch? We shall now examine his reasons in detail.

[52] As we would expect, Troeltsch does not attempt to solve the problem of suffering by reference to the Fall. He regards this ploy as 'very childish and at the level of popular mythology' (*Gl.* 217).

[53] See e.g. *Gl.* 266 ff.; 'Religionsphilosophie' (1904), 128–9; and Köhler 1941, 177, who quotes from a letter from Troeltsch on the subject of miracle. Compare, however, *Abs.* 80 f., for Troeltsch's criticisms of what he saw as an illegitimate kind of appeal to 'internal miracles' in the Ritschlian school.

4

Troeltsch and the 'Cumulative Case' against Incarnational Christology

TROELTSCH'S arguments against incarnational Christology are somewhat scattered among his theological writings. Moreover, some of his points outside the theological corpus are merely implicitly undermining to such a position, and their significance needs to be clarified. In this chapter we shall attempt the task of tidying up after Troeltsch, of arranging his reasons into a 'cumulative case' against incarnational Christology.

The idea of a 'cumulative case' is not of course new, but has been given fresh currency of late by Basil Mitchell (Mitchell 1973, ch. 3). Mitchell defines a 'cumulative case' as one which is 'rational, but does not take the form of a strict proof or argument from probability' (ibid. 39). Mitchell himself applies this approach specifically to the question of the existence of God, but he also argues, to my mind convincingly, that 'typically, theological arguments are of this kind' (ibid.). That is, it is not characteristic in most theological discussions to be presented with a single knock-down proof, whether something logically irrefutable or overwhelmingly probable. More often, collections of points have to be built up, individually perhaps not decisive, but together reinforcing each other. This remains a perfectly rational mode of approach; the opponent, too, can counter rationally by tackling the individual pieces of the argument in turn.

Now this method of argument is surely no less applicable to Christological debate than to arguments for the existence of God.[1] And, further, it is typical of Troeltsch's own procedure: his regular disavowals of incarnational Christology (or of connected doctrines of atonement and redemption) characteristically pile up an accumulation of different arguments, ending almost invariably with the remark that these traditional approaches are

---

[1] For a recent example of this approach levied in *favour* of incarnational Christology, see Brian Hebblethwaite's discussion in Hebblethwaite 1977; in ed. Green 1977, 101–6; and in Hebblethwaite 1980, 152 ff.

now 'impossible'.[2] Troeltsch's conclusion may seem to us over-confident; but his method is in fact none other than that pre-scribed by proponents of the 'cumulative case' method in theology. Thus, we are not here imposing an alien scheme upon Troeltsch's material, but merely implementing and clarifying his arguments out of his own resources.

But we must first define our terms. What do we mean by 'incarnation', and, more specifically, by 'incarnational Christo-logy'? It is possible to locate the crucial defining characteristic of incarnation at a number of different points, which we would do well to distinguish at the outset.

In a very broad sense, first, a *theology* may be 'incarnational' in a way distinct from (though not necessarily exclusive of) an incar-national *Christology*. One might hold, for instance, that it is in God's nature to be (in this looser sense) 'incarnational'. That is, one could argue that it is characteristic of God to reveal himself in and through humanity; God and humanity, far from being logically incompatible, are capable of real intercommunion, indeed of interpenetration. 'Incarnation', on this view, is the profound implication of God in the whole breadth and range of human development. Such, for example, was the sense in which the 'left-wing Hegelians' could accept an 'incarnational prin-ciple', when loosed from Hegel's own insistence on a perfect in-stantiation of the God/man unity in Christ.[3]

But this, admittedly, is not the most normal evocation of the term 'incarnation'. A second way of defining it, again loosely, but now at least attaching it specifically to the person of Jesus, is to say that what (minimally) characterizes an 'incarnational Christology' is the idea of God taking *a special initiative in Jesus for the sake of humankind*. This is admittedly a loose, and thus am-biguous, definition; and yet it is common currency to talk of 'incarnation' in some such terms — as, for instance, God 'cent-ring' his 'initiative' towards humanity or his 'involvement in creation' in Jesus Christ.[4] A definition like this tells us nothing

---

[2] See e.g. 'On Poss.' 30[a], where a collection of arguments are used simultaneously against cosmic redemption theories and against incarnational Christology; also see 'Glaube und Geschichte', *RGG* 1455, § 4; 'Theodizee', *RGG* 1188–9, § 2; and *Gl.* 353.

[3] For a useful review of this theme in the 'Young Hegelians' see Brazill 1970, esp. III ff.

[4] This is John Macquarrie's definition in ed. Green 1977, 143: 'I would think that *at least* three things are implied in the idea of incarnation: (*a*) the initiative is from God, not

specific, we note, about more controversial issues such as the personal pre-existence of Jesus, or the fullness, finality or exclusiveness of the revelation claimed to be found in him. None the less this is a common, if vague, understanding of 'incarnation'.

A third, and more usual, understanding, however, and one which has the most obvious etymological backing, focuses explicitly on the issue of *pre-existence*. 'Incarnation' on this view means Christ's coming into flesh, and thus the defining characteristic of 'incarnational Christology' is seen as the belief in Jesus personally pre-existing his earthly birth in some divine, or quasi-divine, form (usually the Logos).[5]

But different again is a fourth understanding which locates the crucial distinguishing feature of an 'incarnational Christology' in the belief in a *total interaction of the divine and the human in Christ*. On this view the incarnation is that complete self-gift of God in Jesus; it is a divine revelation *quantitatively* superior to others because here God gives himself fully: he gives nothing less than himself, such that one can talk of Jesus as being 'fully God' as well as 'fully man'.[6]

A fifth understanding, however, adds to this[7] the explicit claim of *qualitative* uniqueness in Christ; that is, it understands the 'incarnation' to imply that no other person could ever be like this again, or convey God in this way. The 'incarnation' on this fifth

man; (*b*) God is deeply involved in his creation; (*c*) the centre of this initiative and involvement is Jesus Christ.' Christopher Butler's definition (ibid. 100) is also loosely construed in this way. It is perhaps ironic that most (though not all: Don Cupitt is the obvious exception) of the contributors to *The Myth of God Incarnate* (ed. Hick 1977) could qualify as 'incarnationalists' on this understanding. It is also perhaps worth pointing out that certain key New Testament passages that often figure in debates about 'incarnation' (I have in mind here especially Gal. 4: 4 and Mark 12, which Dunn 1980, 40, has shown to be closely related) can only qualify as 'incarnational' in this somewhat loose sense.

  5 As is assumed throughout, for instance, in the penetrating discussion in Dunn 1980.
  6 See again e.g. Hebblethwaite 1977, 85, and id. in ed. Green 1977, 101; the same defining characteristic is assumed to be the crucial one in Michael Green's first contribution to the same volume: see 17–57, esp. 21.
  7 Some would argue that a 'full' revelation of God (definition 4) necessarily *implies* the claim of qualitative uniqueness (definition 5). See Hebblethwaite in ed. Goulder 1979, 189–91, who takes this view (as implicitly does Michael Green too: see ed. Green 1977, 29: 'God has nothing more to say'). Granted that this remains a debatable question, I think it wise to maintain this distinction between 'full' and 'qualitatively unique' revelations, especially since we shall see that some of Troeltsch's arguments score only against one position and not the other.

view means that Christ is in a category distinct from all other forms of revelation; the divine manifestation in him is thus both exclusive and final: it is qualitatively superior to all others, and it can never be surpassed.[8]

Finally and sixth (and in a somewhat different vein), the term 'incarnational Christology' may occasionally be used interchangeably with 'the Christology of Chalcedon'. On this view it is assumed that adherence to an 'incarnational Christology' is also adherence to the specific technical language of the Chalcedonian Definition. The assent to belief in the 'incarnation' becomes at the same time assent to the substance language of *physis, hypostasis,* and *ousia.* This is a relatively rare, but none the less distinctive and influential, standpoint, of which we also have to take account.[9]

Now what I have been supplying here is simply a list of distinct possible understandings of 'incarnation' which are actually in use and which locate the distinguishing characteristics of 'incarnationalism' in different places. I am not of course claiming that any of these ways of understanding the term are mutually exclusive. (The Definition of Chalcedon, for instance, incorporates, or implies, all of them.) Nor am I trying to prescribe any one of these views as inherently more appropriate to the term than the others. It is sufficient to state that debates for or against 'incarnation' can be deeply clouded and confused by a failure to clarify the precise issue in hand.[10] Troeltsch himself, one must stress, was far from innocent on this score. But the distinctions I have outlined are

---

[8] See e.g. Maurice Wiles's 'stricter' definition of 'incarnation' at the beginning of *The Myth of God Incarnate* (ed. Hick 1977, 1): 'Jesus of Nazareth is unique in the precise sense that, while being fully man, it is true of him, *and of him alone,* that he is also fully God . . .' (my italics). Also see Wiles's remarks in ed. Goulder 1979, 3–5, where he abides by this definition (ibid. 12 n. 4), but admits that there are a variety of 'stopping-points' (ibid. 4) in possible construals of the 'slippery' word 'incarnation' (ibid. 3). My six definitions attempt to locate these 'stopping-points' more precisely.

[9] This is the broad assumption of Christopher Butler's contribution to *The Truth of God Incarnate* (ed. Green 1977, 89–106 and esp. 94–9). See too Macquarrie 1979 for a sensitive reinterpretation of the Definition of Chalcedon which none the less assumes, as a datum, that it is incumbent on Christians to make some positive use of the Definition's language of *ousia, physis,* and *hypostasis.*

[10] This was of course vividly illustrated by the *Myth of God Incarnate* debate, where the original contributors (ed. Hick 1977) were not agreed on what they were rejecting, nor were their accusers (ed. Green 1977) unanimous on what they were defending. This will have emerged from the illustrations used from this contemporary British debate in the preceding footnotes.

none the less of great use in helping to locate what sort of Christology Troeltsch was rejecting; and to anticipate my conclusions here, what I aim to show is that Troeltsch was principally worried only by the claims of a *full* and *qualitatively unique* revelation in Christ which, as we have seen, may be included in the meaning of 'incarnational Christology' (my definitions 4 and 5 above). He was dismissive too, it is true, of Logos Christology in general (definition 3) and of the specific technical language of Chalcedon (definition 6), but these issues were not of such central interest to him. As for the general interpenetration of the divine in the human (definition 1), and the special initiative of God in Jesus (definition 2), Troeltsch's theology does itself qualify, as may already have become apparent, as 'incarnational'. But let us now attempt to bear out these suppositions by examining Troeltsch's 'cumulative case' in detail.

In what follows we shall divide this 'cumulative case' into three parts: first, the arguments that spring from Troeltsch's commitment to *Historismus,* as discussed in Chapter 1; second, the points emerging from his doctrines of God, redemption, and revelation, as described in Chapter 3; and third, difficulties arising directly from Christological reflection. Some of the points in the different sections will clearly interrelate; moreover, the effect may be of a rather over-numerical approach. But the attempt will be worthwhile, I shall contend, if the full range of Troeltsch's objections can be made clear and available.

I. ARGUMENTS ARISING FROM TROELTSCH'S COMMITMENT TO 'RELATIVITY', 'RELATIVISM', AND 'PERSPECTIVISM'

1. In Chapter 1 we analysed such remarks in *The Absoluteness of Christianity* as 'the historical and the relative are identical', and 'history knows only concrete, individual phenomena, always conditioned by their context', and concluded that these amount to a *metaphysic of history* which Troeltsch terms 'relativity' (*Abs.* 89).[11] There is no doubt that this metaphysic plays a very significant role in Troeltsch's rejection of incarnational Christology; but in order to clarify how it does, and what understanding of

---

[11] See above, ch. 1 p. 27.

incarnation is under attack, we need to distinguish the different meanings Troeltsch ascribes to 'absoluteness' in his book *The Absoluteness of Christianity*.[12] Of central concern here are the two understandings of Christianity's 'absoluteness' that Troeltsch is rejecting:[13] the first is the 'supernaturalist' conception of Christianity (and Christ too) as unconditioned by ordinary human history, as areas of direct divine causality, roped off, as it were, from the usual flow of events (see *Abs.* 52); the second is the 'evolutionary' conception of Christianity as 'absolute' in the sense of a full and final (or 'completed', ibid. 51) revelation of God. In this latter view the 'person of Jesus' becomes the 'bearer' and 'point of breakthrough' for the absolute religion (ibid. 50). Both views, however, Troeltsch contends, share an *exclusivistic* conception of Christ and Christianity, as 'the one and therefore the only truth about God and the world' (ibid. 52). But let us consider these views and their implications in turn.

We have already had occasion to examine the nature of Troeltsch's attacks on 'supernaturalism' and 'external' (or overt) miracles.[14] But what it is now important to note is that he particularly associates these with classical forms of incarnational Christology. Thus, in two important parallel passages (written as

---

[12] In the light of the complexities we discovered in ch. 2, it may be useful to know that the material discussed here appears in both edns. of *The Absoluteness of Christianity*.

[13] He does, of course, go on to accept Christianity's 'absoluteness' in his own, modified, sense, as 'the highest value discernible in history' (see *Abs.* 117–18), and also to express (suitably guarded) approbation of religious 'absoluteness' in the rather different sense of personal conviction (see ibid. 137–8).

[14] Troeltsch did not, as we have tried to indicate at a number of points in chs. 1–3, reject 'supernaturalism' in itself, but only what he called the 'exclusive' or (strongly) 'dualistic' forms of it. ('Inclusive' supernaturalism, i.e. the mysterious but irreducible interpenetration of the divine with the human in all the religions, he was, in contrast, insistent on defending. For the distinction, see esp. *ZTK* 1895, 363; *ZTK* 1898, 4 ff., 9; and 'Religionsphilosophie' (1904), 133–4.) The features of 'exclusive' supernaturalism that Troeltsch found objectionable break down, in my view, to the following: (1) the restriction of divine activity to Christianity alone; (2) the claim to find here areas of pure and *unmixed* divine activity; (3) the concomitant assertion of a special divine causality, suspending normal world-order; (4) the screening off of these divine areas from historical critical scrutiny; and sometimes (5) (also termed 'dualism') the belief in an extreme Kierkegaardian disjunction between God and his creation. For a careful recent discussion of Troeltsch on 'supernaturalism', see Apfelbacher 1978, 191–4. Contrast, in English, Quigley's recent article (1983), with its disastrous misconstrual of this theme in Troeltsch, and the claim that for him there is 'no access to any eternal or supernatural order', and that 'all supernatural elements are discarded' (ibid. 23, 25). Quigley also entirely fails to grasp the metaphysical substructure of Troeltsch's thought, in both *The Absoluteness* and his later work (see e.g. ibid. 25 ff., 36).

far apart as 1906 and 1922), in which Troeltsch describes the formation of patristic Christology, he argues that it was only the miraculous element that could guarantee the 'complete revelation' in Christ: 'it was the miracles of salvation history, characteristic of the direct revelation and communication of God, which remained the finally decisive evidence for central religious truth'.[15] Likewise, in *Der Historismus* Troeltsch complains that the early Christian idea of the 'God-Man' cannot yet make room for the post-Enlightenment view of history: 'The centre here is the *miracle* which cannot be touched by real history . . .' (*GS* iii. 14, my italics). And again, in one of his articles for *RGG*, Troeltsch describes, as one of three 'impossible' beliefs, the separation 'from the rest of history' of 'the Bible, Jesus, and the Church as *absolutely different, supernatural entities*' ('Glaube und Geschichte', 1455, § 4, my italics).

Now, while there may be some truth in this charge considered historically (as a reflection on what may have informed the minds of the fathers at Chalcedon), Troeltsch is surely quite misguided in his suggestion that appeals to the overtly miraculous, and to inviolable areas of direct divine activity, need always attend a defence of Chalcedonian Christology, or indeed incarnational Christology in any sense. It is far from clear that this follows.[16] Troeltsch's assault on Chalcedonianism *qua* 'supernaturalism' must thus be adjudged a dubious success; but we have not yet reached the real rub. For it is Troeltsch's attack on the 'evolutionary' concept of the 'absoluteness of Christianity' that reveals the more telling consequences of his metaphysic of history for incarnational Christology.

Here, what Troeltsch is simply unwilling to countenance is the idea that the Absolute (or supreme 'value', or God)[17] could be

[15] 'Religion and the Science of Religion' (1906) in ed. Morgan and Pye 1977, 101. Also see 'Sig HJ' 185: 'the miracle of the God-Man', etc.

[16] e.g. it is possible, clearly, to suggest instead that the full divinity of Christ is apprehended by faith, and does not require overt miraculous signification. Another possibility — not incompatible with this first suggestion — is some kind of kenotic theory. In either or both of these ways a (revamped) Chalcedonianism may do justice to the full 'conditionedness' of Jesus' earthly life — as some of the best subsequent Christological work has shown.

[17] Troeltsch's view of the Absolute in *The Absoluteness of Christianity* in fact takes up into itself both the characteristics of an 'absolute' Christianity that Troeltsch has rejected (i.e. unconditionedness and manifest completeness), but retains these characteristics for the God who will only make his full appearance at the end of time.

fully or finally revealed until the end of time: 'Absolute, unchanging value . . . exists not within but beyond history' (*Abs.*
90); 'the absolute lies beyond history and is a truth that in many
respects remains veiled . . . [It] belongs to the future and will appear in the judgment of God and the cessation of earthly history'
(ibid. 115). This does not, of course (as we have already seen
in previous chapters), disallow the infusion of the Absolute in
'veiled' or 'conditioned' forms in and throughout history (this is
'incarnation' in our first sense); nor does it disallow special
'bursts' of divine activity (*Abs.* 69), or the possibility of Jesus, in
particular, being 'the authentic and living guarantee of the grace
of God' (ibid. 126), or the one who 'renews a weary world' (ibid.
125), or 'the source of all hope of victory' (ibid. 124), in short,
' "God in Christ" . . . the highest revelation of God accessible to
us' ('Sig. HJ' 206). (This would seem to qualify as an 'incarnational Christology' in our second, very loose, sense.) But what is
firmly ruled out, a priori it seems, is any 'incarnational
Christology' in our fourth and fifth senses: the revelation in
Christ may be the highest available to us, but it is not, and cannot
be, a full or final revelation of God. Troeltsch's metaphysic of
history simply forbids that; 'history' contains 'the absolute in the
relative, *yet not fully and finally in it*, but always pressing towards
fresh forms of self-expression' ('Historiography', *ERE* vi. 722[b],
my italics). And thus Jesus must be 'returned . . . to history
where all is finite and conditioned', whereas 'the primitive Christian community had already taken him *out of history* and made him
Logos and God' ('Sig. HJ' 182, my italics). On the same grounds,
Troeltsch objects just as strenuously to any claims for an ontological *exclusivity* in Christ's revelation (be it an incarnational
Christology in question or no): an understanding of the true
nature of 'history', he claims, belies such an alternative; the Absolute manifests itself in all the great religions, but never in more
than 'preparatory' forms (see *Abs.* 99).

    To the extent that these objections to incarnational Christology
rest on a metaphysic which is asserted rather than argued,
Troeltsch's case is, of course, merely question-begging. Not that
the problem is that a metaphysic, as such, is in play (for all
Christologies, explicitly or otherwise, make metaphysical claims
about God's relation to the world); but rather that this particular
metaphysic is here simply assumed as valid. Thus, in *The Ab-*

soluteness of Christianity, at least, Troeltsch's (uncritical) appeals to Strauss on this point ('Strauss . . . has shown clearly and irrefutably—in opposition to Hegel—that no absolutely perfect principle can be realized in history at any single point' (*Abs.* 78)), and his accompanying suggestion that this is a matter of straight logic, rather than metaphysical predilection ('History is no place for "absolute religions" or "absolute personalities". Such terms are self-contradictory' (ibid.)), are very far from instantly compelling.[18] But we must be careful, first, to underline that Troeltsch's untempered enthusiasm for Strauss was characteristic only of his earlier writings; later remarks reveal a much more cautious approbation.[19] And second, we must be wary of assuming (as some critics have done over-hastily[20]) that Troeltsch's full case against incarnational Christology rests here, or that the exposition of his metaphysic of history in *The Absoluteness of Christianity* represents his final word on the matter. On the contrary, as we shall shortly see, these particular metaphysical convictions play a less central part in Troeltsch's later Christological reflections, and are in any case supplemented by other considerations which we may well find more intrinsically convincing. Moreover, as we have already demonstrated in Chapter 2, it is unwise in the extreme to pass judgement on Troeltsch's Christology solely on

[18] We should distinguish, as we shall see again shortly, between two different sorts of 'logical' problem associated with the Chalcedonian idea of the God-Man: (1) the claim (as here) that the concepts 'God' and 'Man' are such that a complete intersection of the two is logically *impossible*; and (2) the claim, also made by Strauss (though here directly reliant on Schleiermacher), that the representation of the God-Man in terms of one *hypostasis* (the Logos) uniting two *physeis* is very *difficult* to make sense of. Claim (1) rests on metaphysical premises which may now appear highly questionable; (2), however, would probably meet with more general sympathetic attention.

[19] For further themes in common with Strauss in Troeltsch's earlier period see again above, ch. 2 p. 66. For signs of later disenchantment see 'Sig. HJ' 186; 'Essence' 135 (1913 edn. only); and the little article 'David Friedrich Strauss' in *Die Hilfe* 1908. The later references show: (1) a continued endorsement of Strauss's acute realization of the problems of historical critical methods for Christology (see also 'Sig. HJ' 192); (2) an emphatic rejection of the 'monism' or 'pantheism' of the latter part of his career; and (3) an interesting silence about the supposed metaphysical impossibility of a God-Man. As we shall show shortly, all the signs are that Troeltsch no longer subscribed (at least with any confidence) to this third tenet in his 'mature' theological period.

[20] See e.g. Robert Morgan's remarks about Troeltsch's rejection of the full deity of Jesus: 'The reason is plainly that the only theological ontology which [Troeltsch] could offer was a religious metaphysics in which a historical figure could not possibly be called God' (ed. Morgan and Pye 1977, 39; see Morgan's similar remarks, ibid. 42, and also in ed. Clayton 1976, 70).

the basis of *The Absoluteness of Christianity*, whatever the particular issue in hand.

2. We move next to the rather different effects on Christology of the *doctrinal relativism* espoused by Troeltsch after about 1913. It will be recalled that Troeltsch's mature stance is that 'the essence of Christianity differs in different epochs' (*AJT* 1913, 13) and that Christianity 'presents no historical uniformity' and gives rise to 'very diverse possibilities and tendencies' (*Chr. Th.* 13). Hence, what is (actually) doctrinally true and valid for one age or denomination may not be so for another. Against Harnack, then, Troeltsch finally relinquishes the idea of some distinguishable constant preserved in all 'true' manifestations of Christianity.[21]

The ramifications of this for incarnational Christology are fairly obvious, though arguably Troeltsch does not himself perceive them quite clearly enough. What this position fundamentally erodes, first of all, is the possibility that any one Christology (incarnational or otherwise) could be binding for Christians *ubique semper et ab omnibus*, and this is obviously a point of far-reaching consequence. But more specifically (and this is where Troeltsch mistakenly overstates his case) his doctrinal relativism makes the specific thought-forms and language of Chalcedon ('incarnation' in our sixth sense) intrinsically unlikely candidates for direct transference into a twentieth-century milieu. That is not to say, as Troeltsch himself should have admitted, that they are impossible candidates; nor that immersion in the history of the Christological struggles of the first five centuries (and indeed beyond) should not be a vital qualifying component, surely, in the breadth of historical work required of anyone involved in the business of reformulating the 'essence'.[22] It is here, however, that Troeltsch can on occasion betray his own best convictions. For it is one thing to say, as he does, that the thought-forms of the early Church seem 'very foreign' ('Sig. HJ 183), and that 'modern religion' must look beyond them 'elsewhere and in a different manner' (*GS* ii. 817) in the business of working out a contemporary Christology; but it is quite another to dismiss such watersheds as Nicaea and Chalcedon as containing '*nothing* . . . for preaching, devotion and catechism'; and to assert that even

---

[21] See above, ch. 1 pp. 30 ff.
[22] Again, see above, ch. 1 pp. 33 f.

'academic training in theology can . . . place it in the background' ('Sig. HJ' 206, my italics). That, as I hope my analysis in Chapter I will have indicated,[23] is out of line with Troeltsch's own convictions about the nature of doctrinal reformulation; and to that extent we may well criticize him for an inadequate admission of the importance of sustained reflection on traditional formulations in any responsible Christological work.[24]

That is not to say, though, that Troeltsch's views on doctrinal relativism do not levy a fairly major assault on 'incarnational Christology' in our sixth sense (the Christology of Chalcedon, *tout court*). And his reflections in *Der Historismus und seine Probleme* on the perspectival nature of all historical judgements[25] clearly add force to this. For since historical work (not just on Jesus, but on the whole vast landscape of Church history) is, according to him, the proper foundation for any doctrinal reformulation, then the new insights that successive new historical 'perspectives' will reveal will clearly affect one's view on the adequacy or continuing validity of patristic Christological solutions.

3. On a slightly different tack, we saw that Troeltsch gave up, in *Der Historismus,* his previous conviction that *social* and *psychological laws* were constant. Although we concluded that this move did not, technically, amount to relativism,[26] it none the less leaves us with a question mark hanging over his doctrine of humanity, and has at least implicit consequences for his case against incarnational Christology. Is there still room, in the last

---

[23] Again, see above, ch. I p. 33, and also p. 43 for the implied view of religious truth, the means to which is at least partly careful historical study.

[24] In part we may perhaps attribute Troeltsch's dismissiveness here to Ritschlian influence: Ritschl himself, after all, regarded Chalcedon as fundamentally misguided in its attempt (in his view) to describe Christ in the terms of 'disinterested scientific knowledge' (Ritschl 1966, 398). This may help to explain, but none the less does not excuse, a latent contradiction in Troeltsch's thinking here. Robert Morgan, however, makes criticisms of a stronger, and to my mind somewhat less justifiable, sort, when he simply dismisses Troeltsch's Christology for having an inadequate 'continuity with past interpretations of the tradition' (ed. Morgan and Pye 1977, 43) and for abandoning the *homoousion,* 'which remains a serviceable criterion of orthodoxy' (ed. Clayton 1976, 74). This criticism, we note, simply assumes this 'criterion of orthodoxy', and thus does not adequately meet Troeltsch on his own ground, where such criteria were precisely the sort of things that could no longer be taken, unquestioningly, to be binding. Whether Troeltsch's reasons for rejecting this particular criterion were good ones is a question that has to be argued out point by point, not prejudged to his disadvantage.

[25] See above, ch. I p. 41.

[26] Again, see above, ch. I p. 41.

works of Troeltsch, for an anthropological constant to which a Christology could apply itself? (This is important, because all Christologies—incarnational or otherwise—imply specific attitudes to the doctrine of humanity, and are implied by them; and certainly the assumption of the Christology of Chalcedon, at least, was that such an anthropological constant could be taken as given.) In Troeltsch's case, at least in the earlier *Glaubenslehre* and the *RGG* articles, it is clear that he also is in favour of some such constant.[27] Humanity, there, is characteristically—and presumably universally—caught in 'bondage to nature' and thus in 'existential anguish', sin, and weakness. Moreover, if we search in Troeltsch's last works, we find that the picture is not drastically changed, despite his increased relativism. In *Christian Thought*, for instance, Troeltsch can still talk of humanity's 'sense of guilt', or its 'egoism obstinately central in the individual self' (*Chr. Th.* 20), without any apparent restriction of reference. None the less, he had already in an earlier lecture (of 1910) cast doubts on the universal applicability of Jesus' revelation on the grounds of 'varieties of possibility for spirtual fulfilment (*Beseelungsmöglichkeit*) among various cultures and human groups' which made it difficult to conceive of Jesus alone as 'the culmination of humanity'.[28] This, it seems to me, amounts to a new argument against the finality and exclusivity of 'incarnational Christology' (in our fifth sense) on anthropological grounds, and is an objection further shored up by Troeltsch's later admissions about the mutability of human psychological and social conditions. Thus, even though Troeltsch's views on a core universal sinfulness (manifested in 'obstinate egoism' and 'guilt') remained constant, his suggestion was that the profound flux and pluriformity of human conditions could none the less undermine the claim that Jesus Christ alone qualified as 'the culmination of humanity' ('On Poss.' 31[b]). Other 'religious life-contexts' could surely produce different human ideals, different 'redeemers and paradigmatic figures' (ibid.).

4. A similar shift of view is of course involved in Troeltsch's move in *Christian Thought* to a new form of relativism with regard to the *truth claims* of the great *world religions*. As we saw in Chapter

---

[27] See above, ch. 3 pp. 88 ff., and the exposition there of the *RGG* article 'Erlösung'.
[28] See 'On Poss.' 31[b], but I have slightly modified the translation.

1, Troeltsch there repudiates his previous claim, made in *The Absoluteness of Christianity*, that Christianity represents the highest religious truth, and now allows that the other great world religions are equally 'true' and 'valid' in their own spheres, all 'perspectives', that is, on ultimate religious truth.[29] There had been hints before this that Troeltsch was losing his certainty of Christianity's 'absoluteness': in the same lecture of 1910 cited just now Troeltsch remarks, for instance: 'The immensity of the world leads us to assume an infinite *plurality of spiritual worlds* . . . There can be no question, therefore, of a cosmic significance of Jesus' ('On Poss.' 31[b], my italics).

Later, in *Christian Thought*, Troeltsch does not even bother to draw the Christological conclusions; indeed, if anything, it is the complete absence of reference to Christ which is noteworthy here. The 'Divine Life' is now deemed to draw all the truths of the world religions into itself; how then could the fullness of this Divine Life be supposed to have manifested itself solely and exclusively in one religious tradition? Once more, then, we have here a merely implicit, but none the less very significant, attack on 'incarnational Christology' (again in our fifth sense) arising from reflection on the world religions and their claims. What I have called Troeltsch's 'metaphysical perspectivism' is the key here: as we saw in Chapter 1, each of the great religions claims a holistic vision of divine truth, but each in fact has its purchase on that reality restricted and distorted to some degree by its perspectival field of vision; hence all claims to final or exclusive revelation in one tradition (let alone in one person) must surely be laid aside.

Now whatever one thinks of this particular solution to the problem of the truth claims of the 'other' religions, it must I think be admitted that Troeltsch had here (in 1923) already highlighted one of the most pressing difficulties (if not the most pressing difficulty) for any future 'incarnational Christology' in this (our fifth) sense.

From here we must now turn to further components of Troeltsch's cumulative case which arise out of his dogmatic material, as considered in Chapter 3.

---

[29] See above, ch. 1 pp. 37 ff.

II. ARGUMENTS ARISING FROM TROELTSCH'S DOCTRINES OF GOD, REVELATION, AND REDEMPTION

We already noted at the end of Chapter 3 some positive ways in which Troeltsch's theology appears to short-circuit the need for an incarnational Christology.[30] Now we must spell out the more negative points. To some extent this will involve overlap with lines of argument already referred to, but here we shall find them clothed in more strictly theological garb.

5. We saw in Chapter 3 that possibly the most fascinating aspect of Troeltsch's *doctrine of God*, but at the same time the one least well expounded and defended, was his defence of a form of 'panentheism'[31] whereby, as an implication, divine freedom and activity is to a degree tempered or restricted by the need for positive human response. It is at least arguable, therefore, that Troeltsch's doctrine of *Selbsterlösung,* and his concomitant commitment to the theme of divine passibility, together imply that God could not have manifested himself fully or finally before the end of time, even had he wished to do so. For if God is only now progressively being 'enriched' by the return of finite beings to him through redemption, as Troeltsch asserts, then perhaps an 'incarnation' involving his full and final richness (our senses 4 and 5) could not yet even constitute a metaphysical possibility. To say this is admittedly only to add speculation to speculation;[32] but it suggests a train of thought which might, had Troeltsch been more explicit, have rounded out in more reflective theological terms the stark metaphysical assertions presented to us in *The Absoluteness of Christianity.*

6. As far as Troeltsch's *doctrine of revelation* is concerned, however, there are two separate and fairly clear considerations which appear to have relevance for his views on the viability of an incarnational Christology.

(i) Troeltsch's doctrine of continuous or 'progressive' revelation, first, brings with it once more a significant questioning of the idea of a final or exclusive revelation in Jesus ('incarnational

---

[30] See above, ch. 3 pp. 101 f.

[31] Troeltsch does in fact use this term, though only once: *Gl.* 176.

[32] Troeltsch's *RGG* article 'Weiterentwickelung der christlichen Religion' is, implicitly at any rate, engaged with this same problem, but gives no further (obvious) clues on the *Selbsterlösung* theme.

Christology', again in our fifth sense). For if God continues to reveal himself through history, Troeltsch urges, does this not undermine the supposition that a final revelation has already occurred in Jesus? As Troeltsch puts it, 'this personality does not stand in isolation. There is a rich extension of historical life which can without hesitation be taken into account with it in determining the Christian idea and filling it with living power' ('Sig. HJ' 202).

The point here is not simply the negative one of a restriction of revelation in Jesus, but more importantly the democratization of revelation to open up a much more positive appreciation of all the saints, sages, and prophets of the Christian (and preceding Jewish) tradition, an appreciation which, Troeltsch freely acknowledges, has especially tended to be suppressed in Protestant Christianity: 'There have always been those . . . who isolate Jesus from the whole preceding and succeeding history, wanting to make him the only support and basis for faith' (ibid. 203). In contrast to this, Troeltsch recommends:

Jesus will not be the only historical fact that is significant for our faith. Other historical personalities too can receive their due . . . There is no need either to stop at the Reformation. Such historical facts can be found right down to the present. (ibid. 201.)

(ii) Individual revelation, in Troeltsch's view of it, also appears to undermine potential appeals to incarnational Christology, but this time in a rather different way. We saw in Chapter 3 that it is this understanding of revelation that is primary for Troeltsch, and that it involves an experiential immediacy which threatens, at least, to remove the need for a Christological reference altogether. That this is not in fact the case in Troeltsch's scheme we shall demonstrate in Chapter 5. None the less, Troeltsch's already-noted mystical tendency,[33] his penchant for emphasizing the 'religious intensification and elevation of the personal life' ('Offenbarung', *RGG* 921, § 4), and the fact that he never, to my knowledge, mentions Christological reflection in the context of his occasional discussions of prayer[34]

[33] See above, ch. 3 pp. 95–6.

[34] See e.g. the discussion of 'inner experience' in 'Religion and the Science of Religion' (1906) in ed. Morgan and Pye 1977, 92. Also relevant (and revealing, surely, of Troeltsch's own spiritual life) is his insistence, *contra* Herrmann, that 'a real, personal, relationship with [Jesus] is not possible' ('Sig. HJ' 197; see also ibid. 188).

all indicate that, as far as his own spirituality is concerned, the idea of the incarnation has no central function for him. Individual religious experience seems to a large extent to be direct and self-authenticating. Experience of this sort is not deemed to require, at any rate logically, any particular Christological presupposition. Thus we have here an ironic reversal of the patristic argument that only the 'incarnation' (understood in its Chalcedonian form) proves mystical experience possible.[35] On this latter view, it is the incarnation that alone opens up the possibility of the divine and human intermingling in religious or mystical experience. But one can only assume that to this Troeltsch would have replied that it reflected too little confidence in personal experience, or that it made a naïve attempt to validate that experience by an indirect route.[36]

7. Next, we must tackle the much larger question of Troeltsch's rejection of traditional theories of *redemption*. While a detailed analysis of this issue cannot here be attempted, it is one that clearly has relevance to the status of incarnational Christology, since the notion of a once-for-all redemption was, historically, the presupposition for Nicaea and Chalcedon, and still remains both an assumption and prop for 'incarnation' (at least in our fourth, fifth, and sixth senses). It is, moreover, over this question of redemption that Troeltsch often waxes most effusive, his arguments pouring out in quick succession.[37] Here, however, we shall attempt to break down a complex (and not necessarily well-ordered) case into clusters of related points. It is inevitable that we should find some overlap here with Troeltsch's more general case against incarnational Christology *per se*: none the less we shall mention the full range of points briefly, so as to give the whole picture.

(i) First, Troeltsch reiterates in this context of redemption the charge that 'history', as he understands it, simply cannot accommodate a 'cosmic salvatory intervention of God into the world' (*Gl.* 22). Similarly, his (assumed) metaphysic of history also informs his regular charge that such a theory of 'cosmic' redemp-

---

[35] This was the argument used most forcefully e.g. by Gregory Palamas in the 14th cent. to support the hesychastic theory of contemplative prayer.

[36] Troeltsch's position does not, however, make historical reference redundant. His position is complicated, but we shall examine it in detail in ch. 5.

[37] See again the passages referred to in n. 2 above.

tion is necessarily attended by an unacceptable appeal to the 'miraculous'.[38] We have already seen reason, however, to question the adequacy of such arguments in their merely asserted form. As such, they just beg the question about the validity of the metaphysic that informs them.

(ii) Troeltsch approaches nearer the heart of the problem, however, when he goes on to spell out in detail some of the implications for traditional atonement theories of a commitment to the historical critical *method*. The root problem here, as Troeltsch highlights, is the shift in post-Enlightenment 'liberal' theology to an excessive, indeed sometimes exclusive, emphasis in Christology on the 'historical Jesus'; once the inputs into Christology get reduced (ostensibly at least) to what is recoverable on historical critical grounds about one contingent, past figure, the attempt from there to whip that figure up into a soteriological archetype of cosmic significance is effectively foiled at the outset: discrete bits of historical information about the earthly career of Jesus of Nazareth simply will not do that job. This, at least as I read him, is what Troeltsch is saying in an extremely acute point made in 1910 and apparently aimed especially at members of the 'Ritschlian' school: 'the attempt', he says, 'associated particularly with liberal theology, to transfer to the human Jesus the role of a universal world-redeemer traditionally assigned by the church to *Christ*, is wholly impossible and fraught with intolerable contradictions' ('On Poss.' 30ᵃ, my italics).[39] Thus, as he puts it elsewhere, it is primarily our post-Enlightenment *'humanly historical* understanding of Jesus' which makes it difficult any longer to conceive of him as a cosmic redeemer on the old model ('Erlösung', *RGG* 484, § 3, my italics). More specifically, though, and as an adjunct to this point, Troeltsch is accustomed to remind us that use of the historical critical method also makes increasingly unlikely the traditional supposition that Jesus himself taught a substitutionary theory of forgiveness of sins, let alone the idea of his own atoning death.[40] Thus even this final

---

[38] See 'Sig. HJ' 185: 'a miracle which makes God change his mind'; see also the objection to God's 'intervention' in 'Erlösung', *RGG*, 484, § 3, and the appeal to the 'unity' or 'homogeneity' of the world in *Gl.* 353, and 'Theodizee', *RGG* 1189, § 3.

[39] Also see e.g. *Gl.* 340.

[40] See e.g. *Gl.* 224, 353–5. This point is still of course open to debate. Much depends on one's evaluation of the authenticity of Mark 10: 45 and the eucharistic words; it must be said that Troeltsch never discusses these problems in detail.

dominical appeal in favour of a theory of cosmic redemption is undercut; and hence Troeltsch perceives in the effects of historical critical work on the Gospels a far more fundamental assault on traditional models of redemption than he thought even his 'liberal' Ritschlian forebears had perceived.[41]

(iii) Troeltsch is much more in tune with his Ritschlian heritage, however, when he comes to rehearse what he calls his 'ethical' and 'religious' objections to traditional theories of atonement. It is almost as if he assumes in his audience here a familiarity with the careful dissection of the satisfaction theory of atonement in Ritschl's *Justification and Reconciliation*.[42] At any rate, Troeltsch does not himself bother to go into the matter in detail; but nor does he care to distinguish systematically between the various (and frankly very different) options in the history of atonement theory. It is rather as if the demerits (as he sees them) of the satisfaction theory transfer automatically to all the others—with the possible exception of the Abelardian solution, for which he has (perhaps predictably) somewhat warmer words.[43] Troeltsch's objections on these 'religious' and 'ethical' grounds, then, are often delivered in short and sharp bursts with little pause for analytical reflection. But the case, I think, breaks down into the following considerations.

Troeltsch rejects the satisfaction theory specifically, first, because he sees it as involving a 'grossly anthropomorphic' and indeed 'legalistic' understanding of God, as one who has to be placated, and who can be made to change his mind.[44] But also, second, he appears to object more sweepingly to any notion of vicarious suffering. This is partly because he finds 'ethically

---

[41] For Ritschl, for instance (who of course also rejected purely objective theories of atonement), it is none the less vital to be able to say that 'it is not the mere fate of dying that determines the value of Christ's death as a sacrifice; what renders this issue of His life significant for others is *His willing acceptance of the death inflicted upon Him . . . as a dispensation of God and the highest proof of faithfulness to His vocation*' (Ritschl 1966, 477, my italics). In this way Ritschl is willing to continue with a sacrificial conception of Jesus' death. But again compare with this Troeltsch's critical remarks in 'On Poss.' 30ª.

[42] This had been attacked first in vol. i of *Justification and Reconciliation*, but is returned to again in vol. iii (see e.g. Ritschl 1966, 263 ff.).

[43] See *Gl.* 115. Here Troeltsch again follows Ritschl (see Ritschl 1966, 371, 473). To what extent Abelard really intended a merely 'subjective' interpretation of the atonement is still however a matter for debate: see the interesting discussion in Moberly 1978, 23 ff.

[44] See *Gl.* 349, 353; 'Sig. HJ' 185.

unbearable' the idea that a supposedly sinless victim should take on him unjustly deserved suffering;[45] but also, from the point of view of the individual's appropriation of redemption, Troeltsch drives home Ritschl's objection that the model of objective vicarious suffering proves 'religiously' or 'ethically' unacceptable (*Gl.* 354; 'Erlösung', *RGG* 484, § 3), because it leaves unclear what part the free response of the individual should play in being redeemed. It is the old paradox of grace and freedom, says Troeltsch (*Gl.* 354); an objective theory of atonement properly implies that all are (objectively) saved (ibid. 353). But what room then for the individual's will to respond?[46]

Again, and connectedly, Troeltsch expands in his *RGG* article on 'Theodizee' on the drawbacks of the conception of the Fall that has characteristically accompanied models of cosmic redemption. It is unfortunate that here again Troeltsch does not distinguish between different possible conceptions of the Fall available in the Christian tradition; hence his assault on 'the church's teaching' actually only scores against a Western (and specifically Augustinian) model. But there is something radically wrong, he says, with the conception of freedom that allows that one creature (Adam) should have had such a devastating effect on subsequent humanity as the myth of the Fall implies. For this one act of 'freedom' by Adam implies the inhibition of real freedom of choice for subsequent individuals; this too, then, is a picture that is 'religiously intolerable' ('Theodizee', *RGG* 1188–9, §§ 2, 3).

Finally, and again reflecting themes in Ritschl,[47] Troeltsch objects strenuously to the antithesis between law and love that he sees at least all substitutionary theories of atonement as assuming.[48] It is that (false) assumption, he says, that shores up this theory of redemption; take it away (as he claims Jesus also did (see *Gl.* 221)), and one is free to develop a much richer understanding of the nature of God's love.[49] One is also loosed from the

---

[45] See 'Erlösung', *RGG* 484, § 3; *Gl.* 224, 353 ('die ethischen Bedenken').

[46] Again see *Gl.* 353, and also 'Glaube und Geschichte', *RGG* 1456, § 4: 'It becomes impossible . . . to view redemption as an act of Christ by which God was affected, leaving our present redemption to consist merely in the appropriation . . . of this act.'

[47] For Ritschl's polemic against the Augustinian view of the Fall, see e.g. Ritschl 1966, 344 ff.; for the rejection of an antithesis between law and love see ibid. 263 ff.

[48] See *Gl.* 221, 224; 'Gesetz: II. Dogmatisch', *RGG* 1383, § 3.

[49] See *Gl.* 222 and also the discussion of Troeltsch's view of divine love above, ch. 3 pp. 96 ff.

contradictions of an atonement theory which represents God first as making impossible demands in the law, and then as releasing his just wrath on an innocent victim out of 'love' for his creation.

(iv) Troeltsch also reinforces his objections to theories of cosmic redemption by an appeal to the 'immensity of the world process' ('Erlösung', *RGG* 484, § 3), the 'continuity' or 'immeasurability' of the 'life of the world' (ibid.; cf. also *Gl.* 353), and the 'eternity of the divine creation' ('Theodizee', *RGG* 1189, § 3). How likely is it, he argues, when one considers the vastness of the universe, and the length of its duration, that one man should redeem it? Indeed, one of Troeltsch's recurrent themes in the *Glaubenslehre* (as we shall have reason to remark again shortly) is the reflection that the universe must be directed towards other ends than simply that of humanity's redemption.[50] Thus, to hold that one man could redeem the world, according to Troeltsch, merely parallels the '*geocentrism*' and '*anthropocentrism*' of a pre-Copernican world-view ('On Poss.' 30ᵃ; 'Sig. HJ' 189). Just as a huge mental adjustment had to be made at the discovery that the earth was not after all at the centre of the universe, so now Christian theology has to admit that its traditional doctrine of atonement is far too restricted in view and application.

(v) Finally, and perhaps most significantly, Troeltsch appeals to the *immanence* of God against traditional views of redemption ('Erlösung', *RGG* 484, § 3; 'Theodizee' 1189, § 3). We have already noted the importance of this point in Chapter 3: if God is held to be continually present in revelatory activity, then redemption becomes an individual experience, recurrently available, and not an act already objectively achieved and then merely 'appropriated' by individual believers. Present experience of redemption must come first, instead of an authoritarian imposition of dogma (see *Gl.* 329). Redemption is no longer 'absolute' (that is, once for all) because it becomes 'drawn into the fluctuations of . . . ordinary spiritual life' ('Half C.' 71). It is turned into 'the idea of a redemptive elevation and liberation of the person through the attainment of a higher personal and communal life from God' ('On Poss.' 27ᵇ), or 'an ever-new work of God upon the soul . . . new in every moment' ('Sig. HJ' 184).

---

[50] See e.g. *Gl.* 255-6.

In sum, Troeltsch concludes that it is God (the Father) who must be considered the redeemer (*Der eigentliche Erlöser bleibt Gott* (*Gl.* 116)). As for Jesus, he does provide 'the possibility of redemption' (ibid.), and is certainly not just an exemplar of moral rectitude; but his death must not be seen as salvific in itself, not as a 'metaphysical-cosmological redemption', but as something that affects us 'psychologically'.[51] These statements as they stand remain elusive, and we shall have more to say about them later. But for the mean time we now see that Troeltsch has claimed, by means of a barrage of different arguments, to undermine very considerably the traditional soteriological prop for 'incarnational Christologies', at least in our senses 4–6. Next, however, we turn to slightly different material, and to some items in Troeltsch's cumulative case arising directly from Christological reflection.

III. ARGUMENTS ARISING FROM CHRISTOLOGICAL REFLECTION

Here it will be necessary to adopt a more consciously chronological approach, as we shall detect shifts and developments in Troeltsch's argument.

8. There was, of course, that note in Troeltsch's earlier Christology (carried over bemusingly, as we saw in Chapter 2, even into the second edition of *The Absoluteness of Christianity*[52]) that echoed the Ritschlian school's distrust of metaphysical dissection in Christology (and in particular that of Chalcedon[53]), and relied instead on a direct experiential relation to Jesus that would render any such niceties of doctrine unnecessary (see again

---

[51] See *Gl.* 79; also see ibid. 103, 115.

[52] See above, ch. 2 pp. 69 f., 76. The passage in question here (*Abs.* 161) is admittedly mainly concerned with repudiating the need for historical critical work on the New Testament in favour of a more direct relationship to Jesus; but I think we can take it that the 'wearisome roads and detours' of 'the study of history' mentioned here would equally include entanglement with the philosophical thought-forms of Chalcedon, granted the close parallelism here to Herrmann's thought. (Also see the later 'Sig. HJ' 206, which says as much more explicitly.)

[53] Ritschl (see n. 24 above) distrusted Chalcedon chiefly because of what he saw as its inappropriately dispassionate, or 'scientific', approach to the person of Christ. Herrmann's rejection of Chalcedon is bound up (somewhat curiously) with his equal aversion to the 'Roman Catholic Church' and 'mysticism': see Herrmann 1909, 32 ff., esp. 34.

Abs. 161). But this, as we saw, was always a jarring note in Troeltsch's position; and certainly from 1909 onwards, Troeltsch explicitly repudiated the possibility of direct 'personal relationships' with Jesus that would purport to short-circuit the need for careful historical work on the Gospels. That is not to say, though, that Troeltsch's distrust of metaphysics where Christology was concerned completely disappeared, and indeed we can say that here is another area where a 'Ritschlian' influence is carried over, even into Troeltsch's later thought. Thus, although he does admit, at one point in the *Glaubenslehre* (*Gl.* 117), that precise metaphysical questions are 'understandable' when Christology is in debate, he himself clearly prefers what he calls a 'historical-psychological' approach, which does not attempt to probe such mysteries. Now whether this methodological standpoint is actually in line with Troeltsch's own Christological assertions we have already seen reason to doubt;[54] moreover it is particularly odd from one whose theology, as a whole, is so explicitly metaphysical in expression. Despite the latent inconsistency here, however, we must for the mean time simply note that this anti-metaphysical tendency is one factor, among many others, in Troeltsch's rejection of (at least) a specifically Chalcedonian Christology.

9. Another argument which we must take as somewhat less than central to Troeltsch's Christological thought is a point made only as a fleeting suggestion in the first edition of *The Absoluteness of Christianity*,[55] but then given considerably more backing in the second edition. This is the proposal that it is the (theocentric) *preaching* of Jesus that should be centrally important for Christians (as, it is implied, was intended by Jesus himself), and not any secondary attempts to bolster him up to the level of unadulterated divinity. Thus Troeltsch argues in one of his additions to *The Absoluteness of Christianity* made in 1911:

... the distinctive difference between the preaching of Jesus and its early portrayal in the faith of primitive Christianity is that Jesus . . . saw absoluteness . . . in the Kingdom of God. On the other hand . . . the early Christians . . . transferred this absoluteness to the person of the Messiah

---

54 See above, ch. 3 pp. 100 f.

55 See *Abs.* 160 (= *A*¹ 127–8): '. . . artificial absoluteness leads us *to distinguish Jesus' message from every early Christian or ecclesiastical apologetic.* It leads us back to the grandeur, breadth, and freedom of Jesus, whose message remains the highest and greatest we know' (my italics).

and Lord. Accordingly, his person became absolutized and the significance now attached to the person of the Redeemer had to be supported by all kinds of scriptural proofs and Gnostic speculations. (*Abs.* 148.)

Now this general line of argument is, of course, especially familiar from Harnack,[56] and in its developed Harnackian form seems to deliver a severe blow to 'incarnational Christology' in all but perhaps our weakest sense (number 2 above). For in Harnack's view, the Gospel was and is the Gospel proclaimed by Jesus, not about him; hence although Jesus himself by no means becomes redundant (this is a common misunderstanding of Harnack) his personal impact and importance consist in his being 'the Way to the Father', rather than strictly ontologically equivalent with the Father.[57]

It is hard to say what weight Troeltsch gave to this line of argument. Despite its brief appearance in *The Absoluteness of Christianity* it seems somewhat out of keeping with both his earlier and his later Christological thought. This is not so much because Troeltsch disagreed with the conclusion (that Jesus must be relegated to something less than full divinity), but because he saw Harnack's direct appeal to the message of Jesus as far too simplistic a Christological gambit. Thus, even by the time of the first edition of his article 'Was heißt, "Wesen des Christentums"?' (1903), Troeltsch could be expressing strong dissatisfaction with Harnack's attempt to encapsulate the essential message of Jesus (let alone that of Christianity) into a simple formulation;[58] and this makes the addition of the paragraph just quoted from the second edition of *The Absoluteness* the more surprising, suggesting as it does a certain affirmation of Harnack's line of approach. When we come to Troeltsch's mature 'dogmatic' work, although the *Glaubenslehre* does mention this appeal to Jesus'

---

[56] See esp. of course Harnack 1901, *passim.* One should however add a reminder that Troeltsch's implied position here would have been crucially different from Harnack's at least in this respect: his admission of the eschatological nature of Jesus' conception of the kingdom.

[57] Harnack 1901, 145; see the whole passage 142–6.

[58] See the strongly implied criticism of Harnack in 'Essence' 153 ff. That does not mean that Troeltsch does not include some warm words for Harnack here too. (See e.g. ibid. 152: 'How much we owe to . . . Harnack'; and, in the 2nd edn, an even more fulsome note of praise is sounded: see ibid. 162, top paragraph, which is only in the 1913 edn. Were these positive asides largely diplomatic?)

message as being the standard contemporary one (*Gl.* 123: 'die heutige Darstellung'), and as cutting through the early patristic entanglements with neo-Platonism by going back to Jesus' own conception of God, it is clear from Troeltsch's other reflections on Christology in this period that the Christological enterprise can never be pruned back to reflection on the historical Jesus and his message alone.[59]

Despite an ambiguous impression here, then (and we shall have reason to return to this problem later), we must admit that the Harnackian objection to 'incarnational Christology' (in all our senses 3 to 6) is at least one strand, if a weak one, in Troeltsch's 'cumulative case'.

10. Another important argument that this time only emerges in Troeltsch's period of mature theological work, however, shows some kinship to Harnack's objections to incarnational Christology, while being levied on different grounds—the grounds of 'social psychology'. This is the apparently reductionist argument, put by Troeltsch in 'The Significance of the Historical Existence of Jesus for Faith' (1911),[60] but also found in at least three other places,[61] that it was the *social* and *psychological* needs in the early Church that led to its assertion of the divinity of Christ. This, then, is an implicit assault on any 'incarnational Christology' that asserts the fullness of divinity in Christ (our fourth sense): it was only the need of the (relatively naïve?) earliest Christians, Troeltsch claims, for a binding point of unity which led them to identify Jesus with God 'in order that he might be an immediate object of faith' (*AJT* 1913, 14). The point here, though not very adequately spelled out, seems to be that while the *centrality* of the person of Christ for the Christian cultus is indeed a 'social psychological' necessity for Christianity's survival at all times, it is a characteristic only of the early Church, or rather pre-Enlightenment, Christian to take that centrality to imply *divinity*—to turn the means of cultic cohesion into an object of worship

---

[59] See e.g. 'Sig. HJ' 200 ('preparation and effects can be drawn into the interpretation'), and the discussion of this issue below, in chs. 5 and 6.

[60] See 'Sig. HJ' 195 ('The need for community and the need for cult had no other means than the gathering to worship Christ as the revelation of God') and 203 ('It was the requirement of community and cult which gave to the personality of Christ its central position').

[61] *ST* 994; *Abs.* 161 ('the very possibility of organized worship' requires reference to 'the great religious personalities': this is in the 2nd edn. only); *AJT* 1913, 14.

(see again 'Sig. HJ' 195, 203). The modern believer, however, can learn to make the distinction between one who reveals God and one who actually is God (*AJT* 1913, 14).

Of course, the question that is most pressing here is whether Troeltsch really means to wield this argument in as reductionist a form as sometimes appears. That is, does he really intend to imply that the only reason for the appearance of a liturgy centred on Christ was the need thus to unite and bind the cult's membership? This interpretation, although suggested by Troeltsch on occasion,[62] is surely scarcely admissible on his own premisses; for in the same essay in which he expounds this theory at greatest length, he also insists with equal urgency on the metaphysical claim that Jesus is the 'highest revelation of God accessible to us' ('Sig. HJ' 206), and the locus at which God is 'made visible' (ibid. 198). These are strong enough reasons in themselves, surely, to account for a community centrally interested in the person of Christ, quite apart from social and psychological considerations.[63] Hence we must construe Troeltsch's meaning a little differently, and more subtly: a community which is to maintain any hope of solidarity, I think Troeltsch means, will find the need for a unifying and 'concrete focus' ('Sig. HJ' 195) in its liturgy inescapable; the figure of Christ, then, is necessarily central to all forms of Christianity, and closely bound up with Christian worship. But early Christianity easily slipped from the (socially and psychologically) necessary worship of God *in Christ* to the worship of Christ *as God*. It is this last move that Troeltsch rejects, viewing it as a slightly naïve and uncritical slide into overstatement, understandable certainly in its desire to make God direct (or 'immediate') to vision, but misguided none the less. That it is misguided, however, surely has to be established on other grounds (by other components of the 'cumulative case'); thus this argument, whatever its merits or failings (and we shall return to it later), has little prescriptive force by itself. At best it may help explain a phenomenon (worship of Christ as divine) which must be evaluated as appropriate or inappropriate on other grounds.

[62] e.g. 'Sig. HJ' 195 ('The original motive responsible for the emergence of faith in Christ' was the need for community and cult); and *ST* 994 ('The only peculiarly primitive Christian dogma, the dogma of the Divinity of Christ, first arose out of the worship of Christ, and this again developed out of the fact that the new spiritual community felt the necessity for meeting together').

[63] For more on this see below, ch. 5.

11. Another line of argument which we are not surprised to find reiterated on a number of occasions (indeed it parallels one of Troeltsch's objections to a cosmic redemption) is the appeal to the profound problems created today for virtually any patristic form of Christology by the application of *historical critical methods* to the Gospels. In the first place, Troeltsch makes the point that the rise of Logos Christology, specifically (our third sense of 'incarnation'), marked the Church's adoption of a primarily speculative mode of Christology which had already loosed itself fatally (in his view) from historical moorings (see 'Sig. HJ' 182; *Gl.* 123). Modern Christology, in contrast, tends to start from the 'humanized' picture of Jesus (see 'On Poss.' 30ª), rather than from Jesus' supposed pre-existence 'out of history' ('Sig. HJ' 182). It is fairly clear from these passages that Troeltsch will not even countenance a theory of Jesus's personal pre-existence, and apparently largely for this reason—the question of Christology's starting-point. Thus he moves a step further than Ritschl, who was still willing to concede a very highly attenuated reinterpretation of it.[64]

But second, and perhaps more importantly, Troeltsch underlines that once this 'humanized' picture of Jesus that historical critical study has brought in is accepted as a Christological starting-point, then all Christological assertions become 'burdened with many critical difficulties' ('On Poss.' 30ª). Implicitly this amounts to a fairly strong assault on specifically Chalcedonian Christology (our sense 6), because divine attributes such as omniscience and omnipotence, for instance (which for the fathers at Chalcedon were, by the principle of the *communicatio idiomatum*, assumed to be enjoyed by Christ in his earthly ministry), become very difficult to square with the 'humanized' picture of Jesus that emerges from honest historical critical work on the Gospels. This is not to say, of course, that some sort of kenotic theory could not help obviate these difficulties, and we must note that this is a possibility that Troeltsch

---

[64] See Ritschl 1966, 471: 'The eternal Godhead of the Son . . . is perfectly intelligible only as object of the Divine mind and will, that is, only for God Himself. But if . . . we discount, in the case of God, the interval between purpose and accomplishment, then we get the formula that Christ exists for God eternally . . . But only for God, since for us, as preexistent, Christ is hidden.' Quite how to take this is obviously a matter of some debate: see Richmond 1978, 200 ff., for an interesting review of interpretations.

does not even care to entertain. Nowhere, for instance, does he discuss the work of such important Lutheran kenoticists as G. Thomasius (*Christi Person und Werk,* 1853); but then we have already seen how hastily dismissive he is of Chalcedon's usefulness for contemporary Christology, in whatever guise. What he is much more interested in here, however, is chiding his German 'liberal' forebears for attempting to smuggle back, under the guise of a new 'historical' or anti-dogmatic approach, the core Chalcedonian affirmation of Jesus' full divinity ('incarnational Christology' in our sense 4). This I think is how we must interpret his (admittedly rather veiled) questioning (*Gl.* 117) of Schleiermacher's solution to the Christological problem: the reinterpretation of Jesus' full divinity in terms of his unique consciousness of God or his 'unity of will (*Willenseinheit*)' with the Father (ibid.). Troeltsch's objection here seems to be that we are unlikely to be able to probe 'the mystery of Jesus' personality' with historical tools any more successfully than with the metaphysical tools of Chalcedon (ibid.). By this Troeltsch does not I think mean that historical critical tools are in principle incapable of establishing conclusions about intentions, or states of mind, or 'personality' in general; but rather, as Troeltsch charged Herrmann, that in the particular case of Jesus it is 'anything but obvious that the religious personality of the historical Jesus can be *fully and clearly known* . . .' ('Sig. HJ' 188, my italics).[65]

What we have here, then, is not a knock-down argument against any form of incarnational Christology, but considerations which present pressing *difficulties* for upholders of a specifically Chalcedonian Christology, difficulties moreover which cannot be said to disappear even when only the bare bones of Chalcedon (the claim for the full divinity of Christ—sense 4) are retained.

12. We must distinguish these worries arising from reflection on the effects of historical critical method from Troeltsch's more strictly theological objections to patristic Christology in general and Chalcedon in particular ('incarnation' in our sense 6). Troeltsch's few discussions of Chalcedonian Christology and its

---

[65] See again above, ch. 2 pp. 73-4 and below, ch. 5, where we shall see that 'Sig. HJ' also contains a (not necessarily convincing) strand of argument which reaffirms the possibility of reaching some certainty at least about the 'basics' of Jesus' personality and teaching.

antecedents are admittedly brief and sketchy;[66] but one or two theologically insightful remarks occur in them which, if oversweeping, are still deserving of mention and reflection.

(i) First, on more than one occasion (*Gl.* 123; *GS* iv. 90), Troeltsch will disparagingly refer to the *homoousios* formula of Nicaea as an attempt to wrench Christian faith back into monotheism after it had already implicitly accepted a neo-Platonist emanationist model of God in the preceding generations. (To make this point, incidentally, Troeltsch seems to assume that any Logos Christology will imply an emanationist view of God (*GS* iv. 90).) But if I have interpreted him aright here, then his first objection appears to be that even the Nicaean foundations of Chalcedon are a fairly shaky and ill-balanced alliance of speculative 'late Platonism' (ibid.) with the strongly monotheistic faith of the apostles (see *Gl.* 122–3).

(ii) Going on from here, Troeltsch then apparently sees Chalcedon itself as an equally botched attempt to marry the Logos of 'Hellenistic' emanationist thought with the 'finite historical personality' of Jesus (*GS* iv. 90), a conjunction that Troeltsch believes could only be brought about by retreating into clouds of impenetrable mystery, obscure formulae, and an effective (if not intended) acceptance of a docetic Christ (ibid. 90–1). That Troeltsch is concerned particularly about the dangers of covert docetism in Chalcedonian Christology emerges fleetingly on other occasions.[67] I think we must take it that his round rejection of the 'dogma of Chalcedon' as 'merely a solemn simultaneous recitation of opposites' (*GS* iv. 91) is a result not just of that fear, but of the accumulation of objections (of which this is but one) to the particular language and philosophical assumptions of Chalcedon that had been so penetratingly posed by Schleiermacher (Schleiermacher 1963, ii. 389 ff.) and often reiterated thereafter. Troeltsch does not even feel bound to rehearse those familiar arguments about the meaning of the word

---

[66] The most important are in 'Religion and the Science of Religion' (1906), in ed. Morgan and Pye 1977, 100–1; 'Sig. *HJ*' 182; *Gl.* 123; *GS* iii. 14–15; *GS* iv. 90–1. It is perhaps surprising to find no sustained discussion in *ST.*

[67] See *GS* iii. 14: the Chalcedonian idea of the God-Man 'cannot be touched by real history, . . . *nor by true finiteness*' (my italics); also see 'Sig. *HJ*' 182, where Troeltsch (implicitly if not explicitly) may also be countering docetism, with his insistence that Jesus be returned to history 'where all is finite and conditioned'.

'nature', and the difficulties of conceiving of one 'person' sharing in 'two quite different natures' (ibid. ii. 393), let alone two wills (ibid. ii. 394). It is, once more, as if Troeltsch simply assumes in his readership an acquaintance with the details of that argument, and that a mere aside about the 'metaphysical-logical problem' of Chalcedon (*GS* iv. 90) will suffice to make the connection. But I think it is important to underline here that we do not find in Troeltsch's brief and admittedly over-crude discussions of Chalcedon (dating roughly from 1911 to 1922) a dismissal of the Definition simply on the Straussian grounds that the 'Idea is not wont to lavish its fulness on one historical exemplar'. That was, certainly, the theme dominant in the earlier *Absoluteness of Christianity*. But the reference to 'metaphysical-logical' problems in these later discussions must be taken to refer to the 'contradictions' discussed in the Schleiermacherian critique, taken up of course by Strauss too,[68] rather than to the fundamental metaphysical objection of Strauss that Troeltsch had earlier asserted with such confidence. The concern is far more with the danger of docetic 'phantoms', or a Christ who is not truly 'finite', than with the blocking off of incarnational Christology on a priori grounds. None the less, the rejection of 'incarnation' in at least our sixth sense (Chalcedonianism) is unambiguous here; and impatience with Logos Christology in general (our sense 3) is also witnessed to.

(iii) If we ask, however, what is Troeltsch's most oft-repeated reason for rejecting incarnational Christology in his mature theological period, we find another strand of argument, which in time completely replaces the Straussian dogmatism of his earlier work. This is a consideration we have already touched on in the context of Troeltsch's rejection of a cosmic redemption: it is the thought of the immensity and duration of the world, a thought which can, to be sure, serve at times to deepen one's sense of religious awe in general (see *Gl.* 64), but when applied to Christology in particular has a definitely undermining effect on claims to a full and final revelation in Christ ('incarnationalism' in our fourth and fifth senses).

This point recurs repeatedly in Troeltsch's writings from 1911

---

[68] See Strauss 1972, 761 ff.

on,[69] and is persistently underlined in the *Glaubenslehre*.[70] In 'The Significance of the Historical Existence of Jesus for Faith' (also 1911) the charge is made with particular pointedness and is worthy of extended quotation:

Man's age upon earth amounts to several hundred thousand years or more. His future may come to still more. It is hard to imagine a single point of history along this line, and that the centre-point of our own religious history, as the sole centre of all humanity. That looks far too much like the absolutizing of our own contingent area of life. That is in religion what geocentrism and anthropocentrism are in cosmology and metaphysics. The whole logic of Christocentrism places it with these other centrisms. We have only to think of past ice-ages which will presumably recur, the effects of the minutest polar variations and the rise and fall of great cultural systems, to judge this absolute and eternal position improbable. ('Sig. HJ' 189.)

We note here then that the Straussian metaphysical considerations have retreated, and with them a certain aspect of Troeltsch's self-confident assertiveness. In this passage 'Christocentrism' (understood here as the claim to a final or exclusive revelation in Christ) becomes just vastly 'improbable' rather than logically or metaphysically impossible; moreover, in the *Glaubenslehre* Troeltsch now tells us that it is considerations about the 'immensity of time' which constitute the *greatest difficulties of all* against the absolutizing of a single moment in history' (*Gl.* 90, my italics). This, then, apparently now represents the central component in Troeltsch's case against 'incarnational Christology', and elucidates for us his mature understanding of the scandal of particularity.[71]

We have now concluded our survey of Troeltsch's 'cumulative case'. We have located the element of questionable metaphysical assertion in it, particularly in the earlier phases; but we have also noted the breadth, subtlety, and variety of arguments with which Troeltsch supplements, moderates, and ultimately replaces the

[69] See *Abs.* 115 f. This last paragraph on p. 115 was only added in the 2nd edn. (in late 1911). Compare this with Troeltsch's earlier confident claims (*GS* ii. 7,8 e.g.) that 'it is unthinkable that something higher than Jesus should emerge, no matter how many new forms and combinations this purely inward and personal belief in God may yet enter'.

[70] For *Gl.* see e.g. 33, 64, 90, 94, 117, 177, 292. Also see 'Glaube und Geschichte', *RGG* 1451–2, §§ 2 f.; 'On Poss.' 31b–32a.

[71] For Barth's reaction to this particular theme in 'Sig. HJ' see the interesting discussion in Groll 1976, 15 ff.

Straussian metaphysical clamp that characterized one phase of his earlier work. Accordingly, it would be quite wrong to judge the success or otherwise of Troeltsch's case against incarnational Christology solely on the basis of the rather crude arguments found in *The Absoluteness of Christianity* or other works of that period (a line of interpretation unfortunately found in such critiques as Ogletree (1965, 74 f.) or Hebblethwaite (1980, 120)). For this was far from Troeltsch's last word on the matter. None the less it must be said that the immediate impression given now, some sixty years later, by this cumulative case is that it has worn very unevenly. On the whole it is at its weakest when arguments from the German post-Enlightenment Christological heritage (whether from Strauss, Schleiermacher, Ritschl, or Harnack) are simply served up without adequate critical reflection; as we have seen, these strands of argument may often beg metaphysical questions, lack convincing support in detail, or even actually contradict other clearly held Troeltschian principles (as we saw in the case of Troeltsch's flippant dismissal of the usefulness of even studying Nicaea and Chalcedon). On the other hand, where Troeltsch presents new arguments of his own, the issues seem to remain as challenging now as then, and to be posed in a particularly acute and penetrating way. Questions about doctrinal relativism, about whether there is any one 'essence' of Christianity (let alone whether it should be identified with Chalcedonianism), about the truth claims of the world religions, about the (comparative) neglect of the doctrine of continuous revelation, or about the theological implications of an expanding universe: all these issues are as pressing now, if not more so, as they were to Troeltsch's theological generation.

Moreover, if we are to be completely fair to Troeltsch, we should note in closing that he makes a significant concession in the *Glaubenslehre* to those who would maintain a more traditional Christology: 'anyone who is able', he says, still to affirm the 'deity of Christ' should by all means do so (*Gl.* 117). How can Troeltsch allow this? It is not, I think, an inconsistency on his part. For it is of course congruent with his position on doctrinal relativism not to expect abiding theological agreement.[72] He does

---

[72] Indeed, the 'perspectivism' that still accompanied Troeltsch's doctrinal relativism at this time (see above, ch. 1) is quite in line with his statement here in the *Gl.* that 'we

seem to allow, therefore, that his own (rationally presented) case against incarnational Christology might well be countered by an alternative position. In the light of this, his occasional retorts that incarnational Christology (or equally, cosmic redemption) is patently 'impossible' must be taken as overstatements on his part. It is, further, of some considerable interest to note that he allows—on one occasion that I have found—that the idea of a cosmic once-for-all redemption undeniably retains its power in the contexts of liturgy, music, or poetry. To listen to Bach, to sing Luther's hymns, to attend a Catholic Mass, is, says Troeltsch, to feel its 'greatness' and 'majesty' (*Gl.* 353).[73]

Despite these concessions, if we are now to sum up Troeltsch's cumulative case, we must recall our earlier distinctions and underline that it is not an incarnational *theology* that he objects to (for God, according to Troeltsch, is constantly immanent in the world; his 'being and continuous creative activity . . . carry the world in themselves' (ed. Robinson 1968, 314–15)). Nor, I think, is 'incarnational *Christology*' in our second, very loose, sense necessarily ruled out by Troeltsch (since Jesus Christ remains 'the authentic and living guarantee of the grace of God' (*Abs.* 126), or the means whereby in some sense 'God is made visible' ('Sig. HJ' 198)). What Troeltsch really cannot countenance,

owe one another nothing except toleration' (*Gl.* 117). Troeltsch's work on *ST* is also important here: his use of Weberian 'ideal types' in his socio-historical survey of Christianity brought him to the recognition that various different 'types' of Christology, too, must always coexist in Christianity (see *ST* 994–5).

[73] What is regrettably absent here, however, is any real spelling out of why and how the narrative structure of a Bach cantata or Passion, the emotional impact of great hymnody or plainsong, or the rhythm and symbolic density of an elaborated liturgy such as the Tridentine Mass, might somehow indicate the psychological need for *one* archetypal figure of redemption. There is much that Troeltsch could have said here (quite in line with his 'social psychological' approach to Christology (see below, ch. 5)) that would have helped elucidate his passing, and otherwise somewhat surprising, remarks against von Hartmann ('Essence' 170–3: see above, ch. 3 p. 90) that Christianity must retain the place for one, personal, figure of redemption: 'the sacrifice of the one for the many'. Perhaps unfortunately, as we have already seen in this chapter, most of Troeltsch's writing on the subject of once-for-all atonement theories was polemical and negative, concentrating on a rejection of the extrinsicism of many traditional theories, and highlighting the impossibility of making Jesus' death, *qua* contingent historical event, into a miraculous cosmic reversal of the state of humanity. But the problem of the 'one for the many' looks quite different when wrested from the historian and given over to the anthropologist, psychoanalyst, literary critic, or music theorist. It is a pity that Troeltsch did not pursue some of these themes further. (But see below, ch. 5, for what he did make of 'social psychological' arguments in relation to Christology.)

however, for the variety of reasons discussed, is the maintenance of any 'incarnational Christology' which asserts a *full*, *final* or *exclusive* revelation of God in Christ (our senses 4 and 5); and along with that goes too a dismissive attitude to the personal pre-existence of the Logos (our sense 3) and the particular language and mode of expression of Chalcedon (sense 6). The bulk of the polemic, however, is weighed against 'incarnationalism' in our fourth and fifth senses; the many constituents of what I have called the 'cumulative case' thus make it impossible for him 'to continue to *deify* Jesus and to assign to him an *absolutely central position*' ('On Poss.' 30ᵃ, my italics).[74]

If, then, Jesus can no longer be 'absolutely central' in this rather precise sense of an exclusive divine revelation, what options remain? It is to this question—to Troeltsch's positive Christological alternative—that we must now turn our attention. And here we shall find that Troeltsch has another way of construing Christ's 'centrality' which he most emphatically endorses—but which involves, as we have already intimated, a slightly novel appeal to laws of sociology and psychology.

---

[74] In the light of the conclusions to this chapter I have to say that I find both Wolfe's attempt (1916; see esp. 202) to demonstrate that Troeltsch's Christology is essentially the same as Paul's and John's, and Apfelbacher's (1978, 229) to show that Troeltsch in no way intends to replace traditional Christology with something 'new', somewhat overzealous defences of Troeltsch's supposed 'orthodoxy'.

5

Troeltsch on the Historical Jesus

THE discussion of Troeltsch's positive contribution to Christology in what I have described as his 'mature' Christological
period will include particular reference to two important essays of
1910 and 1911 ('On the Possibility of a Liberal Christianity', and
'The Significance of the Historical Existence of Jesus for Faith'),
and of course also to the *Glaubenslehre* and relevant articles in
Religion in Geschichte und Gegenwart; but it will also bring into consideration the many Christological asides found in other writings
from about 1909 onwards.[1]

   This Christology can be conveniently considered under two
headings. In this chapter we shall concentrate first on the place
that the historical Jesus holds in Troeltsch's position, and give
predominant (though not sole) place to reflection on the 1911 lecture 'The Significance of the Historical Existence of Jesus for
Faith'. Here we shall see that it is characteristic of Troeltsch's
mature Christology to insist that the historical Jesus is indeed of
some importance for faith, and this reveals what I shall call the
'realist'[2] streak in his Christology: his demand that Christology
be in some sense grounded, at least, in verifiable facts about Jesus
of Nazareth. But this is far from being the whole of Troeltsch's
Christology, as is so often assumed as a result of over-
concentration upon the (admittedly confused) argument of 'The

---

[1] The only exception here is the 2nd edn. of *The Absoluteness of Christianity*, which, as
we have shown in ch. 2, must be treated with caution. For a defence of 1909 as at least a
rough point of demarcation in Troeltsch's Christological thought, see again ch. 3 n. 1.

[2] 'Realist' is of course a dangerously ambiguous word, which I employ only with
some hesitation. I am fully aware of the error of suggesting that discovery (of states of affairs external to the knower) can be kept neatly separate from invention (for a discussion
of this recurring philosophical problem see MacKinnon 1976–7, 1–14, esp. p. 2); yet that
rough distinction (conceived of as 'realism' versus 'idealism') is equally clearly one that
cannot be dispensed with altogether. By the 'realist' streak in Troeltsch's Christology,
then, I mean his claim that there is that of God *to be found* in Jesus, as opposed to projected upon him. I do not, however (as further discussion will show), want to suggest
here a 'naïve realism': Troeltsch does not imply that the divine in Jesus is unambiguously presented. Nor by 'realist' do I intend any of the overtones of 'realistic' (as e.g. in
the phrase a 'realistic hope', i.e. one confident of a successful outcome).

Significance of the Historical Existence of Jesus for Faith'. The other side to his Christology, to my mind potentially much richer and more interesting, though often ignored, consists of what Troeltsch calls his 'Christ-mysticism': his willingness to accept an apparently infinite plurality of Christological interpretations imaginatively and 'lovingly' projected on to Jesus. This second aspect of Troeltsch's Christology we shall leave for discussion in Chapter 6.

I

It will aid the clarity of the presentation to consider Troeltsch's understanding of the significance for faith of history in general and the historical Jesus in particular under four headings, reserving critical comment until the full analysis is complete. In addition, it may be useful to suggest some further distinctions where the highly ambiguous term 'the historical Jesus' is concerned. On this score Troeltsch himself seems blithely unaware of possible confusion, and though obviously familiar with, for instance, Strauss's distinction between the 'Christ of faith' and the 'Jesus of history', or Kähler's even more celebrated disjunction between the 'historical Jesus' and the 'historic (*geschichtliche*), biblical Christ',[3] does not exploit or explore the implication of these or other possibly helpful distinctions. Indeed Troeltsch's 1911 lecture is littered with unexplained references to (in turn) the 'historical existence (*Geschichtlichkeit*) of Jesus', the 'historical Christ', the 'historical person of Christ', the 'image (or symbol) of Christ', the 'person of Jesus', the 'historical personality of Jesus', the 'historic Jesus', and the 'historical Jesus', the meanings of all of which are simply left to the reader to infer from the context.

In the light of this it may be useful at least to distinguish, first, the actual *earthly Jesus*, Jesus of Nazareth himself, from, second, the *historian's Jesus*, by which I mean the historian's attempted

---

[3] For Troeltsch's familiarity with Strauss's distinction see 'Sig. HJ' 192. (Note 4 is added by the editor, but it is clear that it is *Der Christus des Glaubens und der Jesus der Geschichte* which is being referred to.) For Troeltsch's familiarity with Kähler's distinction see his disparaging remarks in a review of a later book by Kähler in *GGA* 1899, 945; see also 'Half C.' 70. (For Kähler's own rehearsal of his distinction see Kähler 1964, 43 f.)

description or reconstruction of the earthly Jesus. While there is obviously only one earthly Jesus, the plethora of historians' reconstructions of him clearly differ enormously in quality and substantial content. Yet the term 'historical Jesus' as such is often used in such a way as to gloss and confuse these two meanings.[4] Moreover, one may sometimes find the term stretched to include yet a third sense (ironic as this may seem in the light of Kähler's sharp distinction between the historian's Jesus and the Christ acclaimed by faith), and that is the sense of *the Gospel portraits of the earthly Jesus*. These, in their different ways, are of course representations of Jesus written from the perspective of faith, yet none the less are deeply concerned (in contrast, for instance, with the Pauline corpus) with the presentation of a vivid and memorable chronology of Jesus' life and death, and with the characterization (however freely and fancifully done) of his earthly career: his teaching, his activity, and the impact of his personality. To the extent that some arguments for the significance of the 'historical Jesus' are actually only demands that Jesus' earthliness be not forgotten (in the face, say, of gnostic or docetic threats), the Gospels themselves are in this sense sufficient bulwarks;[5] and we shall see that (for slightly different reasons) Troeltsch too implies a vital concern for specifically the Gospel accounts of Jesus' life. Quite different in nuance, however, and fourth, is what I shall call the *historic Jesus* (risking the obvious danger of confusion with Kähler's *der geschichtliche Christus*, misleadingly translated 'historic Christ'). By 'historic' I simply mean—as in common parlance—'influential, significant, or of far-reaching consequences'. The perspective here is not that of faith, but (as with the 'historian's Jesus') of dispassionate historical enquiry. The difference from the historian's Jesus (and

[4] I have in mind in particular Bultmann's celebrated essay 'The Primitive Christian Kerygma and the Historical Jesus' (in ed. Braaten and Harrisville 1964, 15–42), where Bultmann's suggestion that the 'historical Jesus' is not identifiable with the 'kerygmatic Christ' is not, it appears, a rejection of the idea that the earthly Jesus and the post-Easter Christ are personally identical, but rather an insistence that the (dispassionate and at the same time fallible) *historian's Jesus* cannot appropriately be the object of faith in the way that the 'kerygmatic Christ' can be. We shall see (esp. in ch. 6) that this distinction between the 'earthly' and 'historian's' Jesus is also useful at certain points in clarifying Troeltsch's position.

[5] See e.g. Käsemann's arguments for the necessity of reference to the 'historical Jesus', argued at least partly on these grounds (against Bultmann) in 'Blind Alleys in the "Jesus of History" Controversy' (Käsemann 1969, 23–65).

it is clearly only a relative difference, not an absolute disjunction) is that here Jesus is viewed in his long-term significance for, say, the development of Western civilization and culture, rather than with the sole intent of singling out what we may reconstruct about his own career and lifetime.

To charge Troeltsch with failing to rehearse these distinctions is not to deny that they are (implicitly at least) important for him. And to demonstrate this, we shall now examine the variety of ways in which the 'historical Jesus' features significantly in his Christological construction.

1. *The significance of Jesus as exponent of the Christian 'principle'*

At one level—that of the history of ideas—it is simple enough to see how Jesus may be regarded in a broad sense as historically 'significant'. This is a non-controversial point, indeed almost a truism; we are talking here of the impact of the 'historic Jesus' in the sense just outlined. Few would deny that Jesus of Nazareth has exercised an immense influence on all Christians, and indeed on Western culture in general. But not all would perhaps be at ease with the language in which Troeltsch characteristically expresses this point. We shall explain this here very briefly.

According to Troeltsch, Christianity may be regarded by the historian as an instance of an 'individual totality' (see *GS* iii. 32 ff.). This language is foreign and perhaps misleading today: to talk of historical processes as 'totalities' may well suggest a rigid or even deterministic attitude to historical development.[6] But this is far from Troeltsch's intention. What he primarily wishes to express by the term is very close to what some contemporary philosophers of history would call 'colligation':[7] that is, to pursue the study of history one has to use concepts like 'revolution', 'renaissance', 'nation', 'religion', 'class', etc., which identify 'continuing processes'.[8] Now it will, of course, as Troeltsch

---

[6] For a slightly more detailed note on what Troeltsch meant by 'individual totality' and for the somewhat misleading use of it in Dennis Nineham's work (Nineham 1976), see my *NZST* article (Coakley 1979, 238 n. 53). The unfortunate overtones of the English word 'totality' have led Michael Pye to make the sensible suggestion that the 'hopeless' word 'totality' be replaced by the term 'complex' (see ed. Clayton 1976, 179 n. 7).

[7] Coined by W. H. Walsh (see Walsh 1976, 59 ff.). But compare his more recent, revised views in 'Colligatory Concepts in History', reprinted in ed. Gardiner 1974, 127–44.   [8] This is Walsh's phrase (ed. Gardiner 1974, 127).

admits, be a somewhat subjective matter for the historian to decide where an 'individual totality' begins or ends (see *GS* iii. 33-4); on the other hand, to identify an 'individual totality' is not just arbitrarily to impose an interpretation on the facts. The historian, claims Troeltsch, looks for a structure 'lying in the matter itself' (ibid. 34), for 'magnitudes which have already coalesced' (ibid. 33).

In the case of Christianity, its point of inception as an 'individual totality' is clear enough: Jesus was, says Troeltsch, the original exponent of a new understanding of God and correspondingly of a new ethical directive.[9] And because all Christians look back to Jesus as their norm and inspiration, Christianity is especially coloured and characterized by the novelty of these original ideas — by its 'fundamental impulse (*Grundtrieb*)', as Troeltsch terms it. Jesus and his message thus constitute the unifying point of reference in the Christian 'individual totality'. But, as we have already noted in another context, even in the first edition (1903) of his important essay 'Was heißt, "Wesen des Christentums"?', Troeltsch stresses, against Harnack, that Jesus' message cannot simply be *identified* with a 'continuum' in Christianity ('Essence' 155). Each generation of Christians has to fashion its own 'essence' of Christianity, and for the most part the demanding eschatological ethic of Jesus tends in one way or another to be tempered or softened. To take Jesus' eschatological expectations for the kingdom seriously, as is characteristic of Troeltsch's mature Christological position,[10] is thus to admit that the essence of Christianity will not be found 'neat', as it were, in the '*onesided* and *abruptly transcendent* ethic' of Jesus himself (ibid., my italics).

[9] For Christianity described as a 'totality' see e.g. 'On Poss.' 32ᵇ; 'Sig. HJ' 206. For Troeltsch on the distinctive characteristics of Jesus' message, see esp. 'Grundprobleme der Ethik', *ZTK* 1902 (and later, with some important revisions, in *GS* ii. 552-672); also see *ST* 51 ff.

[10] See above, ch. 2 p. 72. See again 'Grundprobleme der Ethik', esp. the revised *GS* ii version (Bense 1974 provides a good discussion of this important essay). Also see 'Essence' 154 f. (some of which is again only in the 1913 edn. of this article), and note how Troeltsch continued to stress Jesus' eschatological orientation in his later work: reviewing Archibald-Fuchs in 1915 (*GS* iv. 782), and Wernle (in *TLZ* 1916, 56). Troeltsch's grasp of the importance of eschatology for Jesus shows that Bultmann's criticism of the 'history-of-religions school' (and Troeltsch in particular) for not taking proper account of the eschatological dimension of the New Testament is not quite fair in Troeltsch's case (see Bultmann 1961, 14-15).

Jesus alone cannot account for, or encompass, all the subsequent developments in the Christian 'totality'.[11] None the less, as Troeltsch still insists, 'the importance of the classical, original time always remains in that it calls human hearts again and again *out of all culture and immanence* to that which is above them both' (ibid., my italics). In this sense, at least, Jesus and his message remain historically 'significant' so long as the Christian 'totality' endures.

But to say this is to say something relatively obvious, despite the unfamiliar terminology in which it is couched. Of course the 'historic' Jesus and his message are, and always have been, centrally significant for Christianity. But this leaves the crucial theological point as yet untouched. The question remains (and it was one which Troeltsch had already confronted in his earlier Christological writings[12]) what sense, if any, can be made of the significance of the *person* of Jesus. Is he to be granted only a 'historic' significance as the original bearer of a new religious message; or is he personally, and in some stronger sense, a continuing necessity for Christian faith? Troeltsch has regularly been charged with choosing the former option (see Diem 1959, 7; Müller 1966, 344; Pannenberg 1970, 57; Allen 1980, 55), that is, of effectively loosing Christian faith from any integral connections with the person of its founder. That this option was decisively rejected by Troeltsch in his early essays of 1895–6 and 1898 we have already shown in Chapter 2; but it is no less true of his mature Christology, which rejects the disjunction of *Person* and *Prinzip* perhaps even more vehemently.[13] Now, however, the rejection is on interesting new grounds—those of 'social psychology'.

2. The 'social psychological' necessity for a Christian 'rallying-point' and 'archetype'

It is this line of argument that comes to the fore in Troeltsch's 1911 lecture 'The Significance of the Historical Existence of Jesus for

11 See again esp. 'Essence' 154 f., and the useful note by S. W. Sykes here on the changes for the 2nd edn. (ed. Morgan and Pye 1977, 180–1). Also see the illuminating final section of *ST* 993 ff.

12 See above, ch. 2 pp. 55–6, 61–2.

13 See 'Sig. HJ' 197: Jesus is not 'a purely historical fact, simply clarifying the origins and then no longer essential'.

Faith', written in the wake of Arthur Drews's sensationalist, and quite unconvincing, attempt to demonstrate the earthly Jesus' non-existence (*Die Christusmythe*, 1909). Troeltsch had already in 1910[14] provided a sharp attack on Drews's thesis; but the book continued to act as a catalyst for an interesting range of reactions on the question of faith's relationship to the historical Jesus.[15]

Troeltsch's own contribution vividly shows the effect upon him of his research for *The Social Teaching of the Christian Churches* (which he finished this same year), and of the continuing influence of his friendship with Max Weber, both as a source of bibliography and as a personal stimulus.[16] For now Troeltsch starts with the conviction (rather surprising, perhaps, if one has been previously considering only his analysis of the operation of 'ideas' in history) that what is 'essential' in religion—*das Wesentliche*—is '*not* dogma and idea, but cult and community' ('Sig. HJ' 194, my italics). By 'essential' in this context Troeltsch means that which is necessary for the religion's very survival, and he goes on to make the further claim that it is what he calls a 'social psychological'[17] necessity that every such cult or community be sustained by its members' joint reflection on the figure of the founder.[18] This basic line of argument (though

---

[14] In 'Aus der religiösen Bewegung der Gegenwart', *Die neue Rundschau* 1910, 1169–85 (see esp. 1179 ff.); later in *GS* ii. 22–44 (see esp. 36 ff.).

[15] See Troeltsch's own remarks in 'Essence' 170–1 n. 10 (a footnote added in the 1913 edn. of the article). For helpful discussions in English of the range of reactions to Drews's book see Ogletree 1965, 62 ff.; Gerrish 1975, *passim;* and Rupp 1977, 27 ff.

[16] The footnotes of *ST* regularly reflect views exchanged with Weber or bibliography suggested by him and his wife. For the Troeltsch–Weber friendship (the families lived in the same house in Heidelberg for some years) see Marianne Weber's account (Weber 1975, esp. 228, 279–80).

[17] Troetsch did not coin this term. It was generally current in the early years of the century, and especially among the cross-disciplinary group (including Weber, Troeltsch, and Simmel) who formed the 'Deutsche Gesellschaft für Soziologie' in 1910. More research deserves to be done on the intellectual cross-currents of this group; brief remarks on it however can be found already in parts of two recent contributions to ed. Smart, Clayton, Sherry, and Katz 1985: see 279 ff. (in Roland Robertson's 'Max Weber and German Sociology of Religion') and 325 n. 12 (in Trutz Rendtorff and Friedrich Wilhelm Graf's 'Ernst Troeltsch').

[18] We must read this in the light of Troeltsch's other research at the time. Writing *ST*, for instance, was convincing Troeltsch that perhaps the greatest contemporary danger for Christianity was the threat of radical individualism (see *ST* 991 ff., esp. 1006–7; also see 'On Poss.' 35[b] ff.). The only answer was some sort of resuscitated conception of the 'Church type' (*ST* 1006 ff.). At about the same time too (1910) Troeltsch wrote an article on Schleiermacher ('Schleiermacher und die Kirche' in ed. Naumann 1910) which in more specifically theological terms makes the same point about the need

not the tag 'social psychological') Troeltsch had already experimented with during the previous year of 1910.[19] Here, in fact, the argument breaks down, on inspection, into several constituent parts, which we might do well to disentangle.

It is assumed, first, that it is only the focus on a 'personal life' (as opposed, say, to a set of ethical directives or cultic rites) that can provide the necessary cohesive function in a community; for the picture of a person is concrete and vivid, and thus evokes a psychological dependence not shared by ideas, which are often abstract and difficult. It also has the merits of flexibility, of appeal to the 'imagination and feeling', and, not least, of propagation in the form of community tradition rather than defined formulae ('Sig. HJ' 195; also see *Gl.* 91). Hence, the representation of the Christ figure is assured of keeping Christianity alive in a way that its 'principle' or 'idea' could never be. To be sure, Troeltsch does speak (in the *Glaubenslehre*) of the *Person* and *Prinzip* as being mutually supportive—of having a 'circular' relationship (*Gl.* 346); but when pressed to consider what really counts as far as the ultimate survival of Christianity is concerned, it is clear that the person is far the more significant. Thus, as Troeltsch had already put it in 1910, there is actually '*no other way* to hold together the Christian community of Spirit except through the common confession of Jesus' ('On Poss.' 30[a-b], my italics). He is the 'rallying-point' which alone prevents the community from disintegration. If we ask what Troeltsch means by the 'person', or 'Jesus', here, it is not surely (at least at this stage of the argument) either the earthly Jesus himself or, for that matter, the historian's reconstruction of him. Rather it is (as in the 1911 lecture) the 'image' or 'symbol' of Christ, that is, the picture presented of Jesus' 'personality' in the Gospels (or the *Urbild* of him, as Troeltsch also puts it) which performs the function not only of cohesion but also of continual 'edification' and 'revivification' (see 'Glaube und Geschichte', *RGG* 1448-9, § 1).

This is in a sense a 'Christocentric' position which Troeltsch

---

for a conception of the Church as an 'organism' with a 'radiation from some strong nodal point', i.e. the figure of Christ (see ibid. 28 ff.). This Troeltsch took to be Schleiermacher's particular contribution to a renovation of the idea of the Church. (For an interesting discussion of this somewhat neglected theme in Troeltsch's idea of the Church, see Gerrish 1978, 68 f.)

[19] Esp. in two articles of 1910: 'On Poss.' (see 30[b] ff.); 'Aus der religiösen Bewegung der Gegenwart' (see *Die neue Rundschau* 1910, 1182-3 = *GS* ii. 40-1).

presents, then; there is no question of him abandoning 'the central place of Christ in Christianity'[20] as has sometimes been the charge. But it is a Christocentrism of a rather particular kind, not based on the theological consideration of a qualitatively unique relationship between Christ and God,[21] but on sociological and psychological 'laws'.[22] There is not, he says, any necessity arising out of the concept of salvation *per se* to place Christ in such a central position in cult and teaching ('Sig. HJ' 196–7). What is decisive, on the contrary, seems to be at least two specific kinds of human need (not adequately distinguished by Troeltsch himself): the first for social cohesion, 'community and cult' ('Sig. HJ' 203), and this is presumably a matter for sociological analysis; and the second for an 'archetypal' personality, to act as 'a support, centre, and *symbol* of . . . religious life' (ibid. 202, my italics). This latter area is one for specifically psychological reflection, and the 'symbol' or 'archetype' required here actually turns out to cater, as we have already seen, for a considerable variety of psychological needs: for vividness, for plasticity, for edification, for concreteness, and above all for one single 'focus' and 'centre' of religious attention.

So dense is Troeltsch's argument here, however, and so briefly passed over (see esp. ibid. 195), what we may be almost unaware of the novelty, subtlety, and extraordinary potential of the ground he is breaking. His insistence, for instance, that the biblical portrait of Jesus, *qua* 'archetype (*Urbild*)', is a special 'source of power', and as such an irreducible means of integrating the individual's 'imagination and feeling' (as opposed to merely activating intellectual assent), anticipates themes in Jung's later psychology of religion in a remarkable way, as does his suggestion (here only implicit, but elsewhere somewhat clearer[23]) that it is in the nature of 'symbols',

[20] See Turner 1978, 314.

[21] See above, ch. 4, esp. p. 107.

[22] At the time of writing 'Sig. HJ', Troeltsch was of course fairly confident about the stability of laws of sociology and psychology. See esp. the remarks on p. 202 ('we have a general law at work in all human affairs and applied to religion in particular'), and in *Abs.* 63 ('A true understanding of history presupposes universal structures of law . . . in the form of basic psychological drives and sociological laws . . .'). However, it is worth remembering that Troeltsch became much less confident on this score in *GS* iii. See above, ch. 1 p. 41.

[23] See 'Logos und Mythos in Theologie und Religionsphilosophie', *GS* ii. 816: '. . . Christianity has been able to create large, popular organizations, in which the religious

specifically, to attract a constellation of different (and not necessarily mutually compatible) meanings and interpretations.[24] Likewise, and this time on the sociological front, Troeltsch's insights about the cohesive force of the Christ symbol for the cultus are uncannily close to strands in Durkheim's *Elementary Forms of the Religious Life*, which was only to appear in 1912, a year later than this lecture.[25] Troeltsch goes on, in fact, to suggest precisely the reductionist move also associated particularly with Durkheim, when he asserts that the need for cultic cohesion not only helps to *describe* the centrality of Christ for Christianity today, but actually *accounts for* the role of Christ-centred faith in the first place: 'The original *motive* responsible for the emergence of faith in Christ and for linking the new belief in God to the Christ cult is still operative . . . today' ('Sig. HJ' 195, my italics).[26] Whether Troeltsch really means the point reductionistically (that is, as an assertion that there was no other intrinsic reason for the rise of a Christ-centred cultus except the need for social cohesion) we have already seen some reason to doubt;[27] and we shall return to this theme again shortly in our critical analysis.

3. *The need of faith for 'history' in general*

So far, it will be noted, Troeltsch has only established the need for a symbolic figure ('the image of Christ', 'the archetype') to

---

life could be nourished and need not be suffocated by dogma, ritual, and moralism. For its central *symbol* is not a dogma but rather a living, historical personality that every age *can interpret anew from its own particular historical perspective*' (my italics).

[24] I am not of course claiming that Troeltsch used the word 'archetype' with specific Jungian overtones. (For an example of Jung's use, applied to Christ, and implying the relative unimportance of the 'historical Jesus', see Jung 1969b, 409, from *Answer to Job* (1951).) For Jung's distinction between 'sign' and 'symbol' (the former standing for a known referent, the latter for an unknown one, which thus gathers 'complex meanings') see Jung 1969a, 75 (from 'The Transcendent Function' (1916)).

[25] There is no evidence that Troeltsch had read Durkheim's formative earlier article 'De la définition des phénomènes religieux' (*L'Année sociologique* 1899), which had fore-shadowed the themes of *The Elementary Forms*; but then Weber too is also mysteriously silent about Durkheim. Troeltsch was, however, familiar with Robertson Smith's work (see e.g. *GS* ii. 17), and certainly with Wilhelm Wundt's (see e.g. ibid. 19), and it may be that their influence explains his apprehensions about the cohesive force of religious symbols (or 'totems') as a *sine qua non* of religious life.

[26] See also *ST* 994 quoted above, ch. 4 n. 62.

[27] See above, ch. 4 pp. 126 ff.

perform the functions of cohesion, vivification, and so on, and no logical connection has yet been made with either the earthly Jesus or the historian's Jesus, or indeed with any historical data at all. On the basis of the 'social psychological' laws as presented so far there is apparently no bar to a fictional character performing the function of the cultic archetype, and certainly no reason to assume that the 'quest of the historical Jesus' should be significant for Christian faith. This is not, however, the whole picture.

Troeltsch's broad claim, first (presented primarily in the *RGG* articles 'Glaube' and 'Glaube und Geschichte', and in *Glaubenslehre* §6), is that neither individual redemptive experience on the one hand, nor the upkeep of a religious community on the other, is possible without the mediation of 'historical' data. He does, it is true, make a clear distinction between 'immediate' and 'mediated' religious experience ('Glaube und Geschichte', *RGG* 1456, § 4), the latter being historically imparted, and the former having a certain self-authenticating quality (ibid. and *passim*). But this distinction is never one that can be more than theoretical; in fact, he claims, it is only through the agency of the 'mediated' religious experience that God's present work for the individual is effected (ibid. 1455–6, § 4). It is thus only through the historical heritage presented by the faithful community that one is brought to redemption. Likewise, the community's continued existence is protected only by 'historical' reflection (ibid. 1449, esp. § 1*c, d*). All this explains why redemptive experience can never be solely self-authenticating, that is, without any reference to a religious community or tradition.[28]

But what does Troeltsch mean by 'history' at this level of argument? Do not these claims for its necessity look suspiciously like reworded versions of his argument about 'social psychological' needs? He says, for instance, that faith receives only from *history* its 'power, vitality, definiteness, and capacity to take social organization' (*AJT* 1913, 14–15). The needs that this sort of 'history' caters for, then, turn out to be the familiar 'social psychological' ones—the psychological need of the individual, firstly, for concreteness and a personal symbol of faith, and the social need of the community, secondly, for a public and cohesive

---

[28] On the other hand, the reception of the tradition will always involve a new assimilation of it: 'The historical is involved . . . only insofar as it can be constantly transformed anew into something present' ('Glaube und Geschichte', *RGG* 1454, § 3*c*).

reference point. Thus the demand for 'history' is actually a call for the very same things that the 'social psychological' argument pronounces indispensable.[29] And what is meant by 'history' in this context is something more like shared community folklore or story—with all its attendant qualities of personal appeal, vividness, and imagination—than the scholarly and scientific pursuit of historical data. On other occasions too Troeltsch's use of the word 'history' is almost an equation for what is communal, public, or objectified.[30] Not that this is an unimportant train of thought: it may, for instance, suggest an interesting, but here only implicit, argument for the irreducibility of the story or narrative form in the mediation of religious truth.

But from the force of these arguments alone one would still wonder whether the 'history' thus required need have any rootage in actual fact. Or, if it should happen to take a factual basis, one might ask why some feature of the community's contemporary history, or even the individual's own personal history, might not do very well for sustenance.[31] The 'social psychological' argument has already of course asserted a specific need for the 'image of Christ' in the Christian community ('Sig. HJ' 196); and the requirements Troeltsch makes for 'vividness' and the impact of a 'personality' would suggest here a special focus on the Gospel portraits. But does this imply in addition a need for what I have called the historian's Jesus? Or would not a set of lengendary or fictional stories about Jesus do just as well?

4. *The need of faith for the 'historical Jesus'*

However, this is precisely the point at which Troeltsch insists that

---

[29] This is summed up in ibid. 1450, § 1*e*: 'To abandon *history* would be tantamount to faith's abandoning itself and settling for the fleeting and trivial religious stirrings produced by subjectivity left to its own resources . . . The connection with history . . . was forced by psychological requirements immanent in faith itself' (my italics).

[30] See e.g. *Gl.* 87, and 90: 'The removal of actual history means . . . a decline of the community.' See also *Abs.* 161 (an addition of 1911): 'Insofar as reinforcement from history . . . is needed, and especially insofar as a visualization of its foundation is indispensable to the cohesiveness and propagation of a religious community . . . the religious man will turn back to history . . . but he will not let critical historical scholarship interfere with that visualizing of history whose sole intention is to serve the edification and deepening of the spiritual life.'

[31] Troeltsch does of course hold that these features *are* very important aspects of faith. See e.g. 'Erlösung', *RGG* 486–7, § 7.

historical scholarship is significant for faith. A purely fictional account of Jesus, he claims, would not be good enough to sustain the response of faith: it is 'truly significant' to Christians that behind the biblical portraits of Jesus stands 'the greatness of a superior, and real religious prophet' ('Sig. HJ' 197). Further, it is not only his existence and superiority that are important, but also that he 'thus lived, struggled, believed, and conquered' (ibid.). To this extent, then, at least in principle, Christianity's claims about Jesus involve a historical risk. The historian's Jesus, in our terms, does have to come into play. On the other hand, Troeltsch attempts to limit to some degree the amount of knowledge that must be ascertained: '*It is not a question of individual details* but of the factuality of the total phenomenon of Jesus and the *basic outline* of his teaching and his religious personality' (ibid. 198, my italics).[32] But still, 'This must be capable of being established by means of historical criticism as historical reality if the "symbol of Christ" is to have a firm and strong inner basis in the "fact" of Jesus' (ibid.). Should this venture prove unsuccessful, says Troeltsch, it would be the 'beginning of the end of the Christ symbol amongst scientifically educated people' (ibid.). And their doubts would soon filter down to the less educated elements in the Christian community.

Fortunately, however—or so Troeltsch claims—Christians may set aside these qualms in the confidence that these basic facts are indeed ones on which scholarship will easily reach a 'consensus' (*Gl.* 101; see 'Sig. HJ' 200). And, for 'religious purposes', this proves sufficient (*Gl.* 96-7; see 'Sig. HJ' 200). From here scholars may return to further fact-gathering (with results, however, that will be irrelevant to religious conviction) while lay people may gladly be left to their 'instinctive' feel for what is 'essential' in the New Testament (see *Gl.* 100). Troeltsch's confidence in the 'consensus' of historical scholarship thus provides him with a means of asserting a (circumscribed) dependence of faith on historical facts, but also an effective lack of such dependence.

We should perhaps clarify the precise nature of the 'necessity' for reliance on the historian's Jesus that Troeltsch here proposes. Although he never makes this explicit, there seem to be three

---

[32] Also see 'On Poss.' 31ᵃ; *Gl.* 100 f.

slightly different kinds of claim in operation. The first is the argument that faith would be undermined (and this is to be understood in psychological terms) if it were demonstrated that the earthly Jesus' very existence was a 'pious fraud', or again if certain fundamental (and public) facts in his story (the crucifixion for instance) proved to be figments of the early Church's imagination. These kinds of facts would be ones that any historian—Christian or non-Christian—could tackle equally well.

Second, however, there stands alongside this claim (and not clearly distinguished from it) Troeltsch's insistence that we also be assured by historians of the *quality* of Jesus' person. For it is only the earthly Jesus *qua* 'superior . . . religious prophet' ('Sig. HJ' 197), and *qua* 'embodiment of superior religious power' ('On Poss.' 30^b), that enables us to 'transcend ourselves' and to confess him as 'the source of our religious strengths and certainties' (ibid. 31^a; see 'Sig. HJ' 198). At times this argument here seems to suggest that we need to verify that some sort of new breakthrough in human possibilities has actually been achieved in Jesus,[33] otherwise we could hardly feel confident in our own efforts at self-correction and self-transformation. In this sense, therefore, the historian's Jesus can supposedly provide the 'guarantee and certainty' of religious faith.[34] The 'superior power' that we see in Jesus Christ is a kind of 'security (*Verbürgung*)'.[35]

Slightly different again, however, and third, is Troeltsch's mention of the need to establish the main facts about Jesus' *teaching* (as well as his personality). This seems to imply what we should have a specific interest in this as a guide to our own behaviour and attitudes. It must be admitted, however, that Troeltsch does not always make it clear whether the teaching of the reconstructed historian's Jesus should be allowed a special pride of place in this process of decision (and if so, to what extent) or whether it is the broader Gospel portraits of Jesus that will do just as well. The *Glaubenslehre* and *RGG* articles tend to suggest the

[33] This is suggested by 'On Poss.' 32^a: 'the higher humanity emanating from him.'
[34] Art. 'Religious Principle' in ed. Pelikan 1970, 339. For similar observations see 'On Poss.' 31^a, and 'Glaube und Geschichte', *RGG* 1448 f., § 1*b*.
[35] See again 'Glaube und Geschichte', *RGG* 1449, § 1*b*; 1452, § 3 ('historical forces that . . . guarantee . . . truth'); and 1453, § 3*b*. Also see 'Erlösung', *RGG* 483, § 3 and 485, § 3.

latter;[36] the article on the 'essence' of Christianity, as we have already intimated, the former.[37] But the ambiguity should not so greatly surprise us, granted that we have already clarified about Troeltsch's views on doctrinal and ethical relativism and the business of 'essence' reformulation. Jesus' teaching (assuming we can reconstruct some of it with confidence) can never be taken over into a new setting without due process of readjustment and assimilation. This is especially true, as Troeltsch urged, as regards Jesus' eschatological perspective. But that does not mean that Jesus' actual teaching should ever be ignored, either; nor, I think (but we shall return to this point, since Troeltsch himself was not wholly clear on it), does it imply that the *distinction*, at least, between what was actually present in Jesus' teaching and what has been projected onto it is rendered unimportant or otiose.

II

We must now turn to offer some critical remarks on the position just outlined. An examination of the success of Troeltsch's 'social psychological' argument for the necessity of the Christ figure should come first. The main point of criticism that must be made here is that Troeltsch overstates his case, and so turns a perfectly valid (and indeed most fascinating and insightful) pheno-menological analysis into a set of universal claims.[38] Certainly, religions cannot properly be understood apart from a con-sideration of their cultic make-up and socially binding nature, and of the powers of psychological support they also wield. Cer-tainly too (for this seems to be an important implication of what Troeltsch is saying) the Christian theologian's business of Christological construction should have, as a vital component, a keen interest in such sociological and psychological factors (an interest often devastatingly lacking both then and now). And certainly, again, even at the level of descriptive analysis, it does indeed seem that the Christ figure acts in Christianity as the decisive binding force, very much in the way Troeltsch describes

---

[36] See e.g. *Gl.* 20; 'Glaube und Geschichte', *RGG* 1448, § 1a.

[37] See again 'Essence' 155-6.

[38] For a similar criticism see Ogletree 1965, 72.

it. Still, need he really have invoked a 'law'—questionable in its claim to universality[39]—to make this point? What is presented as a social necessity of unlimited application begins to look suspiciously like an unjustifiable demand to interpret all other religions on the model of Christianity. Why, for instance, should 'all great religions of spirit' be said to centre on the adoration of their founder?[40] Or again, while one need not deny that the concentration on a person has certain obvious popular attractions, is it right to suggest that *only* a person (and indeed only one seminal person) can sustain the faith of a religious movement? Could not a more general mythology, a book, a symbol of some different kind, a system of philosophy, or a whole pantheon of heroes cater for a similar need in another religious context?

What then, is the exact status of this 'social psychological' law? Could it really be intended, for instance, as a means of justifying Christological affirmations in some sense? After all, in one difficult passage we have already remarked upon, the law is actually said to account for the 'motive' to have 'faith in Christ' ('Sig. HJ' 195); but the distinction between needs or motives on the one hand and justifications on the other is here passed over. And whereas it is indeed comprehensible why one might assent to the centrality of the Christ figure on the grounds of the necessity for social cohesion, it is far from clear why this assent should involve one in 'reverence' or 'worship (*Verehrung*)' of the figure, in proclaiming 'faith in' him, or in considering him some particular 'revelation' of God.[41] This, surely, would result in a considerable tension between one's intellectual responsibility and one's cultic affirmations. To the extent that Troeltsch gives this impression, then, we must say that he certainly deserves criticism.[42] 'Social psychological' considerations cannot, alone and in themselves, justify Christological affirmations.

But then, as is so often the case with Troeltsch, we have to do the job of analysing out for him the component parts of his 'social psychology' law before we are in a position to see the various

[39] Troeltsch would presumably have conceded this point by the time he wrote *GS* iii (1922). See e.g. ibid. 45-6, and cf. n. 22 above.

[40] See 'Sig. HJ' 195. Troeltsch however admits (ibid.) that 'religions of nature' operate differently.

[41] See 'Sig. HJ' 206, 195, 196, for these claims.

[42] So e.g. Müller 1966, 343.

functions it is performing. At one level, first, all the points made can simply be taken as explanatory or *phenomenological* ones, aiming, that is, just to describe and highlight, to lay bare some of the more hidden pressures on the Christian cultus and its development. But there is also, and second, a strong current of theological judgement implicit here. And this appears to operate part constructively and part critically, depending on what particular social or psychological pressure is in question. Thus, on the one hand, Troeltsch seems to be not only *describing* the particular needs for cohesion, vivification, edification, flexibility, and the evocation of 'feeling' (all, as we have seen, provided for by the 'Christ symbol') but actively *recommending* them ('Sig. HJ' 195 f.); and the further implication (if I am not reading in too much) would seem to be that such considerations ought to be prime material for any future Christological construction.[43] On the other hand, there is at least one psychological pressure mentioned by Troeltsch, the pressure or desire to make God himself an '*immediate* object of faith' in Christ (*AJT* 1913, 14, my italics), which, as we have already seen in an earlier chapter, Troeltsch apparently feels should not be pandered to.[44] Strictly speaking, 'worshipping' Christ *as* God is a category mistake (ibid.). Thus, not all the operative 'psychological' laws are ones to be encouraged.

From here we must turn to consider the force of Troeltsch's further claim that faith is to some degree reliant on the historian's Jesus, or at least on some central facts about Jesus that the historian may provide. The first point of criticism here, however, is that Troeltsch is far too confident about the 'consensus' that may be reached on these 'facts'. Even if one dismisses the details as irrelevant, to ask for agreement on 'the basic outline of Jesus' teaching and his religious personality' is no small demand. Yet despite his apparent appreciation of the difficulties involved (underlined especially in his important article of 1909, which so sharply attacked Ritschl and Herrmann on precisely this score[45]), Troeltsch could here blithely conclude: 'the decisive chief facts

---

[43] This seems to be the implication of 'Sig. HJ' in general, but esp. of 196–7.

[44] See above, ch. 4 pp. 126 ff.

[45] 'Rückblick auf ein halbes Jahrhundert der theologischen Wissenschaft'. See my discussion above, ch. 2 pp. 73–4. In the revision of this article for *GS* ii Troeltsch added specific reference to Schweitzer's *Von Reimarus zu Wrede* (1906) (see Schweitzer 1966) to

can here be ascertained *with certainty* despite all the questions which remain open' ('Sig. HJ' 200, my italics).

The irony here for Troeltsch is that he is torn, it seems, by a genuine desire to do justice to the (largely uncritical) faith of the ordinary believer, and thus he falls back on a typically 'Ritschlian' gambit—the appeal to 'basic' ascertainable facts.[46] Yet, by his own admission, even in the lecture in hand, this is a ploy with very dubious chances of success.[47] Against Herrmann, who was a champion of precisely this line of argument,[48] Troeltsch at one point objects that 'the burden of the historical Jesus problem is as a matter of experience more likely to shatter faith than protect it' ('Sig. HJ' 189). The assurance of a 'consensus' of opinion looks thin indeed in the light of such admissions.

Moreover, there are other, more specific, difficulties with this line of argument. Troeltsch gives little hint, for a start, what he includes in the category of 'chief facts' of Jesus' 'personality and teaching'. Both terms are vague and all-encompassing, and again reminiscent of Herrmann's polemic; how much ground, one wonders, has Troeltsch actually conceded in letting the 'details' go?[49] In addition, the few passing comments we do get (in the *Glaubenslehre*) on what these 'basics' are for Troeltsch himself, lead into the trickiest possible areas of Jesus' self-consciousness—his sense of vocation (his *Sendungsbewußtsein*) and his unflinching fortitude and certainty in the face of suffering (his *Gewißheit*)[50]—both of which again smack of Ritschlian influence,[51] and read oddly from one who had already expressed severe doubts about the difficulties of 'rummaging about' in

support his remark that 'there have arisen new still unsolved historical problems [sc. about Jesus] which make it very difficult for faith to attach itself to so uncertain a reality' ('Half C.' 70 and 71 n. 5; we should also note however slightly more confident remarks on p. 72: 'when the dust has settled enough will remain of the old picture for Jesus . . . still to be seen as the source and power of faith in Christ and so of Christianity.') None the less, there is still a prima-facie tension between the scepticism of 'Half C.' (and indeed of the much earlier 'Geschichte und Metaphysik', *ZTK* 1898) and the confidence of 'Sig. HJ' 200.

46 This is also remarked upon by Klemm 1974, 190, and Gerrish 1975, 25.

47 See 'Sig. HJ' 183, 188-9.

48 See Herrmann 1909, 85.

49 *Gl.* 101-2 and perhaps 111-12 tell us a little more about what Troeltsch would include in this category.

50 *Gl.* 113, 115.

51 For Jesus' sense of vocation (*Berufung*) as a central tenet of Ritschl's Christology, and for the attendant insistence on Jesus' certainty of the efficacy of his death, see e.g.

Jesus' thought-processes on the evidence available.[52] Further, and similarly, there are the extra difficulties of how far the historian (*qua* historian) is competent to assess the religious quality, indeed 'superiority', of Jesus' ministry, personality, and 'power', as Troeltsch demands of him. Because he is vague in expression, this slide from the realm of the publicly verifiable to that of personal or religious evaluation goes almost unnoticed. Once again, though, one suspects that remnants of Ritschlian influence—this time the 'value-judgement' theory—may still be lurking somewhere in the background.[53]

Moreover, there is apparently yet a further flaw in Troeltsch's presentation. For with the security of the 'consensus' supposedly assured, he proceeds to shilly-shally on the question of whether there really is a historical risk or not. As long as the 'basics' are established, he claims, 'one can say . . . that a part of historical research is . . . *irrelevant so far as religion is concerned*' ('Sig. HJ' 200, my italics). But how, we may ask, could such 'relative' dependence be worked out in practice? If the risk were really affirmed, then one would have to picture scholars in constant debate as to whether certain new conclusions were of real significance for recapturing Jesus' teaching and personality, or whether they could be relegated to the category of 'minor details' (ibid.). It is in order to avoid this, no doubt, that Troeltsch invokes his 'consensus' theory. But at the same time, unfortunately, he *appears* to undermine the claim that a historical 'dependence' exists at all—certainly where the uneducated laity are concerned. They are free to spin out their own personal religious interpretation of Christ, just so long as they can rest easy that the scholars have come to an agreement. What then is the nature and extent of the historical 'dependence' asserted by Troeltsch? Is he not impaled on the horns of an impossible dilemma of his own making—the desire on the one hand to

Ritschl 1966, 546: Jesus' 'communion with God' was 'maintained in the whole course of His life, especially in His willingness to suffer for the sake of His vocation, and in the patience which He exercised even unto death . . . In the course of His life He in the first place demonstrated to men His Father's love, grace, and truth, by exercising His Divine vocation, to found the Kingdom of God, from the same motive of love to men which constitutes God's proper will for the realising of their happiness.'

[52] See above, ch. 2 p. 59.

[53] Ritschl urged that without 'value judgements' there existed no real, or worthwhile, 'historical knowledge': see e.g. Ritschl 1966, 2–3.

be phenomenologically faithful to the 'naïve' beliefs of the unscholarly Christian, and on the other hand to lay down a theological prescription: the dependence of faith on historical criticism? Perhaps after all—as one commentator, B. A. Gerrish, has suggested (Gerrish 1975)—this stress on the historical Jesus is nothing but an unfortunate and inconsistent addendum to Troeltsch's Christology.

It is with an assessment of Gerrish's challenging case that we shall be largely concerned in the rest of this chapter, and this will at the same time clarify our own views on Troeltsch's position. Briefly, Gerrish's thesis is this: Troeltsch's 'social psychological' argument will only serve to affirm the significance of the 'symbol' of Christ (ibid. 24); Gerrish therefore questions Troeltsch's further claim that 'the image has efficacy only so long as the community trusts the basic correspondence of the image to a life actually lived' (ibid. 26). Why even attempt, says Gerrish, to anchor the symbol in the historical Jesus? Why not root it instead in the historical life of the Church: 'the very fact that the symbol is embedded in the life of a community gives it the concreteness and factual givenness which Troeltsch rightly desires' (ibid. 28). Moreover, Gerrish produces evidence from Troeltsch's own theological corpus to back up his point. Granted the emphasis Troeltsch himself places on individual religious experience, on the significance of tradition, and on the part played by the community in mediating redemption, does not his desire to maintain a hold on the historical Jesus point to 'a dissonance within his own thinking' (ibid. 29)?

To this, I shall contend, the answer is no. For despite the many confusions and logical lacunae in the lecture 'The Significance of the Historical Existence of Jesus for Faith', Troeltsch could, on his own premises, have maintained a consistent argument for the significance of faith's reference to the historian's Jesus. Before attempting to demonstrate this, we must however concede to Gerrish several points. First, it is undoubtedly true, as we have emphasized several times already in earlier chapters, that Troeltsch allows present religious experience a decisive role for the individual (see e.g. *Gl.* 47). As he puts it in the essay under review, it is not 'legitimate' to say that

only the recognition of Jesus as divine authority . . . gives the confidence and joy of faith . . . It is rather that our souls are overcome by the grandeur of prophetic Christian faith in God and that this leads to acknowledgment of Jesus, than vice versa. ('Sig. HJ' 189, my italics.)

Second, we have already shown that we agree with Gerrish that Troeltsch's 'social psychological' argument will not, as such, make the logical connection with the historical Jesus that he clearly intends. The social need for cohesion, and the psychological needs for 'vivification', 'edification', 'concreteness', and so on, can be catered for quite adequately by what Troeltsch calls the 'symbol of Christ', that is, in our terms, the biblical (and especially Gospel) portraits of the earthly Jesus. Here, Troeltsch has mistakenly attempted to replace the necessary *theological* argument with an undoubtedly insightful, but nevertheless ineffective, substitute. Third, we also agree with Gerrish that Troeltsch uses the language of 'absolute' or 'inner necessity' for the historical Jesus (a position he himself rejects) in a dreadfully confusing way (see Gerrish 1975, 33 n. 90). We shall return to this point shortly. Similarly, Gerrish is right to accuse Troeltsch of holding a more conservative (or in this case 'Ritschlian') position than he himself appears to concede (ibid. n. 90). And finally, it is true that Troeltsch's thesis implies something of a double standard between historians (or intellectuals) on the one hand, and ordinary run-of-the-mill Christians on the other: for faith does risk reliance on 'a cheerful report from the New Testament scholars' (ibid. 32). Is this risk unendurable, however, as Gerrish seems to think, or simply one of the many dangers to which faith must, in the nature of the case, lay itself open?

To answer this we must examine Troeltsch's argument for the necessity of the historical Jesus from a fresh angle. We shall consider what arguments he could have given to support the significance of the earthly Jesus and thereby of the historian's reconstruction of him, but which for some reason he failed to present *explicitly* in this particular essay.

First, Gerrish would have done well to consider Troeltsch's all-important metaphysical presuppositions. In the terms of Troeltsch's metaphysic of history, no truths or values are available except through history: 'values . . . reside *only* in concrete realities'.[54] In religious terms, that means that faith must be

---

[54] 'Moderne Geschichtsphilosophie' (originally in *Theologische Rundschau* 1904), *GS* ii. 695–6 (my italics). See also *GS* iii. 17, where 'philosophy of history' is defined as 'recognition of the goals of life *out of history*'.

'able to appreciate the significance of the historical and to see in history the forms in which eternal religious truths assert themselves'.[55] There is no question, then, of pushing Troeltsch here in a rationalistic, Kantian, direction, wherein history becomes primarily a means of illustrating eternal truths. This is a very common misconstrual of Troeltsch:[56] but although it may have been true to some extent of his early work,[57] I believe it to be a fundamentally erroneous interpretation of his mature stance. And this is now all the more clearly demonstrated (thanks to the publication of the Troeltsch–Bousset correspondence) by looking at Troeltsch's response to his friend Bousset, who despite the production of an excellent book on the historical Jesus[58] was none the less an exponent of precisely this Kantian line on the issue of faith and history.[59] Writing to Bousset in the wake of the Drews debate, Troeltsch says he cannot accept Bousset's position because it makes Christianity's connection with Jesus more or

---

[55] 'Glaube und Geschichte', *RGG* 1454, § 3*d*. Here Troeltsch considers, and explicitly rejects, Lessings's objection to connecting faith with contingent historical facts (ibid. 1450, § 2*b*). The 'correct view of the relationship of the universally valid to what is historical', he says, will not preclude the supposition that 'the highest and purest religious forces' do indeed 'break through, receive embodiment, and are visibly guaranteed', even in and through 'historical conditionedness and relativity' (ibid. 1453, § 3*b*).

[56] See e.g. Diem 1959, 7; Morgan in ed. Morgan and Pye 1977, 38. Also see, by implication, Fischer 1967, 49. In contrast, Wehrung 1933, 390 f., seems one of the few commentators to have a correct grasp of Troeltsch's position here. (Kant's own position on this point, incidentally, is also slightly more subtle than he is often given credit for: see his occasional suggestion that the rational 'principle' needs to gain a 'public foothold' *in history* if it is to come to fruition or be 'intelligible'; see Kant 1960, 113, 144.)

[57] It seems e.g. to be implied by Troeltsch's essay on Kant, 'Das Historische in Kants Religionsphilosophie' (*Kantstudien* 1904), esp. the closing para. on p. 154. See Wyman 1983 173 ff. for a good discussion of this, and also of Troeltsch's later, revised, view.

[58] *Jesus*, first German edn. 1904 (Bousset 1906, in English). For Troeltsch's positive reception of the book see above, ch. 2 n. 30.

[59] See esp. Bousset 1911 (a lecture for the same conference as 'Sig. HJ'), esp. 15: '. . . Jesus did not only create the symbols of the Gospel in essentials, but became symbol Himself. . . . But this symbolic aspect enables us now also to dispose of all difficulties which resulted especially on the part of exact historical enquiry. . . . The question as to the existence and the possibility of historical recognition no more plays the leading part; for now we need no longer anxiously fix the limits of what might possibly be fiction and frame-work of His people in the characterization of Jesus and what might be reality in the more limited historical sense. We need no longer fear the eventual result of historical investigation that this reality (in its more limited sense) will remain irrevocably and irretrievably lost. At this point . . . all depends on the symbol and the picture, not on final truth and reality. This lies beyond the symbols in the unalterable God-given profundities of human reason, in the eternal worth of the "ideas". The symbol serves as illustration not as demonstration.

less 'accidental'; on this view, he says, 'the Christian character of religion is . . . lost', because it becomes 'passing chance that connects rational truths with the person of Jesus' (Dinkler-von Schubert 1976, 46).[60] For Troeltsch this is quite unacceptable. As we see from his *RGG* article on 'Faith and History', history does not just 'illustrate', but, more significantly, 'reveals' and 'confirms' ('Glaube und Geschichte', *RGG* 1456, § 4). And there is no other source of such revelation and confirmation *except* history.

Thus, *pace* Gerrish and others, we cannot turn Troeltsch into a crypto-Kantian on this point. Nor, on the other hand, is it appropriate to push Troeltsch in a proto-Bultmannian direction, to imply that he saw revelation as residing in atemporal acts of decision and faith which, in a slightly different way, would escape the entanglement with history and historical enquiry.[61] In his skirmish with Gogarten, Troeltsch makes it quite clear that he does not believe in 'supra-temporal moments' of any kind (ed. Robinson 1968, 312). The point is that, against either of these options, Troeltsch saw religious truth as mediated precisely *in* history, and, on occasions, in special, superior, 'bursts' of divine revelation in prophetic personalities.[62] For the Christian, the supreme locus of such truth is Jesus; and thus Troeltsch makes the 'realistic' claim that here, in Jesus, Christians may actually find God more than anywhere else. As he puts it in the very essay in question, Jesus is 'the highest revelation of God accessible to us' ('Sig. HJ' 206), and thus, correspondingly, 'God is made visible by reference to him' (ibid. 197–8; also see 'On Poss.' 30[b]).

---

[60] This letter was written in 1909, in response to Bousset's article 'Kantisch-Friessche Religionsphilosophie und ihre Anwendung auf die Theologie' (in the *Theologische Rundschau* 1909). We should note that whereas Troeltsch in his 'mature' theological period often cites the Kantian view that history can only illustrate, not reveal, truth (representing it as the 'modern' view), he is always careful to go on to distinguish his own position from this (see esp. 'Glaube und Geschichte' in *RGG*). For similar reasons, too, Troeltsch was dismissive of a somewhat different solution to the faith–history problem, in the form of Herrmann's Christology, which Troeltsch thought 'led to a definite religious subjectivism which is mainly concerned with personal religious experience and considers *everything historical as merely stimulation and sign-posts*' ('Half C.' 75, my italics).

[61] Gerrish's last para. (1975, 35) might be open to this construal, but his endorsement of W. Fresenius's position (ibid. 33 ff.) would suggest otherwise. Morgan, however (as we noted in ch. 3), has explicitly suggested that Troeltsch harbours a kind of proto-Bultmannian understanding of revelation: see ed. Clayton 1976, 59 ff. See again my criticisms in Coakley 1977, 327–8.

[62] See *Abs.* 69. This idea does not of course mean, at least certainly not for the mature Troeltsch, that such superior moments of revelation can be 'read off' from history by the uncommitted observer: see again the discussion above, ch. 3 pp. 86–7.

Does this not then provide a clear theological reason for faith's need to relate to the actual earthly Jesus? For what there is to say about Jesus cannot, on Troeltsch's own admission, be reduced to a pragmatic statement about the efficacy of the Christ symbol.[63] If the earthly Jesus is believed to have been the pre-eminent revelation of God, then the desire to recover what one can about him through accurate research is of obvious religious significance. Where Troeltsch is misleading, however, is in his assertion that this is a '*purely* psychological' matter (see *Gl.* 84); in fact the issue leads beyond 'pure' psychology into far-reaching metaphysical claims.[64]

None the less, only my interpretation, surely, explains why Troeltsch can give a pride of place to the earthly Jesus' teaching in his essay on the 'essence' of Christianity. For there Troeltsch argues, as we have already noted, that Jesus' ethic should continue to hold a pre-eminent position in ethical reflection, even if it is too demanding to be followed explicitly. Again, Troeltsch inadvertently provides the reason for this in his essay on the significance of the historical Jesus. The 'divine', he says, 'presents itself in history . . . with the substance of an overarching totality of historical life'. But 'this in turn receives its most *important strength and certainty* from the *historical person* of Jesus' ('Sig. HJ' 206, my italics, and see 'On Poss.' 32[b]). Now surely such a continued reference to the earthly Jesus would only need to be made on the supposition that here was a special, indeed 'superior', revelation of God.

Further, and likewise, it is only if this 'realist' claim is in

---

63 This was what I had originally understood Gerrish's stance to imply (see e.g. Gerrish 1975, 29: 'neither past nor future can invalidate the truth and life which are mediated by the symbol in the present'; and ibid. 35: 'the symbol . . . has the surprising power to speak for itself'). However, other hints in the essay (ibid. 28–9) and subsequent correspondence with Gerrish show that Gerrish himself is motivated not so much by pragmatic considerations as by Reformation principles: the appeal to the 'Word', and the refusal to make faith in any sense a 'work'.

64 It should of course be remembered that, for Troeltsch (as is especially clear in his work in the early years of the century on psychology of religion), psychological considerations are more likely to lead on to metaphysical decisions than not. (See the excellent short discussion of this point in Wyman 1983, 64 ff., esp. 66–7.) On the other hand, we have already noted (see esp. above, ch. 4 p. 124) Troeltsch's reluctance to get involved in metaphysical precision where Christology is concerned. To this extent, then, he does bring on himself the familiar dismissive charge that he has provided no '*substantive* connection between the Christian faith in God and the person of Jesus' (Reist 1966, 192; also see Morgan in ed. Morgan and Pye 1977, 38–9).

operation that Troeltsch's remaining argument for the significance of the 'historical Jesus' holds. This is the supposition—admittedly a debatable one[65]—that the Christian believer only attains real 'strength' and 'certainty' from the ideal presented in Jesus if he knows it is a *real* possibility (see again 'Sig. HJ' 197–8). This is in a way a form of 'psychological' dependence, but it is different, we note, from the psychological needs for 'vivification', 'edification', and so on, which we have seen would be equally well served by a 'symbol'. This, in contrast, demands contact with a historical actuality if it is to be satisfied.[66]

This point need not be laboured further. We now see that although features of Troeltsch's theology do indicate a trend in the direction suggested by Gerrish, there is an important 'realist' strand there also that Gerrish has overlooked.[67] On the other hand, Gerrish is entirely right to highlight the confusion in Troeltsch's argument. To conclude our analysis, therefore, let us now note some of the implications of Troeltsch's position which he was evidently reluctant to concede.

First, as Gerrish too mentions, Troeltsch ends up espousing a position closer to some of his (more 'orthodox', or rather 'Ritschlian') opponents than he apparently intends. Earlier in

---

[65] It is of course quite possible to believe in an 'impossible' ideal. At times this may hold positive attractions. But in practice, and at the phenomenological level, Troeltsch is surely right to say that for most Christians it is important to distinguish between emulating the example of a real man, Jesus, and emulating, say, a fantasy hero such as Batman or Spiderman.

[66] That is not to say that there are not remaining *difficulties* to this argument, which Troeltsch was not, I think, as well alerted to as he might have been. (1) At times, as we have seen, Troeltsch makes as part of the argument an appeal to Jesus having achieved a new breakthrough in humanity (see e.g. 'On Poss.' 32[a]), and this seems to be a hangover from the sort of Christology Troeltsch was espousing about the turn of the century (see above, ch. 2 pp. 66 f., 69). Yet, on his own admission by 1909 ('Half C.' 72), the supposition that Jesus opens up 'a new stage of humanity' is one of the things no longer patent of historical demonstration on the evidence available. So there is a problem of internal consistency here. More importantly, (2) Troeltsch does not adequately face the problem that the sort of things most likely to be 'psychologically' important to Christians in this way (e.g. Jesus' experience in the Garden of Gethsemane, or his demeanour during the cruxifixion itself) are extremely unlikely to be substantiated by historical critical means with any great certainty. None the less there is a remaining force to Troeltsch's argument here which cannot be lightly brushed aside, despite the difficulties and historical risks involved.

[67] Gerrish seems to a degree to have admitted this, implicitly at least, by referring in a more recent essay to Troeltsch's words in *AJT* 1913, 14–15: 'present religious experience continues to receive its life and power from the vital work of history: this it is, *and particularly the prophets and Jesus*, which leads us to God (see ed. Clayton 1976, 110, my italics).

the essay, for instance, he criticizes the Ritschlian school for its argument that Christians would be 'impotent and in despair without the elevating or suggestive impression of the person of Jesus' ('Sig. HJ' 192). Yet one can see almost no difference between this and Troeltsch's own argument that faith only finds 'support and strength' (ibid. 198) in the knowledge that 'a real man thus lived, struggled, believed and conquered' (ibid. 197).[68]

Second, and similarly, Troeltsch gets into an appalling confusion about what would constitute an 'absolute' or 'inner necessity' for the historical Jesus.[69] This position (which he connects for some reason with appeals to the miraculous, with the doctrine of original sin, and with claims for direct personal contact with Jesus[70]) is firmly rejected. The question remains, however, what sort of 'relative' dependence he is maintaining in contrast. Does he think the dependence is 'relative' because it is only (or so he believes) 'social psychological'? Or is it that the 'consensus' on the main facts about Jesus removes what would otherwise be an 'absolute' dependence? A third possibility, however, which is only hinted at,[71] makes the best sense of Troeltsch's position. On this supposition, and as Troeltsch maintains elsewhere,[72] faith is only 'relatively' dependent on the historical Jesus because this dependence is only one component in the complex constitution of faith. Faith is thus not solely dependent on recoverable data about the earthly Jesus (although this is, as we have shown, of considerable significance: theologically, ethically and psychologically). Rather, faith depends on a great variety of things. It rests on the accumulated interpretations of Jesus mediated through the Bible and community for instance, on the community's own contemporary history, ethical strength, and

---

68 Troeltsch does admit the similarity in 'Sig. HJ' 201; where he wants to *diverge* to a degree from the Ritschlians in their presentation of this argument emerges in ibid. 188–9.

69 See 'Sig. HJ' 184, 185, 190, 191.

70 See ibid. 184–5, 197. Again, it is not surprising that Troeltsch has been misunderstood as wanting to sever all integral connections between Jesus and God the Father as a result of his wielding this idea of 'absolute, inner necessity' with such imprecision and (frankly) odd overtones.

71 See ibid. 189 ('Neither is it legitimate to say that only the recognition of Jesus as divine authority and source of certainty gives the confidence and joy of faith') and 200 (Jesus is not the 'sole source of Christian faith's knowledge and its power for life', etc.).

72 See 'Glaube und Geschichte', *RGG* 1437 ff. *passim*; and 'Erlösung', *RGG* 486–7,

§ 7.

unity of purpose, and on the individual's own past history and religious experience. This is why Troeltsch can say, for instance, that it is not *'only* the recognition of Jesus' that 'gives the confidence and joy of faith' ('Sig. HJ' 189, my italics). Likewise, if faith has these manifold props and constituents, it may not so much surprise us that an experience of redemption may occur without reference to the earthly Jesus *per se*. It may be only secondarily, as Troetsch says, that the believer recognizes the theological significance of Jesus as the 'highest revelation accessible to us' ('Sig. HJ' 206), and thus becomes alerted to the vital importance of historical enquiry about him.[73]

A third and final point that must be levied against Troeltsch is one that we have already touched on. We now see that Troeltsch's 'social psychological' argument, for all the novel insights it provides, sends up a smoke-screen which tends to avert the metaphysical questions which Christological claims invariably beg. But will this do? If Jesus is indeed held to be the 'highest revelation accessible to us', or 'the embodiment' of 'the distinctively Christian idea of God' as Troeltsch puts it elsewhere ('On Poss.' 30[b]), then the implications for the doctrine of God must be spelled out systematically and clearly. What does Troeltsch mean by these claims? Whatever he does, it is really no longer possible for him to consider the 'grandeur of prophetic Christian faith in God' in isolation from the 'personality and teaching' of Jesus himself.[74] This, it must be said, is a severe weakness in Troeltsch's position; and it is odd, as we have already suggested, from one whose theology in general is so explicitly metaphysical.

In this chapter we have described and analysed what we have called the 'realist' strand in Troeltsch's Christological thought. But we have so far only just mentioned another feature of his Christology which also makes its appearance in the essay under review. In it Troeltsch can say, for instance, that the Church can 'interpret the picture of Christ in practical proclamation very freely and flexibly, using *everything* that flowed into him and

---

[73] See 'Erlösung', *RGG* 485, § 3: 'The task of theology is . . . limited to the descriptive analysis of the present and ever new process of redemption in its particular moments and *then* to link to it the historical reference backwards to the revelation in Jesus and in the community . . .' (my italics). For further discussion of this theme see below, ch. 6.

[74] See above, ch. 3 pp. 100 f. and n. 50 there.

everything which in the course of thousands of years has been accommodated and loved in him' ('Sig. HJ' 201, my italics). But how is this flexibility to coexist with Troeltsch's insistence on the need to know about the 'historical Jesus'? To this question we turn in our next chapter.

6

Troeltsch and the Many Christs

In Chapter 5 we showed how Troeltsch presents in his lecture on the historical Jesus two theses which are logically distinct. On the one hand, the 'symbol of Christ' is declared necessary both for the community's social cohesion, and for the individual's various needs for an 'archetypal' personality. On the other hand, the earthly Jesus (and hence careful historical reconstruction of him) is also shown to be highly significant: for general *theological* reasons (for here, it is believed, God is most fully seen); for more specific *ethical* reasons (because Jesus' teaching is a vital reference point in Christian ethical decision); and for a *psychological* reason (because of the desire to know that Jesus represents a real human possibility).

But it should be clear by now that Troeltsch does not in any way restrict God's revelatory or redemptive activity to that which may be discovered in Jesus: the 'historical person Jesus' is by no means the 'sole source of Christian faith's knowledge and its power for life' ('Sig. HJ' 200); thus there should be no immediate cause for alarm that 'each age interprets [Jesus] really quite differently and puts its own ideas under his protection' ('Essence' 147).[1] Human 'imagination' ('Sig. HJ' 195 and 'On Poss.' 31[a]) and 'loving' projection ('Sig. HJ' 201) may actually be the mediators of a continuing process of revelation. It is not just the 'historical Jesus' who 'embodies' God ('On Poss.' 30[b]), gives confidence and strength to persevere ('Sig. HJ' 197), and even justifies a posture of veneration ('Sig. HJ' 206)[2]—although he does indeed do all these things. But it is also, and at the same time, the 'infinitely variegated' Christ pictured in the New Testa-

---

[1] This is an addition made in 1913, and doubtless influenced by Troeltsch's work on *ST*, which convinced him of the irreducible diversity of Christian belief. See esp. *ST* 994 f. on the different 'types' of Christology which will always coexist. For more on the significance of 1913 as a Christological turning-point, see the end of this chapter, below.

[2] Robert Morgan's translation of the verb *verehren* here ('Sig. HJ' 206) as 'reverence' rather than 'worship' is I think right in the light of what Troeltsch says about Jesus being not God *simpliciter* but 'the highest revelation . . . accessible to us'.

ment, and then anew by countless successive generations of Christians, who reveals God, elicits faith, is a guarantee and source of strength, and whom Christians join together to worship.[3]

This juxtaposition of themes raises, it seems to me, three pressing problems, which we shall treat in turn. First there is the need to probe more exactly the extent to which the 'historical Jesus' is important for revelation and redemption in Troeltsch's view (granted the apparently unrestricted freedom he allows to later interpretative remodelling[4]), and also to ask what purpose the reconstructed picture of Jesus is deemed to perform. That the 'historical Jesus' is in some sense indispensable for Troeltsch we have already demonstrated; but the precise extent and purpose of Jesus' importance require further clarification. Second, there is the problem of Troeltsch's attempt to find in the tradition's infinitely varied portraits of Christ an identifiable, personal unity. And third (and concomitantly) there is the difficulty of explaining how, and in what sense, this 'Christ' can be described as 'living'.

The first problem, that of the extent and purpose of faith's reference to the historian's Jesus, can best be elucidated by looking at Troeltsch's treatment in the *Glaubenslehre* of the traditional *munus triplex* theme in Christology, much beloved of the Reformers and their successors.[5] Although only briefly enunciated,[6] Troeltsch's presentation could well be said to encapsulate his whole Christology *in nuce*. The first thing that is important here is that, following Ritschl (and indeed Luther and Calvin before him[7]), Troeltsch gives a distinct pre-eminence to the office

---

[3] See e.g. 'Glaube und Geschichte', *RGG* 1448, § 1b, and *Gl.* 19–20, § 1. But then cf. again e.g. 'Offenbarung', *RGG* 921, § 4.3, and *Gl.* 20–1, § 2: here the reference is once more to Jesus. Troeltsch does not see the two themes as incompatible: see e.g. 'Sig. HJ' 200–1, 202–3.

[4] See e.g. 'Sig. HJ' 202: we can use 'full freedom' in adaptation of Jesus to contemporary concerns. Or again see 'Glaube und Geschichte', *RGG* 1454, § 3c: 'The main point, the personality of Jesus, will be interpreted in so universal a manner that faith will continue to be able to link *whatever it regards as sacred and precious to it*, and even future acquisitions will find room in it' (my italics).

[5] There are useful historical surveys of this theme in Ritschl 1966, 417 ff., and Pannenberg 1968, 212 ff.

[6] See *Gl.* 103–4, 116, and 345; also see 'Ämter Christi', *RGG* 213–14, for Troeltsch's little historical survey of the theme.

[7] Luther in fact only discussed two offices, King and Priest, but gave kingship the priority. Calvin's presentation changed and developed somewhat in the course of years, but the basic priority was none the less given to kingship. See Ritschl 1966, 419 ff.

of King over those of Prophet and Priest (*Gl.* 104, 116, and see 91).
Moreover, the way Troeltsch now reinterprets Christ's Kingly
officium as providing a 'rallying-point' for the cultus, and a personal reference point of devotion rather than a dogma (*Gl.* 104),
reminds us of functions well familiar from 'The Significance of
the Historical Existence of Jesus for Faith', which logically require, as we have seen, not the historian's Jesus, but simply the
biblical (and specifically Gospel) portraits of Jesus for their
satisfaction.[8] The pre-eminence, then, that Troeltsch gives to
Christ's Kingship already serves to indicate the rather circumscribed extent to which the historian's Jesus comes into play
in Christological construction.

Moreover, when we turn to look at his treatment of the offices
of Prophet and Priest, we again see that the significance of
reference to the historian's Jesus is relatively limited. As Prophet
Christ reveals God; as Priest he redeems. But in neither function
(both of which, strictly speaking, are for Troeltsch coterminous[9])
is the reference to the earthly Jesus as mediated through research
experientially prior. The process of redemption, for instance, is
something in the first instance mediated by the community 'as if'
(*Gl.* 346) it comes from 'Christ'; this, in turn, drives the believer
back to Christ himself in search of the origins of this redemptive
life-stream.[10] But by 'Christ' here Troeltsch evidently means the
biblical portraits ('das Bild Christi' (ibid.)). Where then does the
reference to the historian's Jesus come in? Only, it seems, in a
secondary and limited way, especially where redemption is concerned. Only, that is, to the extent that the already confirmed
believer feels the need of a degree of 'psychological security',
'strength', and 'certainty' in the business of *imitatio Christi*: the

[8] See above, ch. 5 pp. 141–7. *Gl.* 103 admittedly talks of 'the historical personality of
Jesus' as fulfilling the office of King as well as the other offices; but I think we must take
'historical' in the sense of 'public' or 'objectified' (see again ch. 5 p. 147) in the case of the
kingly *officium*.

[9] See *Gl.* 104, and also 115: the functions of revealing and redeeming in Jesus strictly
speaking coincide (as the revealer of God he leads us to God). This of course parallels
Troeltsch's more general equation of revelation and redemption (see above, ch. 3).

[10] These two points of reference (the present experience of redemption in the community and the reference to the person of Christ) are mutually dependent—or in a
'circular' relationship (see *Gl.* 346 and above, ch. 5 p. 143). As Troeltsch himself
acknowledges (*Gl.* 345, 348), the idea of Jesus being mediated through the community
and thus exercising a real power in redemption is to be traced back to Schleiermacher,
for whom Jesus is not simply a moral exemplar but an actual means of communicating
the power of God.

need, as we have seen enunciated in Troeltsch's 1911 lecture, to have confidence that it is not an unreal ideal that is being pursued ('Sig. HJ' 197, 207).[11]

Likewise, the Prophetic office of Christ as revealer is by no means restricted to what may be reconstructed about Jesus' earthly career (Jesus 'in his earthly appearance' (*Gl.* 346)). Jesus of Nazareth, as a prophet very much in the Old Testament tradition,[12] is to a degree restricted, and certainly deeply conditioned, by his circumstances (*Gl.* 346-7, 114-15, 102); his eschatological message is, as we have seen, sharply 'one-sided' in Troeltsch's view (*Gl.* 347; see 'Essence' 155). Thus, to look for the implications of that revelation expanded and reworked in Paul, Augustine, Luther, and a host of others,[13] and then to feed back those reflections into an (expanding) 'Christ' figure is, for Troeltsch, entirely appropriate,[14] and indeed consistent with his stress on the importance of revelation continuing through history. If again we ask how significant, precisely, the fundamental revelation in Jesus is (and thus, concomitantly, how important the business of historical reconstruction), the answer is, I think, nuanced slightly differently from the case of redemption. Experientially, again, the reference may be secondary;[15] but this time that secondary reference has more than merely psychological import. In that the earthly Jesus 'reveals' God (indeed, it is believed, more than any other person has revealed him[16]), reference to him is of vital interest as the 'source, stability,

[11] In the same lecture Troeltsch of course emphasizes that historical knowledge about Jesus is certainly not the only source of religious strength and confidence (see 'Sig. HJ' 189, 200-1), but an understandable psychological need none the less.

[12] Troeltsch stresses this continuity with the Old Testament prophetic 'ethos' in one of his last essays to make a Christological reference: 'Glaube und Ethos der hebräischen Propheten' (1916) in *GS* iv. 34-65. See esp. 62-3.

[13] See *Gl.* 114-15. 'Sig. HJ' 201 adds that there is no need to stop at the Reformation either: 'Such historical facts can be found right down to the present.'

[14] See e.g. 'Essence' 168: 'The prophetic element in religion belongs not only to the past but also to the present. . . . When we are certain that the spirit of Christ, through history, is speaking a new *word* to us, we do not need to be ashamed to admit that it is a *new* word.'

[15] See e.g. 'Sig. HJ' 206: 'We have resolutely to grasp the divine as it presents itself to us in our time. In our time it presents itself in history and in the connexion of the individual's subjectivity with the substance of an overarching totality of historical life. This *in turn* receives its most important strength and certainty from the historical person of Jesus' (my italics).

[16] See again e.g. 'Sig. HJ' 206, and *Gl.* 346: 'Christ in his historical manifestation is a tremendous revelation of God, of sublime height, gentleness, and power'.

and authority' (*Gl.* 347) of all that is later retrojected on to him, both as an (admittedly elusive) indication of the nature of God, and as a starting-point, at least, of all ethical decisions. All the 'fundamental themes' (*Grundgedanken* (*Gl.* 347)) are there.

This reference to the *munus triplex* discussion leaves us in a better position to clarify the purposes to which Troeltsch wishes to put the historian's Jesus. It is important, first, to note that it does not appear to be his intention in any sense to prove or legitimate faith by reference to historical enquiry about Jesus.[17] Dispassionate historical enquiry (the historian's Jesus *per se*) cannot bring about faith, or provide a compelling 'proof' for it (see *Die Hilfe* 1908, 59[a]). To this extent, then, Troeltsch does not deserve Bultmann's later charge (made against 'liberal theology' in general, but Troeltsch in particular) that the impossible attempt was being made to move *from* historical research *to* faith.[18] Nor, like Harnack (another target of Bultmann's),[19] does Troeltsch attempt to prune back Christological statements to the limits of what the historian can reconstruct about Jesus. For Troeltsch, as we have seen, 'imagination (*Phantasie*)' is in general a positive asset in Christological reflection; whereas for Harnack (as is shown in his celebrated correspondence with Barth) an 'imagined Christ' was precisely what had to be routed in favour of 'reliable … knowledge of this person' (Rumscheidt 1972, 31). Troeltsch, in contrast, explicitly rejects the suggestion that historical enquiry about Jesus should act as a 'fetter' on Christological construction (*Die Hilfe* 1908, 59[a]).

[17] The only strand in Troeltsch's Christological thought that might be taken to suggest this is his (somewhat questionable) insistence in 'Sig. HJ' (see 197) that the historian should be able to verify that in Jesus there was a '*superior* . . . religious prophet'. However, we note that even this reference to the historian occurs once the believer's faith is already established ('Someone who really belongs in his heart to the world of Christian experience' (ibid.)). Thus it is important to underline again here that Troeltsch's Christological 'realism' is not 'naïve': it does not expect to find a supreme act of God umambiguously presented in Jesus. Faith *interprets* historical facts (see *Gl.* 79, 113); it does not 'read off' an obvious, publicly presented, meaning from them (see again above ch. 3 pp. 86 f).

[18] See Bultmann 1969, 30: 'Historical research can never lead to any result which could serve as a basis for faith, for *all its results have only relative validity*.' Bultmann then goes on to discuss Troeltsch's 1911 lecture. (However, cf. again *Gl.* 346 f. for a clearer picture of Troeltsch's views on when and to what extent the reference to the historian's Jesus becomes important for faith. Bultmann would have done well to take the *Glaubenslehre* into account.)

[19] See again Bultmann 1969, 31.

On the other hand, and from the standpoint of faith, we have seen that reference to the earthly Jesus via critical research provides, first where revelation is concerned, vital formative clues[20] as to the nature of God and the foundations of ethical decision, and second, where redemption is concerned, a certain reassurance, or means of 'courage' (*Gl.* 103). Thus, as we saw in Chapter 5, reference back to Jesus both 'reveals and confirms' ('Glaube und Geschichte', *RGG* 1456, § 4), but not, as we now clarify, to the disinterested observer, and not, either, as the *sole* locus of revelation and confirmation (see again 'Sig. HJ' 189). Nor, as Troeltsch sometimes over-excitedly suggests ('Sig. HJ' 198), is it consistent for him to say that either of these functions of the historian's Jesus acts as an absolute *sine qua non* of faith's continuing existence. The 'risk' here, though certainly real, is only a relative one; lack of confirmation would result in perhaps quite radical readjustment, but not actual destruction of faith. It is only Christ *qua* personal 'rallying-point' (that is, in his office as King) who is absolutely indispensable for the survival of Christian faith (see again 'Sig. HJ' 194–5; 'On Poss.' 30[a-b]; *Gl.* 91).

Finally (and this was a point on which Troeltsch was not always at all clear,[21] for reasons we shall shortly chart), reference to the historian's Jesus can also be important in a slightly different capacity, on occasions of debate and disagreement, as a 'criterion' to which all parties can refer for judgement. As Troeltsch puts it in the second edition of 'Was heißt, "Wesen des Christentums"?':

> . . . the original time really is recognised as crucial, and out of this recognition its real and genuine meaning always has some effect on the Christianity of the time. This original history . . . remains the criterion among all confessions, sects and groups, and it is never applied without its real meaning having some inner effects. ('Essence' 147.)

Thus, in the case of a radical departure of Christological interpretation from Jesus' original actions and teaching, the latter

---

[20] Troeltsch liked to talk about the 'classical' phase of revelation in Jesus (see 'Essence' 147), by which he meant 'particularly important' (ibid.) but not *restrictively* normative.

[21] Clarity on this point only really comes in 1913, as I shall explain shortly. Until then, Troeltsch could sometimes imply that any interpretation of Jesus was acceptable (see e.g. 'Sig. HJ' 201) and at other times could indicate the dangers of such unlimited freedom (see e.g. his criticisms of Renan's 'subjectivity' in *GS* ii. 11).

should be given precedence. Both interpretation and the historian's Jesus are important, but 'in their interrelationship the preaching of Jesus is the stronger'.[22]

So far we have indicated at least a potentially consistent understanding of the relationship between the historian's Jesus and the many Christs of faith in Troeltsch's Christology, allowing both for a rich, imaginative diversity of Christological construction and for a dimension of critical reflection on Jesus. Yet there still remain two facets to his Christological thought which are at the very least problematic, and closely related to each other. What, for instance, are we to make of his brief remarks in the 1911 lecture that Jesus (or 'Christ': the two are used here interchangeably) is a *'living,* many-sided and . . . elevating . . . personality'* ('Sig. HJ' 202, my italics), or again, a *'living . . .* indefinable *personal life'* (ibid. 213, my italics)?

There are two new moves here which might appear illegitimate, or at least in tension with what we have already seen of Troeltsch's Christology. The first is the attempt simply to equate the earthly Jesus with all the 'many Christs' of Christian interpretation and thus give to these interpretations some sort of identifiable unity. The second and concomitant claim is that Jesus, as the Christ (or 'symbol of Christ' as in the rest of the 1911 essay), is in some undefined sense 'living', and presently efficacious as a 'personality'. These difficulties and their relation are nicely illustrated in the following memorable passage from Troeltsch's 1910 lecture 'On the Possibility of a Liberal Christianity':

Jesus is the *embodiment of superior religious power, embellished in ever new ways* in the course of thousands of years, whose heartbeat is felt throughout the whole of Christendom, even as the vibration of a ship's engine is felt in every nook of the whole ship. This is why he himself *will always keep on living . . .* and why [prophetic Christian] belief will rise to its full power. . . only by having *such a person to look up to.* But if this is so, then the figure

[22] Of course even this procedure—the use of the historian's Jesus as a 'criterion'—will not produce unambiguous results by any means. Troeltsch's attack on von Hartmann (considerably expanded in the 2nd edn. of 'Essence': see Sykes's remarks in ed. Morgan and Pye 1977, 180–1) well illustrates this. Troeltsch seems to have been unclear whether to attack von Hartmann chiefly on the grounds of (1) erring too far from the earthly Jesus' message (See 'Essence' 172–3), as we might expect from ibid. 147 and 156; or (2) rejecting the importance of the *person* of Christ (ibid. 172–3); or (3) (rather differently) because von Hartmann's reconstruction was not true, and ultimately 'we are concerned not with Christianity but with the truth' (ibid. 175).

of Jesus will *remain alive* and inseparable from the power of the Christian belief in God. ('On Poss'. 30^b-31^a [my italics].)^23

What is evident from this is that, unless Troeltsch can establish that the *embellished* Jesus (the 'symbol of Christ' in his later lecture) is in some sense personally continuous with the earthly Jesus, then it remains unclear how such disparate reflections on the cultic figurehead could properly be said to refer to one identifiable entity. As to the further claim for the autonomous existence of this 'power', the slide from the earthly Jesus to the *totum Christi* is again supposed to smoothe the path. For the Christ figure is apparently 'living' just in so far as it is constantly reworked and 'embellished'; yet the reason that its existence is not merely in the minds of its venerators is that they identify it with the existence of the earthly Jesus (the 'person to look up to'). How then does Troeltsch attempt to establish the identity of the earthly Jesus with the cultic Christ? Although he does not state this explicitly, it appears that he uses three related theological concepts specifically for this purpose. We shall examine them, and their effectiveness, in turn, noting that each owes a particular debt of influence to one of Troeltsch's forebears in the post-Enlightenment theological tradition of Germany.

The first is the ambiguous term 'personality'. On the one hand this is obviously meant to refer to the earthly Jesus, since we remember that the 'personality' of Jesus was one of the things that Troeltsch felt should and could be recovered by historical research (see 'Sig. HJ' 198; 'On Poss.' 31^a). In the *Glaubenslehre* and *RGG*, however (and briefly in the 1911 lecture), it has a much more extended sense, encompassing not only Jesus' person but all the interpretations laid upon it by subsequent Christian generations.^24 It is in fact *this* 'personality' that brings Christians to redemption (see *Gl.* 346, 356; also 'Erlösung', *RGG* 487, § 7). Jesus' historical personality, on the other hand (as we have already noted), is deemed considerably limited by the natural presuppositions of his race and time (*Gl.* 346), and can act only as the 'kernel' of subsequent accretions (see *Gl.* 113).^25

---

^23 Troeltsch was sufficiently fond of this combination of metaphors (the heartbeat and the ship's engine) to use it on other occasions too: see *GS* iv. 71.

^24 See e.g. *Gl.* 91, 346; 'Glaube und Geschichte', *RGG* 1454, § 3*c*; 'Erlösung', *RGG* 487, § 7.

^25 As we have already noted, Troeltsch often appears to give these accretions com-

Now, as Troeltsch himself remarks in his 1911 lecture, the originator of this language of 'personality' as a Christological bridgehead between the past and the present was 'the later ecclesiastical Schleiermacher' (see 'Sig. HJ' 187).[26] But the more immediate exponent of the idea, as Troeltsch also notes (ibid.), was Herrmann, with his talk of the 'Person of Jesus', or Jesus' 'inner' or 'personal life', understood as a 'Power that came into history with the life of Jesus' and still now confronts us (see Herrmann 1909, 291).

The trouble is that this notion of Herrmann's is extraordinarily slippery, as Troeltsch himself was quick to point out (see 'Sig. HJ' 188 f.). His main criticism, as we have had reason to mention before, was that it short-circuited the need for careful critical study of Jesus' earthly personality; this was no way, Troeltsch objected, to blur the distinction between what honestly could be reconstructed about Jesus (the historian's Jesus, in our terms) and what were later addenda; nor was it an appropriate way to avoid admitting that the earthly Jesus is no longer 'directly and personally effective' (ibid. 188).[27] Yet does not Troeltsch's own use of this word 'personality' (especially in his 1910 lecture cited above) invite just these same criticisms? Even if he intended rather different nuances to Herrmann's, as he intimates in his 1911 essay, that is, a 'personality' not directly available but mediated through community tradition (ibid. 189), not all the difficulties are removed. We are still left wondering (as in Herrmann too) whether this 'personality' actually exists, except in so far as it is conjured up in the minds of believers, and whether it is not mere sleight of hand that makes so many divergent conceptions of him into one identifiable entity.

Troeltsch's second means of attempting to identify Jesus with

pletely free rein in their interpretation: see again e.g. 'Glaube und Geschichte', *RGG* 1454, §3c.

26 See e.g. Schleiermacher 1963, ii. 363: 'If . . . the faith of the later generations, and consequently of our own, is to be the same as the original one and not a different faith . . . then it must still be possible to have the same experiences; . . . Our proposition, therefore, depends upon the assumption that this influence of the fellowship in producing a like faith is none other than the influence of the personal perfection of Jesus Himself.'

27 Troeltsch later made a similar criticism of Harnack's Christology: he questioned whether it was 'possible for anyone to orient himself so directly and naively to the figure of Jesus, regardless of all historical criticism' (in 'Adolf von Harnack and Ferdinand Christian Baur', a Festschrift article in honour of Harnack (1921), in Pauck 1968, 113–14).

the many Christs in a way provides an answer to these questions in metaphysical terms but is no less problematic in itself. This time it is the language of the Spirit of Christ (*Geist Christi*) which, as we have already had occasion to mention,[28] Troeltsch also identifies, in Pauline mode, with the Holy Spirit (see *Gl.* 119–21, 125). But the connection asserted here between Jesus' earthly life and the Spirit is mysterious, indeed thoroughly bemusing. The Spirit is variously described as being 'released' by the death of Jesus,[29] or by his suffering (*Gl.* 361), or rather differently, and more subjectively, by the faith of the primitive Christians ('Sig. HJ' 213). At least in the *Glaubenslehre*, however, this Spirit has its 'source, support, and authority' supplied by its historical basis in Jesus, but then after his death becomes the 'principle' of the broadening and deepening Christian movement, capable of transcending the limits of a particular historical life and of making 'Christ' present to successive generations of his followers (*Gl.* 347).

This time, I think, it is mainly the influence of Hegel that looms large,[30] at least where the argument takes an explicitly metaphysical turn, indicating a separate existence for the *Geist Christi* as a force in history. But in general it is left extremely unclear in Troeltsch whether the Spirit is something just borne or entertained in the minds of Christians, and used as another metaphor, perhaps, for the sense of Christian community,[31] or

---

[28] See above, ch. 3 pp. 99 f.

[29] See *Gl.* 121, 347 (note that Troeltsch actually goes well beyond a 'historical-psychological' interpretation of Jesus' death here—cf. ibid. 115—and implies a *metaphysical* result). Also see 'Essence' 149: 'It is no longer the historical Christ, the Christ according to the flesh, who is the basis, but the spirit of Christ which is released when the earthly manifestation is shattered in death.'

[30] For Hegel, Christ's death on the cross (which is of course also God's death) is a necessary stage in the emergence of *true* Spirit: 'The sensuous existence in which Spirit is embodied is only a transitional phase. Christ dies; only as dead is he exalted to Heaven and sits at the right hand of God; only thus is he Spirit . . . To the Apostles, Christ as living was not that which he was to them subsequently as the Spirit of the Church, in which he became to them for the first time an object for their truly spiritual consciousness' (Hegel 1956, 325).

[31] See once more the definition of the Spirit in *Gl.* 347 as 'the animating and driving *force of the community*, a *principle* of the continual widening and deepening of the Christian understanding of God' (my italics). This definition contains both poles of meaning: community spirit and metaphysical 'principle'. Cf. with this however 'Sig. HJ' 203: here it is less clear that the Spirit has a life of its own; rather it is kept alive precisely by a 'succession of strong religious personalites' who draw their prime inspiration from the 'spirit of Jesus' to which they look back.

whether Troeltsch is really claiming that it also has an *independent* metaphysical existence. As Wyman (1983, 87–8) has most acutely pointed out, to the extent that the former alternative is the case, Troeltsch is closer to Schleiermacher in his notion of Spirit; [32] to the extent the latter, there is a definite step towards Hegel. But either way, the relation of this Spirit to Jesus remains problematic. In the *Glaubenslehre*, as we have seen, Troeltsch merely invokes the death of Jesus and its aftermath as sufficient reason for this 'Spirit' (now the 'Spirit of *Christ*') to take on a life of freedom (*Gl.* 347). But he makes no proper attempt to explain this, and without a full Hegelian metaphysical substructure, it tends to look like mere assertion. We might, of course, have expected an appeal to the resurrection at this point, but Troeltsch, as we shall see shortly, shared with many of his 'liberal' forebears a considerable embarrassment on this subject, a subject which he evidently thought historical critical tools could not probe (*Gl.* 112). The result of all this is that the concept of Spirit, or *Geist Christi*, as Troeltsch presents it, appears to provide no more convincing way of connecting Jesus with the many Christs than does the concept of 'personality'.

Troeltsch's third attempt to make this connection is, I think, an extension of his first two, and is perhaps closest to his heart. [33] What he calls his 'Christ-mysticism', with an evident debt this time to Schleiermacher, involves not only the embellishment and expansion of memories of Jesus into the many-sided figure of Christ, but also the assertion of a real 'continuity' between that historical personality and the community that builds itself around

---

[32] See Schleiermacher 1963, ii. 535: 'the expression "Holy Spirit" must be understood to mean the vital unity of the Christian fellowship as a moral personality; and this . . . we might denote by the phrase, its *common spirit*.'

[33] We know from *ST* 996 Troeltsch's preference for 'Spiritual Religion' (the mystic 'type'), which he sees as intrinsically related to 'modern Idealism'. In *ST* 994–5 he describes the 'Christ of mysticism' as 'an inward spiritual principle, felt in every stirring of religious feeling, present in every influence of the Divine Seed and the Divine Spark; this mystical Christ was Divinely incarnate in the Christ of History, but He can only be recognized and affirmed in inward spiritual experience; this principle therefore agrees in general with the "hidden ground" of the Divine Life in man.' Troeltsch is of course here describing a 'type' rather than relating his own views; none the less in the light of what he says in *ST* 996 I think we can take it that it is a position for which Troeltsch has some sympathy. The 'Christ-mysticism' theme in his dogmatic work thus reveals at least a strand of his own personal piety that was directly Christ-orientated. Elsewhere, as we have remarked before, Troeltsch makes no mention of Christ when discussing prayer, and appears to be of a more strictly *theo*centric mystical type.

it (*Gl.* 103; see 'On Poss.' 31ᵃ, 32ᵇ). Thus Jesus himself—Troeltsch does say Jesus here and not Christ—can be said to be present through the mediation of the community.[34] There is a claim made to some real identity between the mystical body and its head: the *caput mysticum* with the *corpus mysticum*.[35] Presumably the origins of this identity must be traced to the disciples' reflection on the human Jesus they had known. Hence Troeltsch can talk of a situation in which 'every believer feels himself to be an emanation from [the] central point', and this central point is evidently the earthly Jesus himself ('On Poss.' 31ᵃ and see 32ᵇ). Or, as he puts it more pictorially in the *Glaubenslehre*, Christian believers are like a searchlight (*Lichtkegel*) always being beamed out anew from a central source, Jesus (*Gl.* 116).

Unfortunately, however, and despite the immediate attractions of this idea, Troeltsch's 'Christ-mysticism' surely begs the questions we have already raised all over again. For is it not by mere fiat that a substantial continuity is asserted between the earthly Jesus and the 'object of [the believer's] . . . imagination'?[36] To 'feel' that one is 'an emanation' from 'this central point' is surely not sufficient reason to assert a real identity. Likewise, the 'Christ' of the believer's imagination may be very far removed from the real earthly Jesus (as Troeltsch himself had to admit when faced with interpretations that he felt had erred too far from the original[37]).

We must conclude that Troeltsch's main bridging ideas of 'personality', '*Geist Christi*', and 'Christ-mysticism' do not seem inherently convincing in their effect, and are also curiously out of line with Troeltsch's insistence elsewhere that there is a place,

---

[34] For the 'Christ-mysticism' see esp. 'On Poss.' (which even claims—somewhat questionably—that this theme carries on the 'innermost motif' of the old 'christological dogma of the church' (p. 32ᵇ)); it is also found in *Gl.* and (briefly) in 'Essence' 147. (It does not appear in 'Sig. HJ'.) For the debt to Schleiermacher, see Schleiermacher's discussion of the 'mystical' apprehension of Christ in community: Schleiermacher 1963, ii. 429 ff. There may well also have been some influence from von Hügel's rather similar concept of the *Christ éternel* as 'the Spirit of community which originates in the historical Christ and brings forth the *corpus mysticum* of the Church'. (See Troeltsch's letter to von Hügel of 22 Oct. 1905 in ed. Apfelbacher and Neuner 1974, 72; Rollmann 1978, 47 also comments on this passage.)

[35] *Gl.* 120: 'Jesus is made present through the faithful and in the community (*Durch die Gemeinde und in der Gemeinschaft*).'

[36] See 'On Poss.' 31ᵃ.

[37] See again e.g. Troeltsch's criticism of Renan and von Hartmann, as cited above, nn. 21 and 22.

and an important if circumscribed one, for careful critical work on the historian's Jesus. All three of these concepts, by contrast, appear to offer beguiling means of circumventing that risky and arduous task, of presenting the believer with a felt effect of the earthly Jesus without entry into the confusing byways of historical criticism. In trying to further this line of approach Troeltsch uses four additional ploys (ploys, now, rather than concepts), which he brings to bear in his attempt to weld Jesus and the many Christs together. It may be as well to look at these briefly in turn, to see if and how they aid his argument.

The first is a line of approach we have already remarked upon in Chapter 5: Troeltsch's emphasis on the possibility of a scholarly 'consensus' on the main facts about Jesus' personality and teaching. Evidently it is the confidence that this procures that leaves ordinary Christians bold in their free play of imagination about Christ (see e.g. *Gl.* 96-7, 100-1). On these grounds, the move from historical scholarship to imaginative reflection is accomplished without undue concern. But we have already questioned Troeltsch's confidence in such a consensus. And indeed, on his own occasional admission, such confidence seems wholly misplaced.[38] Moreover, even if such agreement could be reached, it would still be unclear how this could justify wholly uninhibited eisegesis. This first ploy, then, must be judged a particularly weak one.

Troeltsch's second ploy is only found clearly in the *Glaubenslehre*,[39] and this time involves the appeal to an intrinsic inseparability of fact and interpretation.[40] When the question comes up of the need to establish an 'inner continuity' between

[38] See again above, ch. 5 pp. 152 ff. and n. 45. In addition, it is perhaps interesting to note that, in a relatively late essay of 1916/17 ('Die alte Kirche'), Troeltsch could admit that he still was not sure whether Jesus did or did not think of himself as Messiah (*GS* iv. 71)—an issue surely central to any reconstruction of his personality and teaching. One wonders whether Troeltsch would have by this time been willing to give up his claim to a 'consensus' by New Testament scholars on the basic features of Jesus' life and teaching; see also below, n. 63.

[39] See *Gl.* 101 ff., 114 f. A hint of this argument is also found in 'Half C.' 72: 'Research will make advances and when the dust has settled enough will remain of the old picture for Jesus at any rate still to be seen as the source and power of faith in Christ . . .'

[40] *Possibly* this is a reflection still of the Ritschlian value-judgement theory. (See e.g. Ritschl 1966, 212: there is no 'disinterested' knowledge of God; 'we know the nature of God and Christ only in their worth for us'.) But I am inclined to see more of F. C. Baur's influence with his talk of the historian grasping a 'movement . . . immanent in the subject itself' (*Dogmengeschichte* i/1, 29, cited in Hodgson 1966, 162) and of Paul's theology as

the disciples' apprehension of the historical Jesus and their faith in Christ (*Gl.* 101), the answer, we are told, is never to read into the historical data what is not already latent in the 'nature (*Wesen*)' of Jesus' history (ibid. 115). One should interpret him according to the intrinsic 'sense and spirit' of the facts (ibid. 102, and see 114). Now this in itself is unexceptionable—though somewhat unhelpfully vague. What is more questionable, however, is that Troeltsch appears extraordinarily confident that this has duly been done by previous generations; for what was effected by reflection on him must surely somehow have come 'out of him' ('Es *muß* in ihm gelegen haben, was aus ihm ward' (ibid. 114, my italics). Not only is there a natural unity of fact and interpretation, then, but in the past the Church has apparently been extraordinarily adept at detecting it (see ibid. 114–15).

This latter claim is, however, clearly question-begging, especially since Troeltsch himself urges in the same section of the *Glaubenslehre* that one needs to keep fact and interpretation distinguished *in principle*, precisely lest interpretations be confused with facts.[41] Surely, then, not all the free 'embellishments' made on the figure of Jesus can have been latent in his 'nature'? Again, then, we are faced with an argument that asserts rather than convinces: not all the many Christs 'must' have been latent in Jesus, as Troeltsch surely has to admit, even on his own premises.

Troeltsch's third and fourth ploys, in contrast, bring us right to the heart of the problem, and are closely related to each other. For the real problem, as will now be clear, is a metaphysical one: does Troeltsch wish to grant to 'Christ' (otherwise identified as the evolving Christian *Prinzip*) an independent metaphysical existence, with a life of its own? Or does he not? And for the answer to this, and for Troeltsch's third ploy here, which is his explicit appeal to a modified Hegelian principle of historical development, we must turn once again to the tangled argument of that extraordinarily important essay 'Was heißt, "Wesen des Christentums"?'.[42]

---

being a making explicit of what was already implicit in Jesus (see *Neutestamentliche Theologie* 128, again as cited in Hodgson 1966, 203).

[41] See *Gl.* 100, 102: Troeltsch clearly has Herrmann in mind here, as someone who does not sufficiently distinguish fact and interpretation. Also see 'Half C.' 70, where Troeltsch makes it clear that the question about whether apostolic faith really was in continuity with the 'real Jesus' has to be faced critically.

[42] Once more I refer back to my discussion above, ch. 1 pp. 30 ff.

We recall that, even in the revised 1913 version of this, Troeltsch could still describe the development of Christianity as being the working out of some 'tension' created at its inception. It is this tension in the Christian 'idea', or so he claims, that propels it forward and drives it into constantly new moments of productivity.[43] Thus what has sprung from the original 'central point' of the earthly Jesus has actually 'increased in power through the centuries in which it has made its impact upon world history' ('On Poss.' 31ᵃ). The appeal here, we note, is still to the *self-consistent* evolution of a metaphysical principle: a position which, as we saw in Chapter 1, Troeltsch was eventually to modify. But what we now see is that *while it lasted* it provided the crucial metaphysical underpinning for Troeltsch's attempt to link the many Christs and give them unity and an independent existence.

His fourth ploy, moreover, drew on the understanding of truth that accompanied this. As long as Troeltsch espoused this particular form of teleology, he could regard individual manifestations of Christianity (and thus, concomitantly, individual interpretations of Christ) as contributing to some cumulative—and cosmic—truthfulnesses.[44] But once he was to admit that there might not be any one continuum unifying the many historical forms of Christianity, his understanding of doctrinal truth changed accordingly.[45] And this, implicitly at least, created a crisis for Troeltsch's 'many Christs' theme which I am not sure he ever adequately faced.[46] The loss of a self-consistent teleological force (the Christian *Prinzip*) was at the same time the loss of the in-

---

[43] See e.g. 'Essence' 153–4. Again, I think, we detect shades of F. C. Baur, with his views about the 'antithesis' between Jewish and Pauline tendencies in the early Church (see Hodgson's discussion, 1966, 207 ff.). But, as we have already mentioned in ch. 1, Troeltsch's 1913 revision of 'Essence' begins to show signs of distinct strain in maintaining the Baurian view that there really was one 'principle' or 'essence' working its way out in this development. See the (new) discussion of the real novelty of Paul's message in 'Essence' 149, and the sentence added on p. 152 ('There is no *logically necessary dialectical law* which can be constructed for the step by step emergence of the essence . . .'). Also see *AJT* 1913, 9, for similar sentiments about the real novelty of apostolic faith, 'so strikingly different from Jesus' message about the kingdom of God'.

[44] See e.g. 'On Poss.' 31ᵇ–32ᵃ, for this 'cumulative' conception of religious truth.

[45] See again above, ch. 1 pp. 33 f.: now what is 'true' is true in virtue of a certain *procedure* for ascertaining doctrinal truth, and not necessarily in virtue of any traceable and consistent evolution out of an earlier 'truth'.

[46] Certainly, as we shall discuss in more detail shortly, the 1913 edn. of 'Essence' is a bemusing combination of (1) tacit admission of this crisis and (2) continuance of the old metaphysical confidence.

dependent living 'personality' of Jesus, the *Geist Christi*, and the mysteriously appropriated *caput mysticum*, at least in so far as all these ideas depended on such an assumed metaphysical referent.

We are now in a better position to see what Troeltsch could have meant by talking of Jesus (or Christ) as 'living (*lebendig*)'. As we have already intimated, Troeltsch did not feel able to argue for a living Christ by reference to the resurrection. For the most part this seems to have been because he thought, surely rightly, that the question of Jesus' continued existence after death could not be settled, let alone demonstrated, by reference to historical arguments (see *Gl.* 112): in the words of his interpreter Köhler, the remaining historical 'question mark' here could not simply be turned by faith's fiat into an 'exclamation mark' (Köhler 1941, 69). Typically, though, Troeltsch encourages those who find it in themselves to believe to do so (*Gl.* 112), and this, in itself, should give the lie to those who assume Troeltsch ruled out the resurrection a priori on positivist grounds.[47] However, when Troeltsch does talk in the *Glaubenslehre* about the 'resurrection history' and the 'resurrection appearances' it seems he is referring to the disciples' experiences rather than Jesus', and some sort of 'vision' hypothesis is apparently assumed.[48]

Granted his agnosticism on this score, then, his talk of a 'living' Christ can only be explained in other ways, and the ways chosen by him seem to be three. First, while his metaphysical confidence about the independent *Geist Christi* lasted, here was one obvious way of construing Christ as 'living': the Spirit 'makes Christ present', as he puts it (*Gl.* 347; see also 348 and 360–1). But second, and more cautiously, Troeltsch also uses in the *Glaubenslehre* much the same route taken by Herrmann on this

[47] See Pannenberg 1970, 43 ff., and above, ch. 1 n. 34.

[48] In the *Gl.* see 101, 112, 273 for discussion of the resurrection. Troeltsch does not in any way underestimate its importance for original Christianity ('The Christian believers' faith in God had at first . . . only the concentration of all religious content in a Jesus *transfigured by belief in the resurrection* ('Sig. HJ' 195, my italics)), but he is obviously somewhat at a loss what to make of it for today. The occasional and tantalizing references to Jesus' 'struggle and *victory*' (*Abs.* 162) or to his having 'struggled . . . and *conquered*' ('Sig. HJ' 197) must I think be taken to refer not to his survival of death, but to his moral courage in the face of it (see *Gl.* 115). And in Troeltsch's only article devoted to the subject of Easter, in *Deutscher Wille* 1918, Easter Day simply 'symbolizes' the desperate new hope and light that must overcome the 'night of Good Friday' (ibid. 5), and the need to return to the riches of the Western Christian heritage in the face of the dissolution of falsely optimistic 'monism' (ibid. 5–6).

issue,[49] by talking of Christ's presence in the more stretched or metaphorical sense as mediated through the memory of the Church community.[50] Strictly speaking, on this second option it is only 'as if' Christ is present (ibid. 114, 346) rather than actually so, and, as we have remarked on a number of occasions, Troeltsch is anxious here to distinguish his position from Herrmann's at least on this score: he denies that one can thus magically make the earthly Jesus directly present ('Sig. HJ' 188-9).[51] In the *Glaubenslehre*, however, what I have here distinguished as first and second options are in practice somewhat confusingly intertwined (see e.g. *Gl.* 120), with the result that Troeltsch's critique of Herrmann is not clearly carried through. Third, however (and this brings out an important evocation of the German 'lebendig', which of course means 'lively' as well as 'alive'), we find Troeltsch talking in his more social psychological vein of the 'Christ symbol' as 'lebendig' in the sense of evocative, alluring, or capable of many interpretations (see e.g. *GS* ii. 816, and probably too 'Sig. HJ' 202-3). This is at least part of what he means when he says that the Christ symbol will 'always go on living' (ibid.).

This analysis of Troeltsch's Christological theme of the many Christs has shown that there were two fundamental difficulties with his various attempts simply to equate the earthly Jesus with all subsequent Christological interpretations. The first difficulty, which should have been clear even on Troeltsch's own analysis by 1909 (and the start of his overt criticism of Herrmann's Christology[52]), concerned the need to make a critical distinction, at least, between Jesus as he actually was (approached via careful historical scholarship) and subsequent apprehensions of him. Even in 1910, then, it was odd for Troeltsch to say, as he did at one point, that 'it is . . . neither possible nor necessary to separate what [Jesus] actually was and what the faith of millennia has lovingly projected onto him'.[53] But as long as Troeltsch continued to

---

[49] For Herrmann, we recall, the 'risen Christ' as such is not available; but the 'Person of Jesus' as a life-force in the community can be said to be 'alive'. For this rather curious conjunction of themes, see Herrmann 1909, 209 ff.

[50] See e.g. *Gl.* 101-2, with its talk of the continuing impact of Jesus' 'personality' in the community; and ibid. 120, already cited in n. 35.

[51] Also see 'Half C.' 75.   [52] See again above, ch. 2 pp. 72 ff.

[53] 'Aus der religiösen Bewegung der Gegenwart', *Die neue Rundschau* 1910, 1183 = *GS* ii. 41. Rupp 1977, 32, cites this passage in support of his claim that for Troeltsch 'the

operate with a belief in a self-consistent metaphysical force inherent in Christianity's development (otherwise identified as
'Christ'), this first difficulty was only sporadically enunciated.
This was because the supporting metaphysic appeared to make
such a critical distinction largely unnecessary: it could be assumed, apparently, that the *Geist Christi* had evolved out of Jesus and
continued thus to evolve in manifold apprehensions of him. The
real crisis, then, for Troeltsch's attempt to identify his many
Christs lay in the apprehension of the fallibility of that assumed
metaphysic. And in various ways we do see Troeltsch coming to
terms with this in the turning-point year of 1913.[54] We can see this
happening both in some of the revisions made to the already complex argument of 'Was heißt, "Wesen des Christentums"?', and
also in the more consistently radical article of the same year 'The
Dogmatics of the "Religionsgeschichtliche Schule" ' (*AJT* 1913).

First, Troeltsch now appears to hint an admission that the
many Christs of Christian tradition are only 'one' to the extent
that they all draw their prime inspiration from 'the prototype
found in the person of Jesus' (*AJT* 1913, 21).[55] To claim in the face
of Troeltsch's new doctrinal relativism (see ibid. 12–13) that they
have any other, mysterious unity now becomes inadmissible, and
invites a further error: the assumption that all and any interpretations of Jesus will have some infallible authority.[56] Yet this is of

historical Jesus and the cultic Christ are intimately and inextricably connected as
origin and development — in contrast both to liberal rationalism and historical
positivism'. In general I accept this analysis, but only as long as 'inextricably
connected' at least allows for the *possibility* of a critical distinction between what we may
construct about the earthly Jesus and what came later. This, as I have shown, was,
contra Rupp, necessarily important to Troeltsch, especially in his critique of Herrmann,
and was not sufficiently allowed for in this passage from 1910. His essay of 1909, in
contrast, had certainly affirmed that it was both 'possible' and 'necessary' to
distinguish the earthly Jesus from later Christological reflections.

[54] As we shall see, the acceptance that this marks a turning-point for his Christology
is only rather implicitly indicated by Troeltsch, and was somewhat inadequately
carried through. Thus, despite his 1913 changes to 'Essence' that indicate such a
turning-point (see below), much remains from the 1903 edn. that is now out of line with
the new position.

[55] Also see the new addition in 'Essence' 147: the appeal to Jesus as the only
'criterion' for 'all confessions, sects, and groups'. Elsewhere, however, the 1913 edn. of
'Essence' continues with the language of the 'essence' of Christianity, or the 'Spirit of
Christ', as an independent metaphysical force (see e.g. 130, 168). Hence the confused
impression in this essay.

[56] This point is admittedly only implied. But the addition in 'Essence' 147 once
again bears it out, as well as Troeltsch's lengthy criticism of von Hartmann in the 2nd

course quite out of line with Troeltsch's mature view on the 'essence' of Christianity. From this we know that he regards any doctrinal decision as being both necessarily *critical*,[57] and also necessarily *provisional*.[58]

Along with this, moreover, come indications that Troeltsch is now willing to concede real and startling novelty in some Christological assertions, such that it is far from clear to the exegete how exactly they find their source in Jesus.[59] And finally, as we have already seen, this leads him to insert into 'Was heißt, "Wesen des Christentums"?' a passage suggesting that when there is real dissension between parties on Christology, then is the time to go back to Jesus himself, and to use historical reconstruction of him as the only available agreed 'criterion' ('Essence' 147) as at least a starting-point and shared reference in the process of doctrinal decision.

Were these (admittedly implicit) concessions of 1913 in any sense destructive of Troeltsch's mature Christology? It is true that they effectively destroy his attempts to unify and hypostatize the many Christs into an independent metaphysical entity; it is also true that Troeltsch wrote virtually nothing of a Christological nature thereafter. Yet in large part we may explain this by his move to Berlin and to a chair of philosophy (in 1915), and by the general, and indeed devastating, distraction of the coming World War, which drew Troeltsch increasingly into the realm of politics.[60] On the whole, however, I am inclined to see the changes of 1913—although never clearly carried through—as a strengthening, not a weakening, of Troeltsch's Christological

edn. of the essay (see ibid. 170 ff.). Von Hartmann's interpretation of Christ and Christianity was certainly not one that Troeltsch was prepared to accept as authoritative.

[57] See 'Essence', esp. 137 ff.

[58] Ibid. esp. 162 ('to define the essence is to shape it afresh') and 166 ('every time it is newly created').

[59] See the new additions in 'Essence' 147 ('it is admittedly true that . . . each age interprets [Jesus] really quite differently') and 149, where it is now admitted that the post-Easter Christ 'does not stand in a perfectly clear relationship to the historical Jesus but can only be connected with him *mysteriously*'. Also relevant is *AJT* 1913, 12: 'a genuinely historical point of view reveals to us such a variety of interpretations, formulations, and syntheses that no single idea or impulse can dominate the whole.'

[60] See Robert Morgan's comments, ed. Morgan and Pye 1977, 48: Troeltsch did not wish to abandon theology in moving to Berlin. 'The need to defend German culture during the war and the desperate need for social and intellectual reconstruction afterwards explain the direction of his political writings after 1914.'

position. The loss of faith in an identifiable, distinct, meta-physical entity (the 'essence' of Christianity or the *Geist Christi*) was not of course the loss of faith in a God who works in history in 'Christ'-like ways; and what emerges now are at least consistent guidelines for a 'historicist' Christology which might have been most fruitfully conjoined with Troeltsch's mature, relativist stance on the question of the 'essence' of Christianity.

By way of a brief speculative conclusion to this chapter, then, let us consider what sort of shape that Christology might have taken, what its attendant strengths and weaknesses would have been, and how the insights of Troeltsch's important 1911 lecture and of the *Glaubenslehre* could have been fruitfully conjoined with his reflections on the reformulation of Christianity's essence.

We recall from our analysis in Chapter 1 that Troeltsch's mature position on the 'essence' of Christianity (his thesis of doc-trinal relativism) argues that the theologian should always com-bine reference to objective historical states of affairs with present evaluation and decision. This programme, as we noted, displays Troeltsch's appeal in doctrinal matters both to a form of cor-respondence theory of truth where historical work is concerned, and to a pragmatist theory where individual doctrinal decisions are concerned.[61] We have also noted more recently that Troeltsch allows a certain pride of place to the earthly Jesus' teaching in any particular formulation of 'essential' Christianity.

Now it is simple enough to link these insights to themes enun-ciated in Troeltsch's Christology. From his essay on the significance of the 'historical Jesus' we know that he wishes (despite his occasional apparent disclaimers) to make what I have called a 'realist' assertion about Jesus. It is not simply that the 'symbol of Christ' functions effectively for Christians as a focus of divine revelation (although Troeltsch's insights here on the significance of Christ *qua* symbol and archetype are of rich poten-tial, as we shall reflect further in our Conclusions); the claim is, however, also made that Jesus actually is 'the highest revelation of God accessible to us'. On the other hand, it is not therefore the case that the earthly Jesus is the *last* revelatory word. God's self-revelation, according to Troeltsch, has continued, and continues to this day. Moreover, it is characteristic of Christianity, and in-deed for a variety of social and psychological reasons necessary

[61] See again above. ch. 1 pp. 33 f., 43.

for it, to gather its fresh revelatory insights into the archetypal figure of 'Christ'. Sometimes it draws a new, neglected, item out of the teaching of Jesus and refurbishes it (as with the rediscovery of Jesus' eschatology, for instance); sometimes, however, it 'accommodates' in the Christ figure a contemporary issue which could scarcely have been Jesus' own (as in black theology, to provide a contemporary example of my own). In other words, wherever there is forged, in Troeltschian terms, a new 'essence' of Christianity, there too will be a concomitant Christological statement, owing something to the 'historical Jesus', but much too to issues and insights which arise from a context far removed from Jesus' own. These manifold reinterpretations, then, are Troeltsch's many Christs: Jesus as interpreted anew by 'every age . . . from its own particular historical perspective' (*GS* ii. 816). Each 'Christ' is of course to a degree culturally relative, and thereby represents only a fragmentary and partial insight into the nature of God; moreover other Christs are not guaranteed an identity with it. Yet on the other hand, each such Christ may indeed claim to mediate some revelation of God, God as elusively grasped in Jesus but no less responded to also in the immediate challenges and circumstances of life here and now.[62]

Now it seems to me that two dangers and two advantages accrue for Troeltsch's Christology when his position is reinterpreted along these lines. The two dangers are both 'risks': the risk, first, of some dependence (though, as we have seen, a relatively circumscribed one) on historical critical work for news of the 'historical Jesus', a risk which we saw Troeltsch had tried unsuccessfully to avert.[63] The second risk is, however, more

---

[62] In this sense it was still possible for Troeltsch to maintain a form of 'Christ-mysticism', though in a modified understanding (no longer involving the claim of direct contact with Jesus or a unity of all the many Christs). Such an outlook is in line with sentiments expressed by Troeltsch back in 1902: 'We . . . do not seek to grasp the eternal divine truth in firm forms and do [not aim] at separating the Divine-immutable from the Contemporaneous (*Zeitgeschichtlichen*), but believe that everywhere we seek God in Christ according to our best abilities, [we] have him in the midst of the Contemporaneous' (review of A. Ehrhard's *Der Katholizismus und das zwanzigste Jahrhundert* in *CW* 1902, 467, cited *sic* in Rollmann 1978, 43).

[63] See above, ch. 5 pp. 152 ff., for ambiguities on this point in 'Sig. HJ'. The subtle shifts of 1913 effected in Troeltsch a more consistent acceptance of this element of risk, as seems implied by his important review of Peisker's book *Die Geschichtlichkeit Jesu Christi und der christliche Glaube* (in *TLZ* 1915, 89–91), where Peisker is heavily criticized for attempting to remove faith into an area of 'absolute certainty' immune from historical 'judgements of probability'.

significant: it is the risk of 'doctrinal relativism' *in toto*, the risk of theological error and deviation in the name of change and development. We have seen that Troeltsch was forced to admit this risk by giving up his earlier appeal to a unified development in Christianity's history; he should, however, equally have clarified his abandonment of the idea of a self-consistent 'personality' operating within all Christological reflections.[64] No such appeal could now succeed in softening the blow of doctrinal relativism. But then, as one might respond on Troeltsch's behalf, the 'blow' of doctrinal relativism is also its peculiar strength: the *admission* of the necessarily limited and partial nature of all historically situated doctrinal formulations.[65]

On the other hand, two advantages emerge from bringing Troeltsch's Christological insights into line with his later views on the 'essence' of Christianity. In the first place, the apparently intellectualistic bias of the programme for deciding on 'essential' Christianity is largely corrected.[66] To reflect on the person of Christ, as opposed to considering merely the Christian message or 'idea', would avoid, as Troeltsch puts it, 'the capitulation of faith to the intellect' ('Sig. HJ' 199). Christology, as Troeltsch so rightly perceived, should be interested in charting the effects of an archetypal figure to whom the whole person responds, and where 'imagination' and 'feeling' are given at least equal rights alongside more strictly rational considerations. Further, and as

---

[64] This is not done explicitly. And it is also somewhat bemusing to find Troeltsch (in typically placatory vein) still putting in a warm word for Herrmann's Christology: see *AJT* 1913, 18. However, in continuing to defend the need for a 'personality' here I think what he means is the abiding necessity for reflection on a person (as opposed to ideas alone), and this of course is in line with his new position.

[65] As Troeltsch puts it himself, 'The less effort one spends in self-deceit, trying to find a theoretical escape from subjectivism, the freer one's hands are to set practical limits to it and defuse the danger' ('Essence' 167). Even Barth has to concede that there is a certain strength to Troeltsch's admission of this necessary 'limitation' (Barth 1956, 383).

[66] To this extent S. W. Sykes's objections to Troeltsch's approach as being 'narrow-mindedly theoretical' and 'élitist' (ed. Clayton 1976, 170-1) are over-harsh and misdirected. He does not mention the insights of 'Sig. HJ' in this context, nor the similar observations in 'Logos und Mythos in Theologie und Religionsphilosophie' (1913) (*GS* ii. 805-36; see esp. 812 with its strong criticism of those who ignore the 'souls of the masses'). The writing of *ST* was of course crucially formative for Troeltsch in his realization of the importance of non-intellectual factors in religion, and so it is to post-1911 writings that we need to look for this theme. For further citations and a useful short discussion see' Clayton 1980, 49-50.

an adjunct to this, Troeltsch also rightly saw that the business of Christology is vitally to do with considerations about community, and with what he called the sense of 'mysterious relationship', or interpenetration one with another ('Sig. HJ' 202). The Christ figure both evokes and binds, and in binding surely has the power to unite both the learned and the simpleton. Moreover it is precisely in these less intellectual areas that the simpleton may have something to tell the learned. All Troeltsch's insights from the phenomenology of ordinary believing here, his penetrating, though undeveloped, sociological and psychological considerations about how the Christ figure works in faith, strongly suggest that faith was not after all for him just the preserve of an intellectual élite, busy with its re-evaluation of a Christian 'principle'. At the very least, the data of vibrant ordinary believing have to be primary materials for Christological construction, not just the more rarefied New Testament research, Church history, and philosophy, as Troeltsch would sometimes seem to have suggested. We shall reserve further treatment of this point for the Conclusions.

The second advantage is a connected one. If the 'essence' programme were to become more specifically Christological, it would have to take its cue not simply from Jesus' teaching—from 'the ethic of original Christianity' ('Essence' 185)—but also from Jesus' personal example, and particularly from his suffering and ignominious death. For these features too must surely be central to any Christology with a 'realist' strand such as Troeltsch's, more central indeed than Troeltsch himself seems to have been willing to concede, perhaps partly in over-sensitive reaction to his immediate 'Ritschlian' forebears.[67] In Troeltsch's theological system, God suffers indeed, but we are given no reason to connect this assertion with the Passion of Jesus. It is, we repeat in conclusion, this particular logical gap in Troeltsch's theology, this failure to connect Christological claims with the doctrine of God, that arguably constitutes the most significant flaw in his doctrinal system. Yet it is a gap that he could surely himself have closed, and that his own final position still begged to be closed.

---

[67] As we have noted before, von Hügel remarked in his letter to the *TLS* on Troeltsch's death (von Hügel 1923, 216) that he and Troeltsch could agree that the 'Ritschlian' school (especially Kaftan and Herrmann) indulged in an over-concentration on the Passion of Christ.

For even after the adjustments of 1913, he could provide his own statement of 'essential' Christianity in the following terms:

Christian religious faith is faith in the divine regeneration of man who is alienated from God—a regeneration effected through *the knowledge of God in Christ*. The consequence of this regeneration is union with God and social fellowship so as to constitute the kingdom of God. (*AJT* 1913, 13, my italics.)

And again, bolstering his attack on von Hartmann in the same year, he could insist in the strongest terms that what is 'really essential' in Christianity is 'the recognition of the living, sin-forgiving and sanctifying Father *in Christ*' ('Essence' 173 (1913 edition), my italics).[68] Yet the means of expounding how, exactly, the 'knowledge of God' is given its decisive colouring 'in Christ' was something Troeltsch himself never adequately or systematically provided, for all his insistence on its prime and central significance.

---

[68] Significantly, the 1st edn. of 'Was heißt, "Wesen des Christentums"?' (1903), with its much briefer discussion of von Hartmann, construes what is 'really essential' simply as 'faith in a living, creative, saving and sanctifying God' (*CW* 1903, 683). The crucial 'in Christ' of the 2nd edn. is not present. It might not therefore be fanciful to see in these two hints of 1913 an increasing recognition by Troeltsch at this time of the need to expound his doctrine of God more explicitly in terms of Christ's person (as opposed to just his message), a programme which he never however substantially carried through. (For the ambiguity on this point in the *Glaubenslehre*, see again above, ch. 3 n. 50.)

Conclusions: The Legacy of Troeltsch's Christology

IT remains now only to assemble the various conclusions of this study, and then to indicate a little more fully, in my final paragraphs, what I take to be the possible positive implications of Troeltsch's example for the doing of Christology today.

In the first place, and at the level of detailed Troeltsch scholarship, it has been part of my task in the course of this book to lay bare the questionable grounds on which many of the negative judgements against Troeltsch's Christology have been made. It may be useful to draw these points together in closing. To the extent that Troeltsch has thus been misinterpreted and dismissed, we may already say that his position is worthy of more positive reflection than it is usually allowed. Many, if not most, of these misunderstandings, it should be said, arise from reading Troeltsch out of context or chronological order, or from jumping to conclusions gleaned from only one or two writings, as opposed to considering his complete Christological *œuvre*.

I trust I have successfully shown that Troeltsch does not in any sense advocate a 'Christless Christianity' (Warfield); that he does not deny a 'central place for Christ' (Turner); that he does not make Jesus' *person* dispensable in favour of the Christian *principle* (Pannenberg); that he does not turn Jesus into a teacher about God whom we can then do without (Müller). Nor, I hope I have clarified, does Jesus for him simply 'illustrate' an idea that could be arrived at by other means such as rational reflection (Diem); nor, concomitantly, do Troeltsch's apprehensions of the significance of the 'historical Jesus' for faith represent an unnecessary, and illogical, addendum to his Christological position (Gerrish). Nor, on the other hand, was that position such that a distinction, at least, between the earthly Jesus and later Christological accretions became otiose (Rupp).

Troeltsch does not undermine the possibility of God's revelation in Jesus (Pannenberg); he does not (despite in a way inviting this criticism by confused or inconsistent argument) make Christ's central position in Christianity merely a matter of social or psychological necessity (Bultmann and many others); nor does he (again, despite an admittedly flawed presentation of his position) advocate a Christ with no 'substantive connection' with the Father (Reist). Nor does he reject aspects of traditional incarnationalism simply because of a preconceived metaphysic of history (Morgan, Ogletree), or because of a blind spot about particular sorts of 'supernaturalism' (implied by Hebblethwaite); indeed, he certainly does not reject 'supernaturalism' *in toto* (Quigley, among others), or rule out the possibility of Christ's resurrection a priori (Pannenberg, influencing many subsequent commentators). Finally, and most significantly, the neglected 'many Christs' aspect of his Christology, despite all its difficulties, completely belies the suggestion that Troeltsch has turned Christology simply into reflection about a contingent past 'hero', Jesus (Bultmann, by implication); for this reason it is, I shall argue, misplaced to categorize Troeltsch's Christology as the final dead-end point reached by the German liberal 'historical Jesus' Christologies of the latter part of the nineteenth century (Diem, and virtually all modern historical theologians, most recently McGrath[1]); instead, we must clarify Troeltsch's position as a systematic alternative importantly different from influential 'liberal' forebears such as Ritschl and Harnack, and, as I believe, novel and rich in its potential. To this point we shall shortly return. On the other hand, to end this catalogue of misconstruals, one can scarcely claim (to mention two of Troeltsch's rare defenders) that his Christology is close to Paul's or John's (Wolfe), or that it need in no way oust 'traditional' views of Christ (Apfelbacher).

My first set of conclusions, then, have involved the exorcism of

---

[1] McGrath 1986 only became available in the final stages of the preparation of this manuscript. Since it will doubtless be widely used as a student textbook it is disappointing to find its short section on Troeltsch's Christology (ibid. 82–5; see also 212–16) reiterating many of the usual misconceptions: that Troeltsch's three principles of historical method 'rigorously exclude' 'supernatural elements' (ibid. 83–4), that the centrality of Christ is for him just a matter of 'socio-psychological utility' (ibid. 85), that he dismisses the resurrection, and 'any claim to uniqueness in Jesus' (ibid. 213), and can be listed as one of those who helped to end 'any attempt to find God in Jesus of Nazareth' (ibid. 216). As such, he supposedly marks the final point in 'The Collapse of the Liberal Christology' (ch. 4).

certain clichéd dismissals of Troeltsch's position based on an inadequate grasp of his actual stance. My second set of conclusions
are, in contrast, quite trenchantly critical ones. For I have certainly been concerned to show in this study that Troeltsch's
Christological thinking has many faulty or questionable
characteristics as it stands.

In large part, first, these are failures of consistency, which from
one who charmingly acknowledged that he was not a systematic
thinker (see *GS* iv. 3), and was always unafraid to change his
mind, are perhaps not so unexpected. None the less, the curious,
and unconvincing, backtracking into 'Ritschlian' traits of
Christology in *The Absoluteness of Christianity,* the confusion of the
argument in 'The Significance of the Historical Existence of
Jesus for Faith', and the difficulties inherent in the 'Christ-mysticism' theme of 'On the Possibility of a Liberal Christianity'—
all these have demanded, and deserved, charges of internal
inconsistency.

More importantly, however, we have also noted a series of
more substantial weaknesses in Troeltsch's mature Christology:
his failure to link reflection on Jesus' Passion and death to parallel
themes in his doctrine of God; his avoidance of metaphysical
precision in general where Christology was concerned; his hastily
dismissive reaction to serious study of patristic Christology; his
unconvincing appeal to 'basic traits' of Jesus' life as certain of
historical verification; and his misleading use of the slippery notion of Jesus' 'personality' as an effective means of avoiding the
risks of the historical component in Christological construction.
These are substantial failings on any account. The first area of
weakness is particularly difficult to account for, and must I think
in part reflect an over-reaction against Troeltsch's 'Ritschlian'
forebears and contemporaries. (As von Hügel remarked, he and
Troeltsch could agree in criticizing the Ritschlians for having a
'(violently Pauline) concentration upon only the Passion in the
life of Jesus Christ'.) But what is interesting about all the other
points of weakness is that they, in contrast, are deeply reminiscent of themes in 'Ritschlian' Christology, and also somewhat
out of line with the general logic of Troeltsch's position. One conclusion we might draw here, then, even if it is a slightly over-
simplified or paradoxical one, is that Troeltsch's Christology is at
its weakest precisely where it unthinkingly carries over strands

from the 'Ritschlian' Christology of which Troeltsch was otherwise so critical.

Its strengths, however, its positive scope, or instructive qualities, lie where it transcends what one could have expected from a typical 'Ritschlian' Christology. This is our third area of conclusions, and involves two separate themes for reflection. First, it seems to me that Troeltsch's Christological thinking is instructive, and above all challenging, precisely in the area where it is apparently most negative. By this I mean its perception of the profound difficulties of maintaining a traditional 'incarnational' Christology in the face of certain cumulative aporias of modern theology: historical criticism, historical relativism, the so-called 'other' world religions, an expanding universe, and so on (see above, Chapter 4). As Drescher has justly remarked, Troeltsch perceived 'like no other theologian of his time, the *upsetting* and *urgent* features of the relation between faith and history' (Drescher 1960, 186, my italics). Thus it has been part of my task to spell out these and other 'upsetting' problems raised by Troeltsch, and to suggest that any serious revamping of Chalcedonianism today (which Troeltsch could not countenance himself, but which he was not in principle opposed to) can scarcely afford to ignore his challenges. Simply to dismiss Troeltsch's Christology here for failure to conform to some supposedly timeless standard such as the *homoousion* is thus to evade the issues that he so acutely perceived. Indeed, any contemporary exposition of 'incarnational' Christology for today (whether specifically Chalcedonian or no) will I believe attempt to side-step the problems raised by Troeltsch only at the peril of its own credibility. Thus we have in Troeltsch's example at the very least a potent reminder of the major challenges of modern thought to the time-honoured Christologies of the creeds. As such, his contribution is already of considerable systematic significance.

The other side to Troeltsch's Christology, however, is its more positive, constructive side. This has often been assumed to be negligible, even non-existent; but while it would be absurd to argue that Troeltsch ever produced a fully developed Christology, or that Christology was even at the centre of his life-work and concerns (his own piety was much more naturally theocentric than Christocentric), I hope I have shown that there are strands in his mature Christological thinking that are certainly worthy of further reflection, indeed suggestive of fruitful ways forward through some of the contemporary Christological *impasses* that now exercise us. Let us reflect a little more fully on this in closing.

Two connected points in particular come to mind here. First, it seems that Troeltsch at least sketched a way in which a 'historicist' Christology could both accommodate an appreciation of the seminal importance of the historical revelation in Jesus (appearing in a quite admittedly eschatological garb), and accept the equal significance of the rich imaginative plurality of the 'many Christs' of Christian tradition and contemporary piety. The apparent choice required between these two, the Jesus of history and the Christ of faith (as purveyed so influentially by such as Strauss and Kähler), was as much a Christological bugbear in Troeltsch's generation as it is in ours. Thus, to plot Troeltsch's systematic stance here amid his most immediate influential friends and colleagues, we see Harnack, at one end of the spectrum, advocating a return to the pure unsullied faith of the 'historical Jesus', supposedly untainted by romantic eisegesis or imaginative projection; and Herrmann at least some considerable way towards the other end, with his advocacy of an 'immediate' and apparently self-authenticating relationship with 'Jesus', uncomplicated by the tedium of precise historical scholarship. Troeltsch, as we saw, had time for both of these authors, and yet was sharply critical of them too, for his own alternative refused the disjunction they both implicitly accepted. Instead, he indicated a way in which (as one New Testament scholar has recently put it) 'the religious interpretation of Jesus [could] be *distinguished* but not *separated* from scientific historical research' (Morgan in ed. Morgan and Pye 1977, 223, my italics). Thus was adumbrated a way in which critical new Testament scholarship might come into fruitful and appreciative interplay with the imaginative reflection of the less sophisticated believer.

What this way was, and the methodological *novum* it implied, is the second and final point for reflection here, and it marks Troeltsch's most significant, if undeveloped, legacy to the contemporary Christological task.[2] It also involves some more

---

[2] I have also addressed this theme in my article 'Christologie "auf Treibsand"? Zur Aktualität von Troeltschs Christusdeutung', in ed. Renz and Graf 1987, 338–51.

speculative reflection on the way Troeltsch's Christology might have developed further, had time and opportunity allowed it.

As we have seen, the 'social psychological' approach of his 1911 lecture, and the 'historical-psychological' method of the *Glaubenslehre*, were not always very clearly or consistently presented. Taken together, however, they represent the Christological outcome of the profound change evinced in Troeltsch's theological attitude by the research he had undertaken for the *Social Teaching*. The implication now was that 'productive' Christology could no longer have its inputs and methods restricted solely to the traditional study of the New Testament, patristics, Reformation, and modern Christological thought, indispensable as all these were (and indeed still are). These were necessary, but not sufficient. For completely new avenues of approach were now opening up, courtesy of the burgeoning social sciences, psychology, sociology, and anthropology. It is clear that as Troeltsch immersed himself in the literature of these new disciplines, he glimpsed their attendant Christological possibilities. We glean this in the first place from the terse but prophetic section 'Christian Thought Dependent on Social Factors', at the close of the *Social Teaching* (*ST* 994 ff.). Here Troeltsch not only insists that varying Christologies are bound to reflect to some extent the social and historical conditions of their proponents (and he briefly sketches the sorts of Christological emphasis that tend to attach to the 'church', 'sect', and 'mystic' types of Christianity, respectively); but he also drops pregnant remarks about the vital necessity of keeping the theologian's assertion about Christ closely linked to the mechanics of 'worship' and the 'cultus', which properly speaking are logically anterior to 'philosophical and purely dogmatic considerations' (ibid. 995). Not only that, but here 'unconscious' forces are the overriding ones, 'instinctive' desires and projections arising from the needs of 'cultus' and 'fellowship' (see ibid. 996), and these, the implication seems to be, call for careful analysis and assessment.

If we now add to these brief and elliptical remarks the important linked material in the 1911 lecture, already closely analysed in earlier chapters, we arrive at a programme for Christological work involving not only the hallowed Christological methods of the traditional theological faculties, but, in addition, a major expansion into the methods of the newer social sciences, for the provision of an assessment of the more unconscious forces that may be motivating, and also enriching, Christological expression. Thus, as Troeltsch vaguely intimated, but never fully carried through for himself, a *phenomenology* of faith in Christ should become a new and indispensable preliminary to Christological construction. This could press forward questions about, for instance, the evocation of feeling and imagination in the religious life (and specifically in response to the figure of Christ), the necessity of the narrative or 'mythic' form in religious belief and activity, and the role and centrality of personal cultic 'symbols' or 'archetypes' for both individual and group livelihood.

With such questions as these taken into account, Christological construction would arise out of a productive convergence between the reporting and analysis of popular piety on the one hand, and the more traditional exposition of historical documents on the other. Such an interplay would result (if I may invent such a title) in a sort of *christologie totale*[3]—a product rooted and grounded in the rich variety of ordinary Christ-centred believing, but no less informed by precise and careful historical scholarship. A significant and exciting part of this programme would naturally be selective contemporary 'fieldwork': case-studies, for instance, of the uses of 'Christ' language in differing political and social contexts, or analysis of the range of evocations and feeling associated with the Christ figure in particular individuals' psychological development. The possibilities here are legion, and as yet mostly untried, at least as far as assimilation by the dogmaticians is concerned.

Why is this? If we reflect on the major schools of Christology evidenced in the post-war West, we are struck precisely by the lack of phenomenological interest shown in contemporary 'Christ-centred' belief in all its variety.[4] If anything the trend has been in the other direction, in turning back once again to the 'historical Jesus': most notable is this in Catholic circles, where recovery of the historical Jesus has been a dominant strand in

[3] The parallelism I have in mind here is with the French historiographical method *l'histoire totale* (of which LeRoy Ladurie 1978 is perhaps the most celebrated example), which aims in its historical reconstruction to do justice to the motivations and feelings of every stratum of society.

[4] McGrath's survey of modern Protestant Christology (McGrath 1986) is in itself eloquent testimony to this omission.

post-Vatican II theology. Even where appeals to this criterion have been treated with suspicion (as by those in the Bultmannian tradition, for instance), the familiar disjunction between the 'Jesus of history' and the 'Christ of faith' has been at the basis of discussion. Indeed many of the more celebrated post-war Christological controversies have centred around the issue of whether this disjunction is a real one—whether, that is, some substantial sort of 'continuity' cannot be claimed between Jesus of Nazareth and later Christological ascriptions.

What has been strangely lacking, however, and even more strangely unremarked upon, is any clear *analytical* discussion of what is involved if one opts for 'Christ' over against the 'Jesus of history'. If one decides, that is, that mere historical information is by no means the full stuff of faith, and that historical-Jesus research, for all its seminal significance, must therefore be transcended, one finds oneself invited to make some sort of fideistic lurch into the unknown. Whether for Barthian, Bultmannian, or neo-Chalcedonian reasons, one is launched into an arena where the language of 'Christ' is wielded with dogmatic certainty but almost no clear experiential reference. 'Who or what is Christ?', we may well ask. It is assumed that we know, for we have entered the magic circle of the *cognoscenti*. But do we know? Indeed, are the precise contents of 'Christ' language clear even in Strauss, Kähler, or Bultmann, from whose German Protestant tradition we have inherited the distinction that so exercises us?

It could be argued, then, that our greatest modern Christological aporia is not so much the conjoining, or otherwise, of the 'Jesus of history' and the 'Christ of faith', but a vast and unspoken unclarity about the reference of 'Christ' language *in toto*, a confusion greatly compounded by the divorce between technical theological discourse and ordinary people's cultic behaviour: how, in so many and various ways, they actually apply the language of 'Christ', and what it means to them experientially, morally, sacramentally. Yet surely neither clarity of reflection on this, nor a theological tapping of the imaginative and emotional power inherent in it, can be achieved without the application of the appropriate analytical resources from the newer social sciences. Such at any rate was Troeltsch's intuition.

Yet the resistance to approaches of this sort in theological circles, even over fifty years after Troeltsch's death, still requires some explanation, beyond that of the immediate neo-orthodox backlash against 'liberal' theology in general, now in itself a thing of the past. Perhaps, then, it is largely a matter of inertia, a failure of adjustment to new techniques and methods out of prejudice or laziness. Certainly the widespread ignorance of developments in the social sciences in many theological faculties, even after supposed reforms of syllabuses in this direction, is regularly and dismally witnessed to in the public debates that rock the Churches;[5] for it is, one might suggest, a corollary of this methodological ignorance that the much bemoaned gap between theologians and the laity widens further. The *present* living language of faith in 'Christ', and the tremendous variety of emotional and unconscious drives that attend it, go virtually unanalysed, leaving the laity bewildered and confused, and theologians no less inattentive to the deeper forces that may be motivating them. 'The capitulation of faith to the intellect' is, as Troeltsch justly perceived, the bearer of spiritual desiccation; it is no less, one might add, the promoter of continuing mutual incomprehension between warring ecclesiastical factions.

But sheer ignorance of the methods and literature of the social sciences is naturally not the only problem. There is, more fundamentally, the still prevalent assumption (that Troeltsch unfortunately, as we have seen, did little himself to dispel) that the use of such 'secular' methodologies must inevitably lead to reductionism, to the a priori rejection of the existence of spiritual and transcendent realities working in and through the material studied. That this does not necessarily follow is certainly still a case that has to be argued, and goes beyond the scope of this present study. But it can be remarked that there are now increasing signs, even in the literature of the social scientists themselves, that at last here the tide is turning.[6] That is, practitioners of an-

---

[5] One thinks here especially in Britain of the *Myth of God Incarnate* debate (see again ed. Hick 1977, and ed. Goulder 1979), where neither 'liberal' nor 'conservative' opponents showed any cognizance of the wealth of illuminating literature from cognate social science subjects on the nature and significance of 'myth'. It was as if Durkheim, Freud, Jung, Leach, Lévi-Strauss (to name but a few) had never been. Thus the categories of discussion never moved far beyond that of the old Straussian debate.

[6] On this see e.g. the insightful comments in Hamnett 1986, where he contrasts 'the strongly secularist tone of social science departments in the 50s and 60s' (ibid. 76) with the more recent developments that indicate 'Believers need no longer fear sociology as a threat' (ibid. 77). With this compare Hamnett's earlier article, Hamnett 1973.

thropology and sociology no longer feel themselves inexorably bound to a metaphysic that automatically excludes theism; why indeed should this follow? But nor, it should be underlined, need the assimilation of such Christological 'fieldwork' as we have here advocated require an uncritical acceptance of whatever view of 'Christ' is held by the subjects investigated. One need hardly stress that not all 'cultic' motivations, or psychological 'projections', will be adjudged healthy or laudable. The point is not however to accept whatever material presents itself, but in the first instance to concentrate on becoming more aware of the subterranean forces inherent in it. As Troeltsch too believed, projection (or *Phantasie*) both necessarily attends our reflections on Christ, and also is as capable of being the vehicle of divine revelation as of self-deception and distortion. The issue cannot be prejudged. Only however by becoming more aware of such projection are we in the position to make the assessment. It is as well to be aware of our limitations. That is not to say that God cannot be present in them.

These suggestions can only bear fruit in practice, and that remains a task for the future. All the signs are, however, that had Troeltsch lived and had the opportunity, his Christology would have developed further along such lines as these. Far then from reaching 'a terminal point in the history of theology from which there could be no further progress' (Diem 1959, 9), or simply marking the final 'collapse of the Liberal Christology' in the tradition of the Ritschlian school (McGrath 1986, 68–85), we have in this strand of Troeltsch's Christological work, or so it has been my concern to argue, the seeds of something much more constructive than Troeltsch probably even realized for himself. In a different time and social setting, but now with infinitely richer and broader resources from the social sciences to hand, the challenge remains to implement such a Christology for today.

Bibliography

Following a convention of English Troeltsch scholarship (see ed. Clayton 1976, 196 ff.), this bibliography is divided into three parts: (1) a complete list of works by Troeltsch in the original German consulted in the course of writing this book; (2) a list of works by Troeltsch in English translation used in my research and cited in the text; and (3) a list of all secondary works cited in the text.

The original bibliography of Troeltsch's works by Hans Baron in *GS* iv. 863 ff. is incomplete and misleading, and has now been completely superseded by the excellent new annotated one: ed. Graf and Ruddies 1982. More complete bibliographies of Troeltsch in English translation than can be given here can be found in ed. Clayton 1976, 197 ff., ed. Morgan and Pye 1977, 253 ff., and in *Mitteilungen der Ernst-Troeltsch-Gesellschaft*, 1 (1982), 26 ff. The useful bibliography of secondary works on Troeltsch in ed. Clayton 1976, 200 ff. has now been updated by F. W. Graf's 'Bibliographical Essay' in ed. Smart, Clayton, Sherry, and Katz 1985, 328 ff. The *Mitteilungen der Ernst-Troeltsch-Gesellschaft* report annually on new Troeltsch scholarship in progress.

1. *Works by Ernst Troeltsch* (listed in order of publication)

Vernunft und Offenbarung bei Johann Gerhard und Melanchthon: Untersuchung zur Geschichte der altprotestantischen Theologie (Göttingen, 1891).

'Die christliche Weltanschauung und die wissenschaftlichen Gegenströmungen', *Zeitschrift für Theologie und Kirche*, 3 (1893), 493–528; 4 (1894), 167–231.

'Religion und Kirche', *Preußische Jahrbücher*, 81 (1895), 215–49.

'Die Selbständigkeit der Religion', *Zeitschrift für Theologie und Kirche*, 5 (1895), 361–436; 6 (1896), 71–110, 167–218.

'Christentum und Religionsgeschichte', *Preußische Jahrbücher*, 87 (1897), 415–47.

'Geschichte und Metaphysik', *Zeitschrift für Theologie und Kirche*, 8 (1898), 1–69.

'Zur theologischen Lage', *Die christliche Welt*, 12 (1898), 627–31, 650–7.

Richard Rothe: Gedächtnisrede gehalten zur Feier des hundertsten Geburtstages in der Aula der Universität (Freiburg, 1899).

Review of H. Martensen Larsen, *Jesus und die Religionsgeschichte*

(Freiburg, 1898), in *Theologische Literaturzeitung*, 24 (1899), 398–400.

Review of M. Kähler, *Dogmatische Zeitfragen: Alte und neue Ausführungen zur Wissenschaft der christlichen Lehre* (Leipzig, 1898), in *Göttingische gelehrte Anzeigen*, 161 (1899), 942–52.

Die wissenschaftliche Lage und ihre Anforderungen an die Theologie (Tübingen, 1900).

'Über historische und dogmatische Methode der Theologie (Bemerkungen zu dem Aufsatze "Über die Absolutheit des Christentums" von Niebergall)', *Theologische Arbeiten aus dem rheinischen wissenschaftlichen Predigerverein*, NS 4 (1900), 81–108.

Review of F. R. Lipsius, *Die Vorfragen der systematischen Theologie* (Freiburg, 1898), in *Deutsche Literaturzeitung*, 22 (1901), 72–3.

Review of A. D. Dorner, *Grundriß der Dogmengeschichte* (Berlin, 1899), in *Göttingische gelehrte Anzeigen*, 163 (1901), 265–75.

'Thesen zu dem am 3. Oktober in der Versammlung der Freunde der Christlichen Welt zu haltenden Vortrage über die Absolutheit des Christentums und die Religionsgeschichte', *Die christliche Welt*, 14 (1901), 923–5.

Die Absolutheit des Christentums und die Religionsgeschichte (Tübingen; [1]1902; [2]1912; [3]1929); new edn. of [3]1929 (Hamburg and Munich, 1969).

'Grundprobleme der Ethik: Erörtert aus Anlaß von Herrmanns Ethik', *Zeitschrift für Theologie und Kirche*, 12 (1902), 44–94, 125–78.

'Der Ehrhardsche Reformkatholizismus', *Die christliche Welt*, 16 (1902), 462–8.

'Was heißt, "Wesen des Christentums"?', *Die christliche Welt*, 17 (1903), 443–6, 483–8, 532–6, 578–84, 650–4, 678–83.

Review of H. Weinel, *Jesus im neunzehnten Jahrhundert* (Tübingen, 1903), in *Deutsche Literaturzeitung*, 24 (1903), 2990–3.

'Das Historische in Kants Religionsphilosophie: Zugleich ein Beitrag über Kants Philosophie der Geschichte', *Kantstudien*, 9 (1904), 21–154.

'Religionsphilosophie', in W. Windelband (ed.), *Die Philosophie im Beginn des zwanzigsten Jahrhunderts: Festschrift für Kuno Fischer* (Heidelberg, [1]1904), 104–62; (Heidelberg, [2]1907), 423–86.

Psychologie und Erkenntnistheorie in der Religionswissenschaft: Eine Untersuchung über die Bedeutung der Kantischen Religionslehre für die heutige Religionswissenschaft (Tübingen, 1905).

'Protestantisches Christentum und Kirche in der Neuzeit', in ed. P. Hinneberg, *Die Kultur der Gegenwart: Ihre Entwicklung und ihre Ziele*, i/4 (Berlin and Leipzig, [1]1906), 253–458.

Die Trennung von Staat und Kirche, der staatliche Religionsunterricht und die theologischen Fakultäten (Tübingen, 1907).

'Theodicee', 'Die Gnade', 'Prädestination', *Die christliche Welt*, 21 (1907), 345–50, 473–6, 712–41, resp.

'Die letzten Dinge', *Die christliche Welt*, 22 (1908), 74–8, 97–101.

'David Friedrich Strauss', *Die Hilfe*, 14 (1908), 57–9.

'Rückblick auf ein halbes Jahrhundert der theologischen Wissenschaft', *Zeitschrift für wissenschaftliche Theologie*, 51 (1909), 97–135.

'Aemter Christi', 'Akkommodation Christi', 'Berufung', 'Concursus Divinus', 'Dogma', 'Dogmatik', 'Erlösung', 'Eschatologie', 'Gericht Gottes', 'Gesetz', 'Glaube', 'Glaube und Geschichte', 'Glaubensartikel', 'Gnade Gottes', 'Gnadenmittel', 'Heilstatsachen', 'Kirche', 'Naturrecht, christliches', 'Offenbarung', 'Prädestination', 'Prinzip, religiöses', 'Protestantismus im Verhältnis zur Kultur', 'Theodizee', 'Weiterentwickelung der christlichen Religion', in F. M. Schiele and L. Zscharnack (eds.), *Die Religion in Geschichte und Gegenwart* (Tübingen, ¹1909–14).

'Schleiermacher und die Kirche', in F. Naumann (ed.), *Schleiermacher der Philosoph des Glaubens* (Berlin, 1910), 9–35.

'Aus der religiösen Bewegung der Gegenwart', *Die neue Rundschau*, 21 (1910), 1169–85.

Die Bedeutung der Geschichtlichkeit Jesu für den Glauben (Tübingen, 1911).

'Die Kirche im Leben der Gegenwart', in W. Dilthey, M. Frischeisen-Köhler, and others (eds.), *Weltanschauung: Philosophie und Religion in Darstellungen* (Berlin, 1911), 438–54.

Die Soziallehren der christlichen Kirchen und Gruppen = *Gesammelte Schriften*, i (Tübingen, 1912).

'Logos und Mythos in Theologie und Religionsphilosophie', *Logos*, 4 (1913), 8–35.

Zur religiösen Lage, Religionsphilosophie und Ethik = *Gesammelte Schriften*, ii (Tübingen, 1913).

Review of M. Peisker, *Die Geschichtlichkeit Jesu Christi und der christliche Glaube* (Tübingen, 1913), in *Theologische Literaturzeitung*, 40 (1915), 89–91.

Review of P. Wernle, *Jesus* (Tübingen, 1916), in *Theologische Literaturzeitung*, 41 (1916), 54–7.

'Ostern', *Deutscher Wille: Des Kunstwarts*, 31 (1918), 2–7.

'Die "kleine Göttinger Fakultät" von 1890', *Die christliche Welt*, 34 (1920), 281–3.

Der Historismus und seine Probleme, i: *Das logische Problem der Geschichtsphilosophie* = *Gesammelte Schriften*, iii (Tübingen, 1922).

'Die Krisis des Historismus', *Die neue Rundschau*, 33 (1922), 572–90.

Der Historismus und seine Überwindung: Fünf Vorträge, ed. F. von Hügel (Berlin, 1924).

Aufsätze zur Geistesgeschichte und Religionssoziologie = *Gesammelte Schriften*, iv, ed. H. Baron (Tübingen, 1925).

Glaubenslehre: Nach Heidelberger Vorlesungen aus den Jahren 1911 und 1912. Mit einem Vorwort von M. Troeltsch (Munich and Leipzig, 1925; Aalen, 1981).

Briefe an Friedrich von Hügel 1901–1923, ed. K.-E. Apfelbacher and P. Neuner (Paderborn, 1974).

'Ernst Troeltsch: Briefe aus der Heidelberger Zeit an Wilhelm Bousset 1894–1914', E. Dinkler-von Schubert, *Heidelberger Jahrbücher*, 20 (1976), 19–52.

2. *Ernst Troeltsch in English Translation* (listed in order of publication)

'Contingency', 'Historiography', in J. Hastings (ed.), *Encyclopaedia of Religion and Ethics* (Edinburgh, 1908–26).

'Empiricism and Platonism in the Philosophy of Religion', *Harvard Theological Review*, 5 (1912), 401–22.

Protestantism and Progress: A Historical Study of the Relation of Protestantism to the Modern World (London, 1912; Boston, 1958).

'The Dogmatics of the "Religionsgeschichtliche Schule"', *American Journal of Theology*, 17 (1913), 1–21.

Christian Thought: Its History and Application, ed. F. von Hügel (London, 1923; New York, 1957).

The Social Teaching of the Christian Churches (London, 1931; New York, 1960).

'The Ideas of Natural Law and Humanity in World Politics' (1922), Appendix I in O. Gierke, *Natural Law and the Theory of Society 1500 to 1800* (Cambridge, 1934; Boston, 1957), 201–22.

'Adolf von Harnack and Ferdinand Christian von Baur 1921' (1921), in W. Pauck, *Harnack and Troeltsch: Two Historical Theologians* (New York, 1968), 97–115.

'An Apple from the Tree of Kierkegaard' (1921), in J. M. Robinson (ed.), *The Beginnings of Dialectical Theology* (Richmond, Va., 1968), 311–16.

'Religious Principle' (1913), in J. Pelikan (ed.), *Twentieth Century Theology in the Making* (London, 1970), 334–41.

The Absoluteness of Christianity and the History of Religions, intro. by J. L. Adams (Richmond, Va., 1971).

'On the Possibility of a Liberal Christianity' (1910), in *Unitarian Universalist Christian*, 29 (1974), 27–38.

'The Ethic of Jesus' ([2]1913), in *Unitarian Universalist Christian*, 29 (1974), 38–45.

Ernst Troeltsch: Writings on Theology and Religion, ed. R. Morgan and M. Pye (London, 1977). This includes 'Half a Century of Theology: A Review' ([2]1913), 53–81; 'Religion and the Science of Religion' ([2]1909), 82–123; 'What Does "Essence of Christianity" Mean?' ([2]1913), 124–79; and 'The Significance of the Historical Existence of Jesus for Faith' (1911), 182–207.

3. *Secondary Works*

ABRAHAM, W. J. (1982), *Divine Revelation and the Limits of Historical Criticism,* Oxford.

ALLEN, L. (1980), 'From Dogmatik to Glaubenslehre: Ernst Troeltsch and the Task of Theology', *Fides et historica,* 12: 37–60.

ALTHAUS, P. (1927), review of E. Troeltsch, *Glaubenslehre* (Munich and Leipzig, 1925), in *Theologische Literaturzeitung,* 52: 593–5.

APFELBACHER, K.-E. (1978), *Frömmigkeit und Wissenschaft: Ernst Troeltsch und sein theologisches Programm,* Paderborn.

―――― and NEUNER, P. (eds.) (1974), *Briefe an Friedrich von Hügel* 1901–1923, Paderborn.

AUSTIN J. L. (1962), *How to do Things with Words,* Oxford.

BARNETT, W. R. (1979), 'Historical Understanding and Theological Commitment: The Dilemma of Ritschl's Christology', *Journal of Religion,* 59: 195–212.

BARTH, K. (1933), *The Epistle to the Romans* ([1]1918; ET of [6]1928, London, 1933).

―――― (1956), *Church Dogmatics,* iv/1: *The Doctrine of Reconciliation* (1953; ET Edinburgh, 1956).

BAUR, F. C. (1864), *Vorlesungen über neutestamentliche Theologie,* ed. F. F. Baur, Leipzig.

―――― (1865), *Vorlesungen über die christliche Dogmengeschichte,* i/1, ed. F. F. Baur, Leipzig.

BENSE, W. F. (1974), 'The Ethic of Jesus in the Liberal Christianity of Ernst Troeltsch', *Unitarian Universalist Christian,* 29: 16–26.

BODENSTEIN, W. (1959), *Neige des Historismus: Ernst Troeltschs Entwicklungsgang,* Gütersloh.

BORGER, R., and CIOFFI, F. (eds.) (1970), *Explanation in the Behavioural Sciences,* Cambridge.

BOUSSET, W. (1906), *Jesus* (1904; ET London, 1906).

―――― (1909), 'Kantisch-Friessche Religionsphilosophie und ihre Anwendung auf die Theologie', *Theologische Rundschau,* 12: 419–36, 471–88.

―――― (1911), *The Significance of the Personality of Jesus for Belief: Reprinted from the Report of the Fifth International Congress for Free Christianity and Religious Progress Berlin 1910,* Berlin.

BRAATEN, C. E., and HARRISVILLE, R. A. (eds.) (1964), *The Historical Jesus and the Kerygmatic Christ,* New York.

BRAZILL, W. J. (1970), *The Young Hegelians,* New Haven, Conn.

BRUNNER, E. (1929), *The Theology of Crisis,* New York.

―――― (1934), *The Mediator: A Study of the Central Doctrine of the Christian Faith* ([1]1927; ET of [2]1932, London, 1934).

BULTMANN, R. (1961), *Kerygma and Myth: A Theological Debate,* ed. H. W. Bartsch (London, 1953; New York, 1961).

—— (1969), *Faith and Understanding,* i ([1]1933; ET of [6]1966, London, 1969).

CLAYTON, J. P. (ed.) (1976), *Ernst Troeltsch and the Future of Theology,* Cambridge.

—— (1980), *The Concept of Correlation: Paul Tillich and the Possibility of a Mediating Theology,* Berlin and New York.

COAKLEY, S. (1977), review of J. P. Clayton (ed.), *Ernst Troeltsch and the Future of Theology* (Cambridge, 1976) in *Heythrop Journal,* 18: 327–8.

—— (1979), 'Theology and Cultural Relativism: What is the Problem?', *Neue Zeitschrift für systematische Theologie und Religionsphilosophie,* 21: 223–43.

COLLINGWOOD, R. G. (1946), *The Idea of History,* Oxford.

COLODNY, R. G. (1965), *Beyond the Edge of Certainty,* Englewood Cliffs, NJ.

DALY, G. (1980), *Transcendence and Immanence: A Study of Catholic Modernism and Integralism,* London.

DAVIDSON, D. D. (1973–4), 'On the Very Idea of a Conceptual Scheme', *Accounts of the Proceedings of the American Philosophical Association,* 47: 5–20.

DIEHL, H. (1908), 'Herrmann und Troeltsch', *Zeitschrift für Theologie und Kirche,* 18: 473–8.

DIEM, H. (1959), *Dogmatics* (1955; ET Edinburgh and London, 1959).

DILTHEY, W. (1927), *Gesammelte Schriften,* vii, Leipzig and Berlin.

DINKLER-VON SCHUBERT, E. (1976), 'Ernst Troeltsch: Briefe aus der Heidelberger Zeit an Wilhelm Bousset 1894–1914', *Heidelberger Jahrbücher,* 20: 19–52.

DRESCHER, H.-G. (1957), *Glaube und Vernunft bei Ernst Troeltsch: Eine kritische Deutung seiner religionsphilosophischen Grundlegung,* n.p.

—— (1960), 'Das Problem der Geschichte bei Ernst Troeltsch', *Zeitschrift für Theologie und Kirche,* NS 57: 186–230.

DREWS, A. (1909), *Die Christusmythe,* Jena.

DUNN, J. D. G. (1980), *Christology in the Making: An Inquiry into the Origins of the Doctrine of the Incarnation,* London.

DURKHEIM, E. (1899), 'De la définition des phénomènes religieux', *L'Année sociologique,* 2: 1–28.

—— (1965), *The Elementary Forms of the Religious Life* (1912; ET London, 1915; New York, 1965).

DYSON, A. O. (1968), 'History in the Philosophy and Theology of Ernst Troeltsch', D.Phil. thesis, Oxford.

—— (1969), *Who is Jesus Christ?,* London.

—— (1974), *The Immortality of the Past,* London.

FEYERABEND, P. (1975), *Against Method,* London.

FISCHER, H. (1967), *Christlicher Glaube und Geschichte: Voraussetzungen und Folgen der Theologie Friedrich Gogartens,* Gütersloh.

FORT, G. VON LE (1965), *Hälfte des Lebens,* Munich.

FRANKENA, W. K. (1973), *Ethics* (Englewood Cliffs, NJ, ¹1963, ²1973).

FRESENIUS, W. (1912), 'Die Bedeutung der Geschichtlichkeit Jesu für den Glauben', *Zeitschrift für Theologie und Kirche,* 22: 244–68.

GARDINER, P. (ed.) (1974), *The Philosophy of History,* Oxford.

GERRISH, B. A. (1975), 'Jesus, Myth, and History: Troeltsch's Stand in the "Christ-Myth" Debate', *Journal of Religion,* 55: 13–35.

_____ (1978), *Tradition and the Modern World: Reformed Theology in the Nineteenth Century,* Chicago and London.

GIERKE, O. (1957), *Natural Law and the Theory of Society 1500 to 1800* (Cambridge, 1934; Boston, 1957).

GOULDER, M. (ed.) (1979), *Incarnation and Myth: The Debate Continued,* London.

GRAF, F. W., and RUDDIES, H. (eds.) (1982), *Ernst Troeltsch Bibliographie,* Tübingen.

GREEN, M. (ed.) (1977), *The Truth of God Incarnate,* London.

GRESCHAT, M. (ed.) (1978), *Theologen des Protestantismus im 19. und 20. Jahrhundert,* ii, Stuttgart.

GROLL, W. (1976), *Ernst Troeltsch und Karl Barth: Kontinuität im Widerspruch,* Munich.

HAMNETT, I. (1973), 'Sociology of Religion and Sociology of Error', *Religion,* 3: 1–12.

_____ (1986), 'A Mistake about Error', *New Blackfriars,* 67: 69–78.

HARNACK, A. VON (1901), *What is Christianity? Sixteen Lectures delivered in the University of Berlin during the Winter-term 1899–1900* (1900; ET London, 1901).

HARTMANN, E. VON (1874), *Die Selbstzersetzung des Christentums und die Religion der Zukunft,* Berlin.

_____ (1882), *Die Religion des Geistes,* Berlin.

_____ (1905), *Das Christentum des neuen Testaments* (Sachsa im Harz, ²1905).

HARVEY, V. A. (1967), *The Historian and the Believer: The Morality of Historical Knowledge and Christian Belief,* London.

HASTINGS, J. (ed.) (1908–26), *Encyclopaedia of Religion and Ethics,* Edinburgh.

HEBBLETHWAITE, B. L. (1977), 'Incarnation: The Essence of Christianity?', *Theology,* 80: 85–91.

_____ (1980), *The Problems of Theology,* Cambridge.

HEGEL, G. W. F. (1956), *The Philosophy of History,* ed. K. Hegel (1840; ET London, 1857; New York, 1956).

HERRMANN, W. (1909), *The Communion of the Christian with God Described on the Basis of Luther's Statements* ([1]1886; ET of [4]1903, London, 1909).

HICK, J. (ed.) (1977), *The Myth of God Incarnate*, London.

HODGSON, P. C. (1966), *The Formation of Historical Theology: A Study of Ferdinand Christian Baur*, New York.

HORTON, R., and FINNEGAN, R. (eds.) (1973), *Modes of Thought*, London.

HÜGEL, F. VON (1904), 'Du Christ éternel et de nos christologies successives', *La Quinzaine*, 58: 285–312.

—— (1923), 'Ernst Troeltsch: To the Editor of the Times', *The Times Literary Supplement* (29 Mar.), 216.

IGGERS, G. G. (1968), *The German Conception of History: The National Tradition of Historical Thought from Herder to the Present*, Middletown Conn.

—— (1973), 'Historicism', in P. P. Wiener (ed.), *Dictionary of the History of Ideas*, ii (New York), 456–64.

JUNG, C. G. (1969a), *The Structure and Dynamics of the Psyche* (*Collected Works*, viii; London, [1]1960, [2]1969).

—— (1969b), *Psychology and Religion: West and East* (*Collected Works*, xi; London, [1]1958, [2]1969).

KAFTAN, J. (1896), 'Die Selbständigkeit des Christentums', *Zeitschrift für Theologie und Kirche*, 6: 373–94.

KÄHLER, M. (1964), *The So-called Historical Jesus and the Historic, Biblical Christ* (1896; ET ed. C. E. Braaten, Philadelphia, 1964).

KANT, I. (1960), *Religion Within the Limits of Reason Alone* (1793; ET La Salle, Ill., 1934; New York, 1960).

KASCH, W. H. (1963), *Die Sozialphilosophie von Ernst Troeltsch*, Tübingen.

KÄSEMANN, E. (1969), *New Testament Questions of Today*, London.

KLAPWIJK, J. (1970), *Tussen historisme en relativisme: Een studie over de dynamiek van het historisme en de wijsgerige ontwikkelingsgang van Ernst Troeltsch*, Assen.

KLEMM, H. (1974), 'Die Identifizierung des christlichen Glaubens in Ernst Troeltschs Vorlesung über Glaubenslehre', *Neue Zeitschrift für systematische Theologie und Religionsphilosophie*, 16: 187–98.

KÖHLER, W. (1941), *Ernst Troeltsch*, Tübingen.

KUHN, T. S. (1962), *The Structure of Scientific Revolutions* (Chicago, [1]1962, [2]1970).

LAKATOS, I., and MUSGRAVE, A. (eds.) (1970), *Criticism and the Growth of Knowledge*, Cambridge.

LEE, D. E., and BECK, R. N. (1953–4), 'The Meaning of "Historicism"', *American Historical Review*, 59: 568–77.

LeRoy Ladurie, E. (1978), *Montaillou: Cathars and Catholics in a French Village 1294-1324* (1975; ET London, 1978).

Lessing, E. (1965), *Die Geschichtsphilosophie Ernst Troeltschs*, Hamburg and Bergstedt.

Livingston, J. C. (1971), *Modern Christian Thought: From the Enlightenment to Vatican II*, New York.

Loisy, A. (1912), *The Gospel and the Church* (1902; ET New York, 1912).

Lukes, S. (1974), 'Relativism: Cognitive and Moral', *Proceedings of the Aristotelian Society*, suppl. 48: 165-89.

McGrath, A. E. (1986), *The Making of Modern German Christology*, Oxford.

MacKinnon, D. M. (1976-7), 'Idealism and Realism: An Old Controversy Renewed', *Proceedings of the Aristotelian Society*, NS 77: 1-14.

Macquarrie, J. (1979), 'Foundation Documents of the Faith: iii. The Chalcedonian Definition', *Expository Times*, 91: 68-72.

Mannheim, K. (1936), *Ideology and Utopia*, New York.

_____ (1952), *Essays on the Sociology of Knowledge*, ed. P. Kecskemeti, London.

Meiland, J. W., and Krausz, M. (eds.) (1982), *Relativism, Cognitive and Moral*, Notre Dame, Ind.

Meinecke, F. (1972), *Historicism: The Rise of a New Historical Outlook* ([1]1936; ET of [2]1946, London, 1972).

Meyerhoff, H. (ed.) (1959), *The Philosophy of History in Our Time*, New York.

Mitchell, B. (1973), *The Justification of Religious Belief*, London.

Moberly, E. R. (1978), *Suffering, Innocent and Guilty*, London.

Moltmann, J. (1967), *Theology of Hope: On the Ground and the Implications of a Christian Eschatology* (1964; ET London, 1967).

_____ (1974), *The Crucified God: The Cross of Christ as the Foundation and Criticism of Christian Theology* ([1]1972; ET of [2]1973, London, 1974).

_____ (1981), *The Trinity and the Kingdom of God* (1980; ET London 1981).

Morgan, R., and Pye, M. (eds.) (1977), *Ernst Troeltsch: Writings on Theology and Religion*, London.

Müller, G. (1966), 'Die Selbstauflösung der Dogmatik bei Ernst Troeltsch', *Theologische Zeitschrift*, 22: 334-46.

Naumann, F. (ed.) (1910), *Schleiermacher der Philosoph des Glaubens*, Berlin.

Niebuhr, H. R. (1924), 'Ernst Troeltsch's Philosophy of Religion', Ph.D. thesis, Yale.

Nineham, D. (1976), *The Use and Abuse of the Bible*, London.

Ogletree, T. W. (1965), *Christian Faith and History: A Critical Comparison of Ernst Troeltsch and Karl Barth*, New York.

PANNENBERG, W. (1968), *Jesus: God and Man* ([1]1964; ET of [2]1966, London, 1968).

—— (1970), *Basic Questions in Theology*, i (1967; ET London, 1970).

PAUCK, W. (1968), *Harnack and Troeltsch: Two Historical Theologians*, New York.

PELIKAN, J. (ed.) (1970), *Twentieth Century Theology in the Making*, London.

PHILLIPS, D. Z. (1965), *The Concept of Prayer*, London.

—— (1970), *Faith and Philosophical Enquiry*, London.

—— (1976), *Religion Without Explanation*, London.

QUIGLEY, M. A. (1983), 'Ernst Troeltsch and the Problem of the Historical Absolute', *Heythrop Journal*, 24: 19–37.

QUINE, W. V. (1960), *Word and Object*, Cambridge, Mass.

RAND, C. G. (1964), 'Two Meanings of Historicism in the Writings of Dilthey, Troeltsch, and Meinecke', *Journal of the History of Ideas*, 25: 503–18.

REIST, B. A. (1966), *Toward a Theology of Involvement: The Thought of Ernst Troeltsch*, London.

RENZ, H., and GRAF, F. W. (eds.) (1982), *Troeltsch-Studien*, i: *Untersuchungen zur Biographie und Werkgeschichte*, Gütersloh.

—— (1987), *Troeltsch-Studien*, iv: *Umstrittene Moderne: Die Zukunft der Neuzeit im Urteil der Epoche Ernst Troeltschs*, Gütersloh.

RESCHER, N. (1978), 'Philosophical Disagreement: An Essay towards Orientational Pluralism in Metaphilosophy', *Review of Metaphysics*, 32: 217–51.

RICHARDSON, A. (1964), *History, Sacred and Profane*, London.

RICHMOND, J. (1978), *Ritschl: A Reappraisal. A Study in Systematic Theology*, London.

RITSCHL, A. (1966), *The Christian Doctrine of Justification and Reconciliation*, iii ([1]1874; ET of [3]1888, Edinburgh, 1900; Clifton, NJ 1966).

RITSCHL, A. (1972), *Three Essays: Theology and Metaphysics; 'Prolegomena' to the History of Pietism; Instruction in the Christian Religion*, Philadelphia.

ROBINSON, J. M. (ed.) (1968), *The Beginnings of Dialectical Theology*, Richmond, Va.

—— and COBB, J. B. (eds.) (1967), *Theology as History* (New Frontiers in Theology, iii; New York).

ROLLMANN, H. (1978), 'Troeltsch, von Hügel, and Modernism', *Downside Review*, 96: 35–60.

RORTY, R. (1980), *Philosophy and the Mirror of Nature*, Oxford.

RUMSCHEIDT, H. R. (1972), *Revelation and Theology: An Analysis of the Barth–Harnack Correspondence of 1923*, Cambridge.

RUNZO, J. (1986), *Reason, Relativism and God*, London.

RUPP, G. (1977), *Culture-Protestantism: German Liberal Theology at the Turn of the Twentieth Century*, Missoula, Mont.

SCHIELE, F. M., and ZSCHARNACK, L. (eds.) (1909–14), *Die Religion in Geschichte und Gegenwart* (Tübingen, [1]1909–14).

SCHLEIERMACHER, F. D. E. (1963), *The Christian Faith* (1821–2; ET Edinburgh, 1928; in 2 vols., New York, 1963).

SCHWEITZER, A. (1966), *Geschichte der Leben-Jesu-Forschung* ([1]1906 (as *Von Reimarus zu Wrede*); [2]1913, [6]1950; Munich and Hamburg, 1966).

SEEBERG, E. (1926), review of E. Troeltsch, *Glaubenslehre* (Munich and Leipzig, 1925), in *Deutsche Literaturzeitung*, 47: 2127–33.

SLEIGH, R. S. (1923), *The Sufficiency of Christianity: An Enquiry concerning the Nature and the Modern Possibilities of the Christian Religion, with Special Reference to the Religious Philosophy of Dr. Ernst Troeltsch*, London.

SMART, N. (1973), *The Phenomenology of Religion*, London.

—— CLAYTON, J., SHERRY, P., and KATZ, S. (eds.) (1985), *Nineteenth Century Religious Thought in the West*, iii, Cambridge.

STACKHOUSE, M. L. (1961–2), 'Troeltsch's Categories of Historical Analysis', *Journal for the Scientific Study of Religion*, 1: 223–5.

STEINER, G. (1975), *After Babel*, London.

STRAUSS, D. F, (1972), *The Life of Jesus Critically Examined* ([1]1835; ET of [4]1840, ed. P. C. Hodgson, London, 1972).

—— (1977), *The Christ of Faith and the Jesus of History: A Critique of Schleiermacher's Life of Jesus* (1865; ET Philadelphia, 1977).

TRIGG, R. (1973), *Reason and Commitment*, Cambridge.

TURNER, G. (1978), 'Ernst Troeltsch and the Study of Religion', *New Blackfriars*, 59: 312–18.

WALSH, W. H. (1976), *An Introduction to Philosophy of History* ([1]1951, [3]1967; NJ and Sussex, 1976).

WARFIELD, B. B. (1912), 'Christless Christianity', *Harvard Theological Review*, 5: 423–74.

WEBER, MAR. (1975), *Max Weber: A Biography* (1926; ET New York, 1975).

WEBER, M. (1963), *The Sociology of Religion* (1922; ET of [4]1956, Boston, 1963).

WEHRUNG, G. (1933), *Geschichte und Glaube: Eine Besinnung auf die Grundsätze theologischen Denkens*, Gütersloh.

WEISS, J. (1971), *Jesus' Proclamation of the Kingdom of God* (1892; ET London, 1971).

WIENER, P. P. (ed.) (1973), *Dictionary of the History of Ideas*, New York.

WILES, M. F. (1967), *The Making of Christian Doctrine*, Cambridge.

WILSON, B. R. (ed.) (1970), *Rationality*, Oxford.

WINCH. P. (1958), *The Idea of a Social Science*, London.

WOLFE, G. E. (1916), 'Troeltsch's Conception of the Significance of Jesus', *American Journal of Theology*, 20: 179–204.

WYMAN, W. E. (1983), *The Concept of Glaubenslehre: Ernst Troeltsch and the Theological Heritage of Schleiermacher*, Chico, Calif.

Index